Mastering
the Art of
Baking

Classic to Contemporary
A Complete Step-by-Step Guide

Anneka Manning

Mastering
the Art of
Baking

Contents

Introduction 6

Basics 8

Biscuits, Meringues & Slices 56

Cakes 114

Muffins, Scones & Quick Breads 156

Breads & Rich Yeast Breads 194

Pies & Tarts 252

Pastries 296

Desserts 336

Conversion charts 380

Index 382

Introduction

There is no denying that baking is one of the more technical, and often the most challenging, forms of cooking. But it can also be one of the most rewarding.

The heavenly aroma of a freshly baked coffee and walnut cake, snowy white clouds of vanilla meringue, the buttery richness of a perfect brioche straight from your oven all contribute to a fulfilling baking experience. *Mastering the Art of Baking* will guide you through more than 280 fabulous and highly approachable recipes each accompanied by clear instructions, step-by-step photography and expert tips.

Learn how to make sourdough (the cheat's way), traditional Indian naan, crumpets and Italian grissini, and serve up rich fruit cake, to-die-for jam-filled doughnuts, perfect scones and chocolate cinnamon babka. The easy-to-follow pastry recipes will have you making your own puff, choux and shortcrust like a professional (with minimal fuss), ready to create more-ish sausage rolls and meat pies, pretty fruit tarts or even an impressive croquembouche.

This comprehensive collection of classic recipes together with essential information about ingredients, equipment and techniques will guide you through the wonderful, but sometimes daunting, world of baking with ease so you can reap the rewards that successful home baking brings.

Basics

Common ingredients

Baking powder is a leavener that is used to help aerate mixtures. It is a combination of bicarbonate of soda (baking soda), cream of tartar (or other acidic powder) and usually cornflour (cornstarch) or rice flour (to absorb moisture). To make your own, combine ½ teaspoon cream of tartar, ½ teaspoon cornflour and ¼ teaspoon bicarbonate of soda to replace 1 teaspoon of commercial baking powder.

Bicarbonate of soda, also called baking soda, is not only a component of baking powder but can also be used as a leavener in its own right. It is activated with the aid of an acid, so is therefore used in mixtures with an acidic ingredient such as buttermilk, yoghurt, sour cream, citrus juice and even molasses. It is important to cook these mixtures as soon as possible, because the bicarbonate of soda is activated as soon as it comes into contact with the acidic ingredient — if the mixture is left to sit, it won't rise as much as it should and the end product will have a coarser, more open texture.

Butter adds flavour, shortness/tenderness and colour. When it is beaten, air is incorporated which, in turn, helps leaven baked goods as they cook. It can also be rubbed into flour or melted and mixed with other ingredients. Unsalted butter is sweeter than salted and gives you more control over the amount of salt in your baking — you can add as much as you want. If you are creaming butter, make sure it is softened by standing at room temperature for at least 30 minutes before using. If rubbing into dry ingredients, make sure it is chilled.

Buttermilk, a cultured milk, is made by adding souring agents to milk. It adds a subtle acidity to cakes and batters, such as pancakes, and is used in conjunction with bicarbonate of soda (baking soda), in goods such as soda bread and scones. Its acidity reacts with the alkaline properties of the soda to provide a particularly good lift. To make your own buttermilk, add 1 tablespoon of fresh lemon juice to 300 ml (10½ fl oz) of regular milk.

Cocoa powder is the unsweetened ground powder made from grinding the cocoa solids when the cocoa butter (the fat) is removed from cocoa beans. Sift it before using to remove any lumps. Sweetened cocoa powder is sold as drinking chocolate. Dutch cocoa is considered the best quality cocoa powder, having a rich and intense flavour and a dark colour.

Cornflour, also known as cornstarch, is made from corn or maize (gluten-free) or wheat (labelled as wheaten cornflour). In baking, it is used in small quantities to replace plain (all-purpose) flour to give a lighter texture.

Cream is used sometimes in baked goods to enrich and tenderise. The fat content of cream determines how rich it is and also its whipping characteristics — the higher the fat content, the easier it will be to whip and the thicker it will be when whipped (low-fat cream won't whip at all). Double (thick/heavy) cream has a 48 per cent butter fat content and is the thickest type of cream. Pouring cream, also known as whipping or single cream, has a fat content of 35 per cent. Thickened cream, also known as whipping cream, is pouring cream with gelatine added to thicken it slightly and make it more stable. It is ideal for whipping. Sour cream adds a pleasant acidity, and richness, to dishes.

Eggs enrich, give structure, bind, lighten, tenderise and add flavour to baked goods. Store them, pointed end down, in their original carton in the refrigerator. Bring eggs to room temperature before using — if you're short on time, you can put them in a bowl of lukewarm water for 10 minutes. All the recipes in this book use 59/60 g (2¼ oz) eggs.

Flour provides the basic structure for the majority of baked goods. Self-raising flour is simply plain (all-purpose) flour with baking powder added. To make your own, add 2 teaspoons baking powder to 150 g (5½ oz/1 cup) plain flour and sift several times before using.

Honey and golden syrup are used to sweeten baked goods, such as rich hot puddings, tarts, cakes and biscuits.

Milk is often used in cakes, puddings, breads and quick breads to help moisten and bind the dry ingredients, and to prevent the final baked product being heavy and dry. Always use full-cream cow's milk in baking recipes unless otherwise specified.

Oil is often used in recipes that don't rely on air being incorporated into butter by the creaming method. Baked goods made with oil tend to store better and stay moister than those made with butter. Oils used in baking generally have a mild flavour, such as sunflower, vegetable and light olive oils.

Salt is mainly used in baking as a seasoning and flavour enhancer. Always add a little salt (usually about ½ teaspoon) to baked goods if using unsalted butter.

Sugar adds flavour, moisture and tenderness to baked goods. Granulated sugar is the most commonly available, but caster sugar, with its fine grains that dissolve quickly, is a better choice for baking. Icing sugar is powdered white sugar and is available as pure icing sugar or icing sugar mixture, which has a little cornflour (cornstarch) added to prevent lumps. Light brown sugar is fine, granulated sugar with molasses added to enrich the flavour. Dark brown sugar has even more molasses added. If you want to substitute brown sugar for white, or vice versa, measure out the same weight (grams or ounces), rather than volume (cups).

Vanilla is used in various forms. Natural vanilla extract and vanilla essence are concentrated flavours derived from vanilla beans. Buy pure essence or extract and avoid those labelled with 'artificial' or 'imitation' as they don't contain any real vanilla. Thick vanilla bean paste is also available and offers a convenient way of adding vanilla seeds to recipes. If using vanilla beans, wash and dry the pod thoroughly after use and place it in a container of sugar to subtly flavour it.

Yeast is a biological (naturally occurring) rising agent. Dried yeast is available in sachets or small containers from supermarkets in the baking section. Fresh (compressed) yeast is available from selected health food stores and delicatessens, and needs to be mixed with lukewarm water to activate it before mixing with dry ingredients. Although it is not strictly necessary, we advise activating dried yeast to ensure it is still alive. Instant dried yeast is completely interchangeable with active dried yeast, another form of dried yeast that does require activation.

Baking equipment

Ovens

Not all ovens cook in the same way so it is important to get to know your oven and make your own adjustments to recipes if necessary. Even when an oven is accurately calibrated its temperature may be slightly out. Use a good-quality oven thermometer to monitor the temperature regularly and make sure the seals are in good order to prevent heat escaping.

Fan-forced or convection ovens, which use a fan to circulate the heat, cook at a higher temperature and more quickly than conventional ovens. The recipes in this book have been tested in conventional ovens — if cooking in a fan-forced oven, decrease the oven temperature by 20°C (68°F) and check regularly towards the end of cooking as the time may need to be reduced by 10–20 per cent.

When baking in a conventional oven place cakes in the centre of the oven and swap multiple trays of biscuits around halfway through cooking to ensure even cooking. If you have two cakes in the oven at once, make sure there is plenty of room between them to allow the heat to circulate evenly.

Measuring

Accurate measuring, whether by weight or volume, is essential for success when baking. Always use one set of measurements when preparing a recipe — metric (grams and ml) or imperial (oz and fl oz) by weighing, or measuring by volume (cups).

Measuring cups are used to measure dry or non-liquid ingredients. They are generally available in plastic or metal and in sets of 60 ml (2 fl oz/¼ cup), 80 ml (2½ fl oz/⅓ cup), 125 ml (4 fl oz/½ cup) and 250 ml (9 fl oz/1 cup) measures. Spoon the ingredient into the cup until heaped, then, without compressing it, run a flat-bladed knife across the top to level. All cup measures in this book are level, not heaped.

Measuring jugs are used to measure liquids. Look for a glass or see-through jug with clear markings and a good spout.

Measuring spoons are used to measure small amounts of both dry and liquid ingredients. They are available in sets that generally include a ¼ teaspoon, ½ teaspoon, 1 teaspoon and 1 tablespoon. One teaspoon equals 5 ml in volume. Tablespoons, however, can come in either 15 ml (½ fl oz/ 3 teaspoon) or 20 ml (¾fl oz/4 teaspoon) volumes. This book uses 20 ml tablespoons. Check your tablespoon volume and if you are using a 15 ml tablespoon, add an extra teaspoon

for every tablespoon of the ingredient specified in the recipe. This is particularly important for ingredients such as baking powder and bicarbonate of soda (baking soda). All tablespoon and teaspoon measures in this book are level — use a flat-bladed knife to level ingredients, as for cup measures.

Scales, electronic versions in particular, are the most accurate way of measuring dry ingredients, such as flour or sugar, and non-liquid, soft ingredients, such as yoghurt or jam. Electronic scales are now affordable and are an invaluable addition to your kitchen. Most give metric and imperial weights, and let you switch between the two. They may also let you 'zero' the reading so you can measure several ingredients in the same bowl one after another, which is handy for one-bowl mixes.

Mixing

Bowls are fundamental to baking and it is important to have a good selection of sizes. Stainless-steel bowls are versatile and durable and are good conductors of heat and cold. Ceramic and glass bowls are sturdy and are also suitable for heating and melting ingredients. Plastic bowls aren't a good choice for mixing as they absorb flavours and become greasy over time.

Electric mixers offer an easy, efficient way to cream butter and sugar, whisk egg whites and combine batters.

Hand-held electric beaters have detachable beaters and sometimes whisk attachments, and a range of speeds. They are relatively inexpensive, store easily and can be used to whisk or beat mixtures. They are also needed if whisking or beating a mixture over a saucepan of simmering water. However, they aren't suitable for heavy-duty mixing, such as bread doughs, and are not as efficient as the stand versions.

Electric mixers that are mounted on a stand have a bowl that screws into the stand and usually come with a range of attachments such as a beating paddle, whisk and dough hook. Like hand-held beaters, they have a range of speeds, but their motors are more powerful and therefore able to cope with larger and thicker mixtures.

Buy the best quality mixer you can afford.

Food processors are invaluable when baking, from finely chopping nuts to making breadcrumbs and even pastry.

Buy the best quality food processor you can afford, and ensure it has a large bowl. A **mini food processor** that will cope with small quantities is also a good investment.

Bakers' friends

Baking beads/weights are small re-usable ceramic or metal weights that are used when blind baking pastry. You can use dried beans or rice instead, but proper weights are handy.

Cake testers are thin metal or bamboo skewers. Metal ones are available from kitchenware stores and are the best option as they won't leave large holes in your baking. The skewer is inserted into the centre of a cake and if it's cooked, it will be clean when withdrawn (unless otherwise stated in the recipe).

Large metal spoons are useful for folding dry ingredients into a mixture or folding in whisked egg whites without losing the incorporated air.

Non-stick baking paper or silpat mats can be used to line baking trays as an alternative to greasing and flouring them. Silpat mats are available from speciality kitchenware stores and can be used time and time again. Wash in hot soapy water and dry thoroughly before storing.

Oven thermometers are important kitchen gadgets. Not all ovens are calibrated and are likely to be at least a couple of degrees out. 'Hot spots' are also common. A thermometer will allow you to check if your oven is accurate and adjust the temperature if necessary. Move the thermometer around in the oven when set at the same temperature and note the reading to check if you have any 'hot spots'. There is no need to remove it from your oven between oven uses.

Palette knives can be bought in various sizes and degrees of flexibility. They have a thin flat blade with a rounded end that makes them useful for transferring biscuits from a tray to a rack, loosening cakes from tins and spreading icing (frosting).

Pastry brushes have natural, nylon or silicone bristles and are used to glaze tarts, brush egg wash onto pastries and doughs, and grease cake tins. Have a few brushes of varying sizes and wash and dry them thoroughly before storing. Avoid cheaper brushes as they tend to shed their bristles.

Piping (icing) bags and nozzles/tips are used to pipe meringue or biscuit mixtures into shapes, to pipe cream, buttercream or other icings (frostings) and to decorate with icing. Various bags and sizes and shapes of nozzles are available. Make sure the bags are cleaned well and dried completely before storing.

Rolling pins should be straight, solid and long enough to roll out a full quantity of pastry or dough without marking the surface with the ends. A good size is about 45 cm (17¾ inches) long and 5 cm (2 inches) in diameter. Wood is preferable to ceramic or marble, as it can hold a fine layer of flour on its surface that will help prevent the pastry or dough sticking. The best ones are made of hard wood with a close grain and very smooth finish. Clean it by wiping with a damp cloth — never immerse a wooden rolling pin in water.

Ruler Keep a ruler or measuring tape in your utensil drawer for checking tin or cutter dimensions, lining tins and checking the thickness of pastry or biscuit doughs.

Saucepans and frying pans are great supportive equipment when baking. They are used for everything from pan-frying fruit to deep-frying fritters, making caramel, cooking stirred custard, syrups and sauces, and poaching fruit. Have a selection of different sizes for a variety of uses. A heavy frying pan with a heatproof handle is perfect for making tarte tatin as it can be used for both the stovetop and oven.

Sieves are used to sift flour to help incorporate air, to combine ingredients evenly, such as flour and cocoa powder or baking powder, and to dust flour onto a work surface before rolling out pastry or kneading dough. They are also used to dust icing (confectioners') sugar or cocoa over baked goods.

Spatulas can be made of silicone, rubber or plastic. Silicone and rubber ones are more flexible, however rubber ones tend to absorb colours and flavours more readily. Spatulas are used to fold and combine mixtures and scrape them from bowls, blenders and food processors. Have a few different sizes and shapes for various tasks.

Timers are necessary for accurate timing and to prevent food burning. Digital timers are more accurate than mechanical ones. Many ovens have inbuilt timers.

Whisks are used to incorporate air into a mixture, remove lumps and combine liquid mixtures, such as eggs and oil. They come in all shapes and sizes — a large and small wire balloon whisk will usually cover all required tasks.

Wooden spoons are used to mix, beat and stir. They are particularly good for mixtures being heated in a saucepan and 'heavier' mixtures that require stirring or beating.

Cutting and grating

Graters come in many different shapes and sizes, from the traditional box grater to rasp-shaped Microplanes. They have various perforations of different sizes designed for specific uses, from finely grating citrus zest and nutmeg to coarsely grating chocolate and cheese. Look for a grater with a variety of perforations or have a couple on hand for different tasks.

Knives should be sharpened regularly and washed by hand (rather than putting them in the dishwasher) to help retain their sharpness and to prevent chipping of the blade. Make sure they are always dried thoroughly before storing. An all-purpose cook's knife is handy for chopping ingredients such as chocolate, nuts and dried fruits. A paring knife can be used to trim pastry, cut fruit and make small incisions. A long serrated knife is best for cutting cakes into even layers (see page 131), slicing biscotti between bakings, and cutting cake and bread into portions.

Pastry and biscuit cutters also come in a variety of shapes and sizes, from simple plain and fluted rounds to more intricate designs such as numbers, letters and novelty shapes. Metal cutters generally have a better edge than plastic ones, giving a cleaner cut without having to apply much pressure. Wash and dry cutters thoroughly before storing. (Metal ones are best dried in a low oven.)

Scissors are another useful utensil when baking, for tasks such as cutting out baking paper when lining cake tins and snipping pastry for decorations. It is a good idea to have a good-quality pair in the kitchen to use solely for cooking.

Bakeware

Baking trays Choose the largest trays that will fit in your oven and make sure they are solid so they don't buckle. Have two or more trays so you can cook a few batches at once.

Cake and loaf (bar) tins come in various sizes, shapes and finishes. It is important to use the size and shape specified in the recipe or the outcome of your baking may be affected. The type of metal that tins are made from and their finish will affect the way they conduct heat and therefore cook. Shiny bakeware will deflect heat and prevent scorching, whereas dark, matt, non-stick bakeware will absorb and hold heat more readily, giving a darker, slightly thicker, crust. Choose good-quality tins, preferably with straight sides, and prepare them as instructed (see pages 122–23). All the tins in this book have been measured at the base, with the exception of kugelhopf tins, which are best measured across the top.

If a tin is marked with a diameter measurement, measure it to ensure it's correct (there are a number of spring-form tins available, for example, that are incorrectly marked).

Dariole moulds and ramekins are mostly available in metal or ceramic form and are used to make individual puddings.

Muffin tins generally come in three sizes – Texas or large (250 ml/9 fl oz/1 cup), medium (80 ml/2½ fl oz/⅓ cup) and mini (20 ml/¾ fl oz/1 tablespoon).

Ovenproof dishes are used to cook oven-baked puddings in, and also to make a water bath for delicate desserts that need gentle cooking (roasting pans can also be used for this).

Patty pan tins are used to make cupcakes and other small cakes. They have either a flat or rounded base.

Pie and tart (flan) tins come in a range of shapes, sizes, depths and finishes. They often don't need greasing before using as the pastry's high butter content prevents it sticking. Tart tins with removable bases ('loose-based') are often used as they allow tarts to be removed easily. Like all cake tins, pie and tart tins should be cleaned in hot soapy water and dried thoroughly (preferably in a low oven) before storing.

Pizza stones are large, flat slabs of unglazed earthenware used for cooking pizzas. Other breads, especially free-form rustic loaves, can also be baked on a pizza stone. The stone evenly distributes heat and absorbs water so it encourages a very crisp base. Pizza stones need to be placed in a cold oven and then heated, as sudden changes in temperate can cause them to crack. Don't use detergent to clean them, simply scrub the cooled stone with a dry brush instead.

Pudding basins are generally used for steamed puddings and are available in ceramic or earthenware form, as well as metal. Metal basins often come with a handy lid that clips into place, while the ceramic or earthenware basins need to be sealed tightly with foil before steaming your pudding.

Ring, kugelhopf and angel food cake tins have a central tube, which forms the cake or bread mixture into a ring shape that enables it to cook relatively quickly and evenly. Ring and kugelhopf tins can't be lined so it is best to grease them well and lightly dust with flour (if specified in the recipe), as detailed on page 122. Angel food cake tins don't need to be greased, lined or floured.

Spring-form tins have a removable base that is released when a sprung latch on the side is opened. You will need to use a spring-form tin when making delicate cakes, such as flourless ones, or cheesecakes that can't be upturned onto a wire rack. Make sure the latch is strong so the base and side fit snugly together — this will prevent any leaking. Turning the base upside down before locking it in place will create a base without a lip, which will make removing the cake easier.

Freezing

Most baked goods can be frozen for up to 3 months. Unfilled and/or un-iced cakes, biscuits, slices, quick breads, breads and tarts freeze better than those with decorations and/or fillings. Cakes and biscuits decorated with fondant, glacé or royal icing; cheesecakes; baked goods that are meringue-based; and recipes with cream-based fillings will not freeze well.

Before you wrap baked goods for freezing, always make sure they have cooled completely. Then, wrap them well in plastic wrap before sealing in a double layer of foil, a freezer bag or a snap-lock bag (make sure you expel as much air as possible) to prevent them losing moisture while in the freezer. Small baked goods, such as biscuits, slices and cupcakes, can be placed in an airtight container, layered with freezer wrap or non-stick baking paper, and then sealed. Label and date clearly before putting them in the freezer.

Uncooked pastry (see pages 28–43) and biscuit doughs without a leavening agent can also be frozen successfully. Shape, roll or cut biscuit dough and freeze on baking trays. Once frozen, pack into airtight containers, separated by freezer wrap or non-stick baking paper, or in freezer bags. Bake the biscuits straight from the freezer, adding about 5 minutes extra to the cooking time.

Thaw other baked goods at room temperature or in the fridge and bring to room temperature before serving. Try to avoid thawing them in the microwave, as they can defrost unevenly and 'toughen' in the process.

Basic mixing techniques

Melt and mix *(cakes, biscuits, slices, quick breads)*

This is the quickest and easiest method for combining ingredients.

1 Mix the dry ingredients together and then make a well in the centre.

2 Melt the butter (and other ingredients, as instructed) and cool, if specified. Pour the wet ingredients into the well in the dry ingredients and use a wooden spoon to stir until well combined. This can also be done in a food processor, using the pulse button.

Creaming *(cakes, biscuits, slices)*

The creaming method is used to beat butter and sugar with an electric mixer (although you can do it with a wooden spoon and a lot of muscle) to change the consistency of the mixture, incorporate air and, in turn, help the cake, biscuits or slice rise slightly during baking.

1 The butter should be softened, but not melted. Combine the butter, sugar and any specified flavourings (such as vanilla or grated citrus zest) in a suitable-sized mixing bowl.

2 Use an electric mixer to beat the ingredients. For best results, don't take shortcuts — keep beating until the mixture is creamy, increased slightly in volume and paler in colour. The sugar should have almost dissolved. Other ingredients will now be either beaten, stirred or folded in before baking.

Rubbing in *(biscuits, slices, scones, quick breads, pastries)*

Rubbing in should be done quickly and lightly, so the butter doesn't melt. It helps if your hands are cool — run them under cold water on a hot day if necessary.

1 The butter is usually chilled, but not always, for this method. Cut it into small, even-sized pieces.

2 Use your fingertips to rub the butter into the dry ingredients until the mixture resembles fine or coarse breadcrumbs, as specified. (This method can also be done in a food processor, using the pulse button.) Other ingredients are usually stirred in after this, using a flat-bladed knife or wooden spoon.

Folding *(cakes, meringue mixtures)*

Folding involves incorporating one mixture into another. It is often used to combine a light, aerated mixture (such as whisked egg whites) with a heavier mixture (such as melted chocolate and butter) or when flour is incorporated into a creamed butter mixture so as not to toughen it before baking.

1 Add the lighter mixture to the heavier mixture in batches. Use a large metal spoon or spatula to cut through the centre, then turn the spoon and draw it up around the side of the bowl.

2 Give the bowl a turn and repeat the folding, making sure you reach right down to the base of the bowl to make sure the mixtures are evenly combined and there are no pockets of either mixture left. Fold until the mixtures are just combined. Do not beat or stir at any stage, as incorporated air will be lost and/or the mixture will toughen.

Whisking *(cakes, meringue mixtures)*

This technique is used when the recipe requires air to be incorporated into eggs or egg whites. Eggs and egg whites should be at room temperature, as this enables them to hold more air than when they are chilled. Use a mixing bowl that is clean, dry and the appropriate size for the quantity of eggs or egg whites to be whisked. Use an electric mixer with a whisk attachment for the greatest efficiency, though a balloon whisk can also be used if you prefer.

Eggs and sugar

1 When whisking eggs with sugar, such as for the base for a sponge cake, whisk until the mixture has increased in volume and is very thick and pale. The recipe will usually specify that the mixture needs to be whisked until a ribbon trail forms when the whisk is lifted. This method is sometimes done in a bowl over a saucepan of simmering water so the eggs cook and thicken while being whisked.

Egg whites

1 When whisking egg whites, for a cake or to make meringue, whisk until soft or firm peaks form, depending on the recipe.

2 If whisking in sugar, add it gradually, a spoonful at a time, while whisking constantly. Continue whisking until all the sugar has been incorporated, the mixture is very thick and glossy and the sugar has dissolved. You can check this by rubbing a small amount of the mixture between your fingers.

Icings

Vanilla buttercream

PREPARATION TIME 5 minutes

COOKING TIME nil

MAKES about 1 cup, enough for 12 cupcakes or a 22 cm (8½ inch) cake

100 g (3½ oz) unsalted butter, softened slightly
1 teaspoon natural vanilla extract
160 g (5¾ oz/1⅓ cups) icing (confectioners') sugar, sifted
Milk (optional)

1 Use an electric mixer to beat the butter and vanilla in a small bowl until pale and creamy *(pic 1)*.

2 Gradually beat in the icing sugar, about 60 g (2¼ oz/½ cup) at a time, until well combined *(pic 2)*.

3 Test the consistency *(pic 3)*. If the buttercream is too thick, beat in a little milk, 1 teaspoon at a time, until it reaches the desired consistency.

VARIATIONS

Chocolate buttercream: Sift the icing sugar with 30 g (1 oz/¼ cup) unsweetened cocoa powder. Makes about 1¼ cups.

White chocolate buttercream: Beat in 50 g (1¾ oz) white chocolate, melted and cooled, after adding the icing sugar. Makes about 1¼ cups.

Orange buttercream: Omit the vanilla. Fold in ½ teaspoon finely grated orange zest after adding the icing sugar.

Maple buttercream: Reduce the icing sugar to 150 g (5½ oz/1¼ cups). Beat in 2 tablespoons maple syrup after adding the icing sugar.

Hazelnut buttercream: Replace 20 g (¾ oz) of the butter with 80 g (2¾ oz/¼ cup) chocolate hazelnut spread. Reduce the icing sugar to 150 g (5½ oz/1¼ cups). Beat in 1 tablespoon Frangelico after adding the icing sugar.

Citrus buttercream: Beat in 2 teaspoons finely grated lemon or orange zest after adding the icing sugar. Tint with yellow or orange food colouring, if desired.

Coffee buttercream: Dissolve 1 teaspoon instant coffee granules in 1 teaspoon boiling water, then cool. Beat into the buttercream after adding the icing sugar.

Raspberry jam buttercream: Omit the vanilla. Fold in 1½ tablespoons raspberry jam (not a reduced-sugar variety) after adding the icing sugar.

Nut buttercream: Omit the vanilla. Fold in 1½ tablespoons very finely chopped pistachios or roasted, skinned hazelnuts after adding the icing sugar.

Spiced buttercream: Omit the vanilla. Fold in ½ teaspoon ground cinnamon or mixed (pumpkin pie) spice after adding the icing sugar.

Glacé icing

PREPARATION TIME 5 minutes

COOKING TIME 2 minutes

MAKES about ¾ cup, enough for 12 cupcakes or a 22 cm (8½ inch) cake

180 g (6¼ oz/1½ cups) icing (confectioners') sugar, sifted
20 g (¾ oz) unsalted butter
1 tablespoon water

1 Put all the ingredients in a heatproof bowl over a saucepan of simmering water (make sure the base of the bowl doesn't touch the water) *(pic 1)*.

2 Stir until the butter has melted and the icing (frosting) is glossy and smooth *(pic 2)*. Use immediately.

VARIATIONS

Citrus glacé icing: Replace the water with 1 tablespoon orange, lemon or lime juice and add 1 teaspoon finely grated orange, lemon or lime zest. Tint with yellow, orange or green food colouring, if desired.

Coffee glacé icing: Replace the water with 1 teaspoon instant coffee granules mixed with 1 tablespoon boiling water.

Chocolate glacé icing: Add 2 tablespoons sifted unsweetened cocoa powder with the icing sugar and increase the water to 2 tablespoons.

1 Beat the butter and vanilla in a small bowl until pale and creamy.

2 Gradually beat in the icing sugar until the mixture is well combined.

3 Use a flat-bladed or palette knife to test whether the buttercream is a spreadable consistency.

> **TIP** This buttercream and all the variations can be kept, covered, in the refrigerator for up to 30 minutes before using. If storing for any longer, set aside at room temperature to soften before using. The texture and consistency of the buttercreams will be affected if refrigerated for more than 30 minutes.

1 Put the icing sugar, butter and water in a bowl over a saucepan of simmering water.

2 The icing is ready to use when the butter has melted and the mixture is glossy and smooth.

Shortcrust pastry

A very high butter content and the addition of egg yolk gives shortcrust pastry and sweet shortcrust pastry the characteristic melt-in-the-mouth texture and rich flavour. These pastries aren't difficult to master, but there are a few basic rules to note when making them. The pastry should be kept as cool as possible at every stage of the process — if it becomes too warm at any point, the finished result will be heavy and greasy. The pastry will also become difficult to work with if it becomes too warm. As with all pastries, care must be taken not to overwork it when mixing and rolling out or it may shrink and toughen during cooking. Always rest the finished pastry in the refrigerator before rolling it out and again when it is in the tin(s) before baking. This assists in preventing shrinkage and toughening of the pastry.

1 Rub in the butter using your fingertips, with your palms facing upwards so you can lift and aerate the flour mixture.

2 Use a flat-bladed knife to gradually incorporate the liquid ingredients into the dry ingredients until a coarse dough forms.

3 Knead the dough lightly, just a few times, until it is smooth.

4 Shape the dough into a disc and wrap in plastic wrap.

Shortcrust pastry

PREPARATION TIME 10 minutes
(+ 30 minutes chilling)

MAKES enough to line a shallow 24 cm
(9½ inch) fluted tart (flan) tin or four
8 cm (3¼ inch) fluted tart tins

260 g (9¼ oz/1¾ cups) plain
  (all-purpose) flour
½ teaspoon salt
125 g (4½ oz) chilled unsalted
  butter, cubed
1 egg yolk
2 teaspoons lemon juice
1 tablespoon chilled water,
  approximately

1 Sift the flour and salt together into a large bowl. With your palms facing upwards, use your fingertips to rub in the butter, lifting the flour mixture up as you rub to aerate it, until the mixture resembles fine breadcrumbs *(pic 1)*.

2 Make a well in the centre of the dry ingredients. Whisk together the egg yolk, lemon juice and water. Add to the dry ingredients and use a flat-bladed knife to gradually incorporate until a coarse dough forms, adding a little more water if necessary *(pic 2)*.

3 Press the dough together — it should be soft, but not sticky. Turn it out onto a lightly floured, cool work surface and lightly knead just a few times, until the dough is smooth *(pic 3)*.

4 Shape the dough into a disc and then wrap in plastic wrap *(pic 4)*. Place in the refrigerator for 30 minutes to rest before rolling out and using as desired.

VARIATIONS

Parmesan shortcrust pastry: After rubbing in butter, add 35 g (1¼ oz/⅓ cup) finely grated parmesan cheese.

Herb shortcrust pastry: After rubbing in the butter, add 1 tablespoon finely chopped chives and 1 tablespoon finely chopped basil leaves.

Sweet shortcrust pastry

PREPARATION TIME 10 minutes
(+ 30 minutes chilling)

MAKES enough to line a shallow 24 cm
(9½ inch) fluted tart (flan) tin, four
8 cm (3¼ inch) fluted tart tins or
24 patty pan holes

225 g (8 oz/1½ cups) plain
  (all-purpose) flour
30 g (1 oz/¼ cup) icing (confectioners')
  sugar
½ teaspoon salt
125 g (4½ oz) chilled unsalted butter,
  cubed
1 egg, lightly whisked
Chilled water (optional)

1 Sift the flour, icing sugar and salt together into a large bowl. With your palms facing upwards, use your fingertips to rub in the butter, lifting the flour mixture up as you rub to aerate it, until the mixture resembles fine breadcrumbs *(pic 1)*.

2 Make a well in the centre of the dry ingredients. Add the whisked egg and use a flat-bladed knife to gradually incorporate until a coarse dough forms, adding a little water if necessary *(pic 2)*.

3 Press the dough together — it should be soft, but not sticky. Turn it out onto a lightly floured, cool work surface and lightly knead a few times, until the dough is smooth *(pic 3)*.

4 Shape the dough into a disc and then wrap in plastic wrap *(pic 4)*. Place in the refrigerator for 30 minutes to rest before rolling out and using as desired.

VARIATIONS

Almond shortcrust pastry: Replace 75 g (2¾ oz/½ cup) of the flour with 50 g (1¾ oz/½ cup) almond meal and reduce the butter to 100 g (3½ oz).

Brown sugar shortcrust pastry: Replace the icing sugar with 65 g (2¼ oz/⅓ cup, lightly packed) light brown sugar.

TIP Both shortcrust pastries can be made up to 3 days in advance and stored, wrapped in plastic wrap, in the refrigerator. Set aside at room temperature to soften slightly before rolling out. Uncooked pastry can be frozen, wrapped well in plastic wrap and then sealed in a freezer bag, for up to 4 weeks. Place it in the refrigerator to thaw completely, rather than leaving it out at room temperature.

Pâte brisée (rich shortcrust pastry)

In pastry making, the rich, crumbly texture and tenderness of good pastry is what is referred to as 'short'. Pâte brisée is an excellent, all-purpose rich pastry that is well suited to savoury tarts and pies as it contains no sugar. It is slightly richer than regular shortcrust pastry, which usually has a strict ratio of 1:2 for fat to flour. The ratio here is slightly higher. You can replace half the butter with lard if you like — lard gives pastry an even more flaky and tender quality than butter and has an incomparably rich flavour.

PREPARATION TIME 10 minutes (+ 30 minutes chilling)

MAKES enough to line a 26 cm (10½ inch) tart (flan) tin

....

250 g (9 oz/1²/₃ cups) plain (all-purpose) flour
Pinch of salt
175 g (6 oz) chilled unsalted butter, chopped
60–80 ml (2–2½ fl oz/¼–⅓ cup) chilled water, approximately

1 Combine the flour and salt in a large bowl. Add the butter and use a pastry scraper or pastry cutter to cut the butter into the flour until the butter is the size of small peas. With your palms facing upwards, use your fingertips to rub in the butter, lifting the flour mixture up as you rub to aerate it, until the mixture resembles fine breadcrumbs.

2 Form the mixture into a mound, then make a well in the centre. Add 60 ml (2 fl oz/¼ cup) of the chilled water and use the fingertips of one hand to swirl the liquid in the well, bringing the flour mixture gradually in contact with the liquid until the liquid is evenly distributed. You will have a ragged heap of dough (*pic 1*).

3 Starting at the furthest side of the heap and working away from you, use the heel of your hand to smear the mixture forward (*pic 2*) in a quick, smooth, sliding action, continuing until all the mixture has been smeared and a dough starts to form. Add a little extra chilled water if a smooth dough doesn't begin to form. (The amount of water required will depend on how dry your flour is and how humid the air is.) You may need to repeat the smearing process two or three times until the mixture comes together smoothly.

4 Gather the dough together and press into a disc, about 2.5 cm (1 inch) thick (*pic 3*). Wrap in plastic wrap and refrigerate for 30 minutes to rest before rolling out and using as desired.

> **TIP** For a richer pastry, reduce the chilled water to 1–2 tablespoons and add 1 chilled egg, whisked lightly with 1 chilled egg yolk, to the well. Add a little extra chilled water later, if needed.

1 After using your fingers to swirl the flour mixture gradually into the liquid you will have a ragged heap of dough.

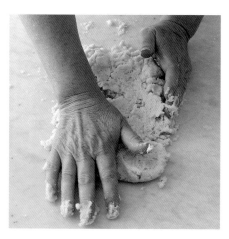

2 Use the heel of your hand to smear the mixture forwards in a quick, smooth, sliding action until a dough starts to form.

3 When the mixture comes together smoothly, gather it together and press into a disc, about 2.5 cm (1 inch) thick.

Pâte sucrée

Pâte sucrée has a wonderful biscuit-like flavour and texture, and is generally used for sweet tarts with fillings that don't require baking, such as fruit tarts. The dough is very fragile and easily over-handled, which makes it too soft to work with. If your pastry becomes too soft to roll, wrap it in plastic wrap and refrigerate for 15 minutes. Avoid using too much flour when rolling, as it can be absorbed into the pastry and make it heavy when cooked. Use a clean pastry brush to brush any excess flour from the dough.

PREPARATION TIME 10 minutes (+ 30–45 minutes chilling)

MAKES enough to line a 24 cm (9½ inch) fluted tart (flan) tin, four 8 cm (3¼ inch) tart tins or ten 6 cm (2½ inch) tart tins

250 g (9 oz/1⅔ cups) plain (all-purpose) flour
½ teaspoon salt
110 g (3¾ oz/½ cup) caster (superfine) sugar
150 g (5½ oz) unsalted butter, cut into 1.5 cm (⅝ inch) cubes and left at room temperature for 10 minutes
3 egg yolks, lightly whisked

1 Sift the flour and salt together into a large bowl. Stir in the sugar. With your palms facing upwards, use your fingertips to rub in the butter, lifting the flour mixture up as you rub to aerate it, until the mixture resembles fine breadcrumbs *(pic 1)*.

2 Make a well in the centre of the dry ingredients. Add the egg yolks *(pic 2)* and use your fingertips to gradually incorporate until a coarse dough forms.

3 Turn the dough out onto a lightly floured, cool work surface. Quickly and lightly knead the dough *(pic 3)* to distribute the butter and eggs evenly, until it is smooth. Shape into a disc and wrap in plastic wrap. Refrigerate for 30–45 minutes to rest before rolling out and using as desired.

VARIATION

Chocolate pâte sucrée: Reduce the flour to 225 g (8 oz/1½ cups). Sift in 30 g (1 oz/¼ cup) unsweetened cocoa powder with the flour and salt.

> **TIP** This pastry can be rolled and placed in a tin, then frozen. There's no need to thaw it before baking.
> In hot weather, it helps if all the ingredients are chilled, even the flour.

1 With your palms facing upwards, use your fingertips to rub in the butter, lifting the flour mixture up as you rub to aerate it.

2 Make a well in the centre of the dry ingredients and add the egg yolks.

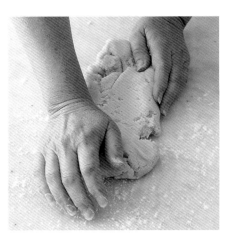

3 Turn the dough out onto a lightly floured, cool work surface. Quickly and lightly knead the dough until it is smooth.

Making shortcrust pastry in the food processor

PREPARATION TIME 10 minutes
(+ 30 minutes chilling)

MAKES enough to line a shallow 24 cm
(9½ inch) fluted tart (flan) tin or four
8 cm (3¼ inch) fluted tart tins

....

260 g (9¼ oz/1¾ cups) plain
   (all-purpose) flour
½ teaspoon salt
125 g (4½ oz) chilled unsalted
   butter, cubed

1 egg yolk
2 teaspoons lemon juice
1 tablespoon chilled water,
   approximately

1 Put the flour, salt and butter in a food processor and process until the mixture resembles coarse breadcrumbs *(pic 1)*.

2 Add the egg yolk, lemon juice and water and use the pulse button to process briefly until the dough just starts to cling together, adding a little

more chilled water to the dough if necessary *(pic 2)*.

3 Press the dough together — it should be soft, but not sticky. Turn it out onto a lightly floured, cool work surface and lightly knead a few times, just until the dough is smooth.

4 Shape the dough into a disc and then wrap in plastic wrap. Place in the refrigerator for 30 minutes to rest before rolling out and using as desired.

Rolling out shortcrust pastry

1 Remove the pastry from the refrigerator and, if necessary, set aside at room temperature for 20–30 minutes or until it is slightly pliable so it can be rolled out easily. Lightly flour a rolling pin and work surface (preferably a cool one, such as a slab of marble, to prevent the pastry becoming too warm). Always roll from the centre of the pastry out to the edges and in the same direction, turning the pastry regularly to ensure it is rolled evenly and doesn't stick to the work surface. Roll until the pastry is the desired thickness, usually 3–5 mm (⅛–¼ inch) *(pic 1)*.

2 It is not necessary to grease a tart (flan) tin when baking shortcrust pastry, even if it's not a non-stick one, as the high butter content in the pastry will prevent it sticking. The easiest way to transfer the rolled dough to the tin is to carefully, and loosely, roll it around the rolling pin and lift it over the tin, then carefully unroll it *(pic 2)*. If using small individual tins, cut a suitable-sized portion of the dough before rolling it around the rolling pin.

3 Use your fingers to carefully press the pastry into the base and side of the tin, making sure it is pressed right into the base edge *(pic 3)*.

4 Use the rolling pin to roll over the top of the tin to trim the excess pastry *(pic 4)*. Alternatively, use a small sharp knife to cut outwards along the edge of the tart to trim any excess pastry.

1 Process the flour, salt and butter until the mixture resembles coarse breadcrumbs.

2 Add the egg yolk, lemon juice and water and pulse just until the dough starts to cling together.

1 Always roll from the centre of the pastry out to the edges and in the same direction. Turn the pastry often to ensure it's rolled evenly.

2 Carefully and loosely roll the pastry around the rolling pin and lift it over the tin, then carefully unroll it.

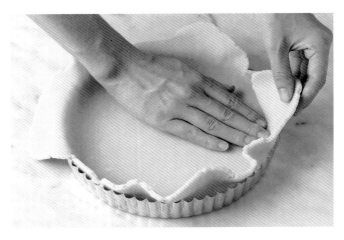

3 Use your fingers to carefully press the pastry into the base and side of the tin, making sure it's pressed right into the base edge.

4 Roll the rolling pin over the top of the tin to trim the excess pastry.

Blind baking

Shortcrust pastry shells need to be partially or completely cooked before the filling is added to make them crisp and prevent them becoming soggy once the filling is added. The technique used for this is called 'blind baking'. The uncooked pastry shell is covered with a piece of non-stick baking paper and then filled with ceramic or metal baking beads (raw rice or dried beans can also be used). The weight of the beads prevents the base from puffing and the sides from slumping during cooking. Whether the pastry is partially or completely cooked depends on the filling you are going to add. Moist fillings that will be baked in the pastry shell (such as baked custard-based fillings or frangipane) require the pastry to be partially cooked. Fillings that won't be baked (such as pastry cream) need to go into pastry shells that have been completely cooked and cooled.

1 Chill the prepared pastry shell until firm — this helps prevent shrinkage during baking. Place the pastry-lined tin on a baking tray. Preheat the oven to 220°C (425°F/Gas 7) or as specified.

2 Take a square of baking paper large enough to cover the base and sides of the shell generously. Fold it in half twice, so you end up with a small square. Fold the square in half diagonally to make a triangle, then again to make a thin triangle with a tail. Cut the tail off,

then open it out — you should have an octagon about 5 cm (2 inches) larger than the diameter of the tin. Place it inside the pastry shell to cover, pressing it gently into the edge of the tin *(pic 1)*.

3 Fill the pastry shell three-quarters full with baking beads, raw rice or dried beans to weigh the pastry down, making sure they reach right to the sides *(pic 2)*.

4 Bake the shell in the preheated oven for 10 minutes. Reduce the oven

temperature to 190°C (375°F/Gas 5), or as instructed in the recipe, and bake for a further 5 minutes or until the pastry is partially cooked and pale gold. Lift out the paper and weights *(pic 3)*. Use the pastry shell as directed.

5 If cooking the shell completely, return it to the oven and cook for a further 8–12 minutes or until golden and cooked through *(pic 4)*. Set aside on a wire rack until cooled before removing from the tin and filling.

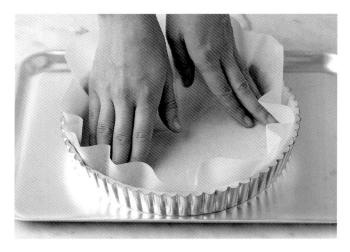

1 Open out the paper octagon and place it inside the pastry shell to cover, pressing it gently into the edges of the tin.

2 Fill the pastry shell three-quarters full with baking beads.

3 Remove the beads from the pastry shell by lifting out the paper.

4 If cooking the shell completely, it needs to be golden and cooked through. Cool it completely in the tin before filling.

Puff pastry

Mastering the art of puff pastry demands no more than practice and patience, but your efforts will be well rewarded. Most commercial varieties are made using margarine and other vegetable fats, and because these have a higher melting point than butter they make the pastry rise more spectacularly. However, the flavour of a home-made version using good-quality unsalted butter far outweighs this. Each time you roll the pastry before folding, it should be three times as long as it is wide. Try to keep the edges straight, using a palette knife to straighten them if necessary. The palette knife also comes in handy for loosening the pastry if it sticks to the work surface when rolled. This recipe gives 81 layers, while extremely fine puff pastry made by a skilled pâtissier can have up to 730 layers! Make sure you chill the pastry between folds, as instructed, to allow it to rest.

PREPARATION TIME 45 minutes
(+ 1 hour 20 minutes chilling)

MAKES about 550 g (1 lb 4 oz)

....

225 g (8 oz/1½ cups) plain
   (all-purpose) flour, sifted
½ teaspoon salt
200 g (7 oz) unsalted butter,
   softened slightly
90 ml (3 fl oz) chilled water,
   approximately

1 Combine the flour and salt in a large bowl. Cut 25 g (1 oz) of the butter into small pieces and add to the bowl. With your palms facing upwards, use your fingertips to rub in the butter, lifting the flour mixture up as you rub to aerate it, until the mixture resembles fine breadcrumbs. Sprinkle over the water and mix with a flat-bladed knife, using a cutting action, until a coarse dough forms. Use your hands to lightly knead, adding a little extra chilled water if necessary, until a soft, but not sticky, dough forms.

2 Shape the dough into a rectangle, about 10 x 15 cm (4 x 6 inches), then wrap in plastic wrap and refrigerate for 20 minutes to rest and firm slightly.

3 Check that the remaining butter is the same pliable consistency as the dough — if it looks oily, it is too soft and needs chilling.

4 Turn the dough out onto a very lightly floured work surface and use a rolling pin to roll it out, always rolling away from you, to a 12 x 36 cm (4½ x 14¼ inch) rectangle (*pic 1*). Use the rolling pin or your hands to shape the butter into a square, slightly less than half the size of the dough, and place over half the pastry (*pic 2*), leaving a border of about 1 cm (½ inch). Fold the edges up and over the butter (*pic 3*), then fold the uncovered pastry over the butter to fully enclose (*pic 4*).

5 Use the rolling pin to gently tap the pastry widthways to form neat ridges (*pic 5*). Without turning the pastry, roll it out, always rolling away from you, until it forms a neat rectangle, about 12 x 36 cm (4½ x 14¼ inches) (*pic 6*). Take care to keep the sides and ends straight, using a palette knife to straighten them if necessary.

6 Fold the bottom third of the pastry over (*pic 7*), then the top third over (*pic 8*) to form a parcel shape. Turn the pastry 90 degrees (*pic 9*), then use the rolling pin to gently tap the pastry widthways to form neat ridges again. Roll the pastry out, always rolling away from you, until it forms a neat rectangle, about 12 x 36 cm (4½ x 14¼ inches). Repeat the folding process, but do not tap to create ridges. Wrap in plastic wrap and refrigerate for 20 minutes.

7 Repeat this process twice; rolling, then turning, then rolling and resting the dough in the refrigerator. This gives a total of 6 rolls and folds (note that encasing the butter in the dough initially does not count as a roll or fold). Refrigerate for 20 minutes before using.

1 Use a rolling pin to roll out the dough to a long rectangle.

2 Place the butter over one half of the pastry, leaving a 1 cm (½ inch) border.

3 Fold the edges of the pastry up and over the butter.

4 Fold the uncovered pastry over the butter to fully enclose.

5 Use the rolling pin to gently tap the pastry widthways to form neat ridges.

6 Roll the pastry out, always rolling away from you, until it forms a neat rectangle.

7 Fold the bottom third of the pastry over.

8 Fold the top third of the pastry over to form a parcel shape.

9 Turn the pastry 90 degrees.

Flaky pastry

Flaky pastry is like a less refined version of puff pastry. It is traditionally used in recipes where lift and delicacy are required but not to the degree that 'proper' puff would afford, such as in pasties, meat pies, sausage rolls, cream horns and fruit turnovers. Large lumps of butter are smeared over the detrempe (the name given to the initial dough mixture), then the butter is layered with the detrempe through a repeated sequence of rolling and turning. The detrempe needs to be rested well before the butter is incorporated or the finished pastry will be tough. It is also important not to stretch the detrempe or the pastry will shrink when baked. If the pastry starts to feel too soft while you are rolling it or the butter starts seeping out, place it in the refrigerator to allow the butter to firm slightly. Always rest the pastry when directed to ensure it remains tender and doesn't shrink when baked.

PREPARATION TIME 45 minutes
(+ 1 hour 10 minutes chilling)

MAKES about 550 g (1 lb 4 oz)

....

225 g (8 oz/1½ cups) plain
   (all-purpose) flour, sifted
Pinch of salt
170 g (5¾ oz) chilled unsalted
   butter, chopped
90 ml (3 fl oz) chilled water,
   approximately

1 Combine the flour and salt in a large bowl. With your palms facing upwards, use your fingertips to rub in half the butter, lifting the flour mixture up as you rub to aerate it, until the mixture resembles fine breadcrumbs. Sprinkle over the chilled water and mix with a flat-bladed knife, using a cutting action, until a coarse dough forms. Use your hands to briefly knead, adding a little extra chilled water if necessary, until a firm and pliable, but not sticky, dough forms *(pic 1)*.

2 Shape the pastry into a rectangle about 2 cm (¾ inch) thick, wrap in plastic wrap and refrigerate for 30 minutes to rest.

3 Turn the dough out onto a lightly floured work surface and use a rolling pin to roll out, always rolling away from you, to a rectangle, about 12 x 26 cm (4½ x 10½ inches) *(pic 2)*. Dot half the remaining butter evenly over two-thirds of the pastry *(pic 3)*, then use a palette knife to spread it out, leaving a 2 cm (¾ inch) border and one-third of the pastry uncovered. Fold over the unbuttered third of pastry *(pic 4)*. Fold the remaining buttered pastry over the top *(pic 5)* to form a parcel shape *(pic 6)*. Turn the pastry 90 degrees *(pic 7)*, then gently press the edges with a rolling pin to seal *(pic 8)*.

4 Roll the pastry out, always rolling away from you, until it forms a neat rectangle, about 12 x 36 cm (4½ x 14¼ inches). Repeat to fold, turn and

seal the edges again. Wrap the pastry in plastic wrap and place in the refrigerator for 20 minutes to rest.

5 Roll the pastry out, always rolling away from you, until it forms a neat rectangle, about 12 x 36 cm (4½ x 14¼ inches). Dot the remaining butter evenly over two-thirds of the pastry and smear as before. Repeat to fold, turn and seal the edges, then roll out again and fold, turn and seal once more. Wrap in plastic wrap and refrigerate for 20 minutes before using.

1 The dough should be firm and pliable, but not sticky.

2 Use a rolling pin to roll out the dough to a long rectangle

3 Dot half the remaining butter evenly over two-thirds of the pastry.

4 Fold over the unbuttered third of pastry.

5 Fold the remaining buttered pastry over the top.

6 The pastry will form a neat parcel shape.

7 Turn the pastry 90 degrees.

8 Use a rolling pin to press the edges of the pastry to seal.

Rough puff pastry

Rough puff is basically a 'cheats' version of puff pastry. Large lumps of butter are tossed through the dough and the dough is then rolled and folded to intersperse the butter through the dough. This results in layers that are formed somewhat randomly and as a result the dough will rise to about twice its thickness when baked, which is much less than true puff pastry. It will also rise more unevenly than puff pastry. While not as elegant as puff pastry, rough puff is a great choice for pie toppings or pastries such as sausage rolls. It is a good substitute when you don't have the time required to make puff pastry.

PREPARATION TIME 30 minutes
(+ 1 hour chilling)

MAKES about 550 g (1 lb 4 oz)

....

250 g (9 oz/1²/₃ cups) plain
    (all-purpose) flour, sifted
Pinch of salt
150 g (5½ oz) unsalted butter,
    cut into 1 cm (½ inch) pieces,
    softened slightly
100 ml (3½ fl oz) chilled water,
    approximately

1 Combine the flour and salt in a large bowl. Add the butter and toss to coat in the flour. Sprinkle over the water and mix with a flat-bladed knife, using a cutting action, until a coarse dough forms *(pic 1)*. Use your hands to lightly knead, adding a little extra water if necessary, until a soft, but not sticky, dough forms *(pic 2)*.

2 Shape the dough into a rectangle, about 10 x 15 cm (4 x 6 inches) and 2 cm (¾ inch) thick *(pic 3)*. Wrap in plastic wrap and refrigerate for about 20 minutes. Do not chill the pastry for too long, as it will make the butter too hard and the pastry will tear when rolled and folded.

3 Turn the dough out onto a very lightly floured work surface and use a rolling pin to roll out the dough, always rolling away from you, to a 12 x 36 cm (4½ x 14¼ inch) rectangle *(pic 4)*. Use the rolling pin to gently tap the pastry widthways to form neat ridges *(pic 5)*. Use a palette knife to straighten the edges if necessary *(pic 6)*.

4 Fold the bottom third of the pastry over *(pic 7)*, then the top third over *(pic 8)* to form a parcel shape. Turn the pastry 90 degrees *(pic 9)*, then use the rolling pin to gently tap the pastry

widthways to form neat ridges again. Roll the pastry out, always rolling away from you, until it forms a neat rectangle, about 12 x 36 cm (4½ x 14¼ inches). Repeat the folding process, but do not tap to create ridges. Wrap in plastic wrap and refrigerate for 20 minutes.

5 Repeat this process once more; rolling, folding and turning, then rolling, folding and resting the dough in the refrigerator. This gives a total of 4 rolls and folds. Refrigerate for 20 minutes before using.

1 Mix with a flat-bladed knife, using a cutting action, until a coarse dough forms.

2 Use your hands to gently knead until a soft, but not sticky, dough forms.

3 Shape the dough into a rectangle, about 10 x 15 cm (4 x 6 inches).

4 Roll out the dough, always rolling away from you, to 12 x 36 cm (4½ x 14¼ inches).

5 Use the rolling pin to gently tap the pastry widthways to make neat ridges.

6 Straighten the edges with a palette knife if necessary.

7 Fold the bottom third of the pastry over.

8 Fold the top third of the pastry over to form a parcel shape.

9 Turn the pastry 90 degrees.

Leavened puff pastry

Mastering this pastry is immensely satisfying, because the results are so exceptional. It's really no more challenging to make than puff pastry — the technique of rolling and turning the dough to layer the butter and detrempe is exactly the same, only this dough is leavened with yeast and therefore includes rising time. It results in a crisp, buttery, flaky pastry you'll recognise as that which is used for croissants. The croissant, whose name translates as 'crescent', is associated with France but it actually originated in Austria and was introduced to France in the 19th century. It became immensely popular there, and in the 1970s the rest of the world caught on to its charms thanks to the advent of industrial manufacturing methods. However, as with many foods, croissants that are made by hand are far superior.

PREPARATION TIME 55 minutes
(+ 2½–3 hours proving and
1½ hours chilling)

MAKES 800 g (1 lb 12 oz), enough to make 10 croissants (see page 312)

60 ml (2 fl oz/¼ cup) warm water
9 g (¼ oz/2½ teaspoons) dried yeast
250 ml (9 fl oz/1 cup) warm milk
1 teaspoon sugar
500 g (1 lb 2 oz/3⅓ cups) plain
  (all-purpose) flour
1 teaspoon salt
310 g (11 oz) unsalted butter, softened
  slightly so it is firm but pliable

1 Put the warm water in a small bowl. Sprinkle over the yeast, then set aside for 6–7 minutes or until foamy. Mix in the milk and sugar.

2 Combine the flour and salt in a large bowl. With your palms facing upwards, use your fingertips to rub in 60 g (2¼ oz) of the butter, lifting the flour mixture up as you rub to aerate it, until the mixture resembles fine breadcrumbs. Make a well in the centre, add the milk mixture and stir, gradually incorporating the dry ingredients, until a soft, sticky dough forms.

3 Turn the dough out onto a lightly floured work surface and knead for 5 minutes or until smooth and elastic. Place in a lightly oiled bowl, turning to coat in the oil. Cover the bowl with plastic wrap and set aside in a warm, draught-free place for 1½–2 hours or until doubled in size (*pic 1*).

4 Knock back the dough with just one punch to expel the air. Cover the bowl again and set aside in a warm, draught-free place for another hour to rise. Knock back the dough once more (*pic 2*). Shape the dough into a thick rectangle (*pic 3*), wrap in plastic wrap and refrigerate for 30 minutes to chill.

5 Turn the dough out onto a cool, lightly floured work surface and use a rolling pin to roll out, always rolling away from you, to a 16 x 32 cm (6¼ x 12¾ inch) rectangle, about 8 mm (⅜ inch) thick (*pic 4*). Take care to keep the sides and ends straight, using a palette knife to straighten them if necessary. Dot the remaining butter evenly over two-thirds of the pastry, then use the palette knife to spread (*pic 5*), leaving a 2 cm (¾ inch) border and one-third of the pastry uncovered.

6 Fold over the unbuttered third of pastry (*pic 6*). Fold the remaining buttered pastry over the top (*pic 7*) to form a parcel shape. Use your fingers to press the edges to seal (*pic 8*). Turn the pastry 90 degrees (*pic 9*). Carefully roll the pastry out on a lightly floured work surface, always rolling away from you, until it forms a neat rectangle, about 16 x 32 cm (6¼ x 12¾ inches). Repeat the folding to make a parcel shape again. Wrap in plastic wrap and refrigerate for 30 minutes.

7 Repeat this process once more: place the pastry on a lightly floured work surface, with the folded edge on your left, and roll, fold and turn, then roll and fold again. This gives a total of 4 rolls and folds. Wrap the dough in plastic wrap and refrigerate for 30 minutes or until firm before using.

1 Set the dough aside until doubled in size.

2 Knock back the dough.

3 Shape the dough into a thick rectangle.

4 Roll the dough out to a 16 x 32 cm (6¼ x 12¾ inch) rectangle.

5 Spread the remaining butter over two-thirds of the pastry.

6 Fold over the unbuttered third of pastry.

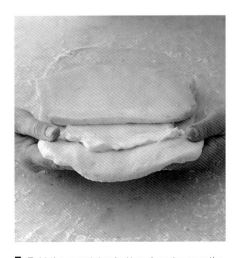

7 Fold the remaining buttered pastry over the top to form a parcel shape.

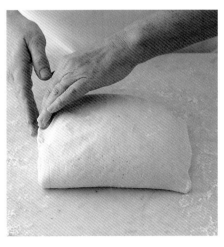

8 Press the edges to seal.

9 Turn the pastry 90 degrees.

Choux pastry

Choux pastry (pâte à choux) consists of a cooked dough, which makes it unique in the pastry world. It is believed that a 16th-century chef working for Catherine de Medici, the Italian-born French queen, created it and then the celebrated pastry chef Antonin Carême used it to make the éclair and croquembouche some 200 years later. Choux pastry contains no leavener, but rises by the action of the steam that forms when it is in the oven. While it is not difficult to make, the pastry's success depends on a few crucial elements: the flour and butter must be weighed accurately; the egg needs to be added gradually because the amount needed will vary according to the strength of your flour and the rate at which it absorbs liquid; and the oven door must not be opened (no peeping!) or it will not rise properly. Choux pastry is used for éclairs, profiteroles, gougères, paris brest, beignets and fritters.

PREPARATION TIME 20 minutes

COOKING TIME 7 minutes

MAKES enough for 12 éclairs or about 30 profiteroles

....

½ teaspoon salt

1½ teaspoons caster (superfine) sugar

125 g (4½ oz) plain (all-purpose) flour, sifted

60 g (2¼ oz) unsalted butter, chopped, at room temperature

3–4 large eggs, lightly whisked

1 Combine the salt, sugar and flour in a bowl and set aside. Put 150 ml (5 fl oz) water and the butter in a medium saucepan and bring slowly to the boil; the butter should melt before it comes to the boil (*pic 1*).

2 Working quickly, remove the saucepan from the heat, add the flour mixture all at once and stir vigorously with a wooden spoon to combine (*pic 2*). Return the saucepan to low heat and cook, stirring vigorously, for about 1 minute or until the mixture forms a smooth, thick mass that comes away from the side of the pan (*pic 3*). Do not overbeat the mixture or the pastry will not rise properly.

3 Transfer the mixture to the bowl of a stand mixer fitted with the paddle attachment and set aside for 5 minutes or until cooled slightly. Gradually add the egg, beating constantly and ensuring it's mixed in well before adding more (*pic 4*). Continue beating in the egg until the mixture is glossy and falls heavily from the beaters (*pic 5*). The mixture should fold in on itself when cut through with a spatula (*pic 6*). You may not need all of the egg.

4 The pastry can be baked immediately, as directed in the specific recipe, or covered tightly and refrigerated for up to 24 hours. Bring to room temperature before using.

TIP To make choux pastry by hand, allow it to cool until warm in the saucepan, then use a wooden spoon to beat constantly while gradually adding the egg, ensuring it's mixed in before adding more. Continue beating in the egg until the mixture is glossy and falls heavily from the spoon.

If making a double quantity of choux pastry, you will need to cool the mixture for longer before adding the egg, as the larger quantity means it will hold the heat well and you don't want the egg to cook. Set it aside for up to 10 minutes and then beat for 2–3 minutes once the egg is added.

1 The butter should melt before the mixture comes to the boil.

2 Add the flour mixture all at once and stir vigorously with a wooden spoon to combine.

3 Cook, stirring vigorously, until the mixture forms a smooth, thick mass that comes away from the side of the pan.

4 Gradually add the egg, beating constantly and ensuring it's mixed in before adding more.

5 Continue beating in the egg until the mixture is glossy and falls heavily from the beaters.

6 The mixture should fold in on itself when cut with a spatula.

Piping/shaping choux pastry

Choux pastry is easy to deal with as, unlike conventional pastries, if you have made it to the correct consistency it won't shrink or toughen in the oven. It does help to use a piping (icing) bag for many choux-based recipes as this will provide the neatest and most consistent shapes. Due to the heat and consistency of the mixture, you will need a good-sized strong bag, available from kitchenware stores.

1 Nozzles tend to be made of plastic and are either plain or fluted. They also come in various sizes. It's best to have a variety of nozzles to suit different recipes.

2 Place the nozzle in the bag, then fold the bag back over one hand to open it out.

3 Spoon enough choux pastry into the bag to fill it about halfway — do not overfill or the mixture could come out the top of the bag.

4 Twist the bag lightly so it feels tight and the pastry is firmly contained. Use the hand you write with to firmly grip the bag where it is twisted and use your other hand to gently hold the nozzle to guide it.

5 Hold the bag firmly and on a slightly diagonal angle, with the nozzle nearly touching the lined tray. Apply gentle pressure with the hand that is gripping the bag to push the pastry out through the nozzle, moving the bag smoothly at the same time to create a line (for éclairs or paris brest). For profiteroles, hold the nozzle directly over the tray and pipe small rounds.

6 When you have finished piping the shape, pipe back a little onto the shaped pastry to avoid a peaked end. If you do end up with ends that stick out, push them down gently with a damp finger. If you need a particular size, shape or length of pastry, mark it on the baking paper in pencil and then turn the paper over before piping. Allow about 1 cm (½ inch) for spreading. For more rustic pastries, scoop up some pastry with a spoon and scrape it off into a neat pile using another spoon.

Using filo pastry

Filo pastry is wafer-thin and requires specialist knowledge and technical know-how to make by hand, so commercial filo is most suitable for home-baking. The sheets are very dry, so filo pastry is always baked in layers, with melted butter brushed generously between each. It is important to work with one sheet at a time and keep the remaining sheets covered with a damp tea towel (dish towel), as the pastry dries out quickly upon contact with air and becomes brittle. Filo is available both chilled and frozen, though the frozen variety is more fragile and can be difficult to work with.

1 Keep the sheets of filo in a neat stack covered with a damp tea towel, within easy reach.

2 Place one sheet on a work surface and brush all over with melted butter.

3 Place another sheet over the top to neatly cover, then brush that sheet with butter. Continue stacking and brushing the filo until you have the number of layers the recipe requires.

4 If the recipe requires you to cut the stack into smaller pieces, use a large sharp knife.

Bread and pastry definitions

Baking blind The pre-baking (either completely or partially) of a pastry shell. The pastry is placed in the tin, then covered with baking paper and filled with baking beads, dried beans or uncooked rice to provide weight before being pre-baked. This prevents the pastry from puffing up at the base or slumping at the side.

Cartouche A round of baking paper that is placed directly on the surface of crème pâtissière, custard and similar mixtures, to prevent a skin forming. A cartouche is cut to cover the surface area exactly, so it is particularly effective. A piece of plastic wrap can also be used.

Crimp A technique that seals the edges of pastry and also creates a decorative finish. It can be done using the tines of a fork or your fingertips (each recipe will specify which to use).

Crumb The technical term for the creamy-coloured, fluffy, soft interior of a loaf of bread, not individual 'crumbs'.

Crust The golden, firm, and sometimes crisp, exterior of a loaf of baked bread.

Detrempe When making laminated pastries (flaky, puff, rough puff, and so on), flour, water and a small amount of fat are initially mixed to form a firm dough, called the detrempe.

Egg wash A mixture of egg or egg yolk and a small quantity of water or milk that is whisked until smooth and brushed over raw pastry or bread dough to give a shine once cooked.

Glaze Applying a liquid to buns or pastries to create a shiny surface. Glazes can be applied before cooking — a mixture of egg yolk and milk (egg wash) is commonly used or it can be beaten egg white or just milk — or after baking, such as sieved, warm apricot jam or a thick sugar syrup.

Gluten The protein in flour that gives baked bread its structure. Gluten is developed by adding water to flour, then working the mixture (kneading) to develop a gluten network.

Greasing This prevents a baked item sticking to the tin or baking tray during cooking. Oil or soft or melted butter can be used and should be applied very thinly to the tin or tray. Sometimes tins are lightly dusted with flour after greasing.

Kneading The action of firmly working bread dough with your hands just after it is mixed to build a network of gluten.

Knock back Using your fist to punch a risen dough to expel air and deflate it. Only one punch is required.

Laminated pastries This term includes pastries whose delicate, airy qualities are achieved by the careful layering of butter and dough, such as puff and flaky pastries. When they are baked, the liquid in the butter converts to steam, which creates lift. The process of rolling and folding the layers of butter into the dough is called 'laminating'.

Piping Forming neat lines or shapes of a mixture using a special piping (icing) bag fitted with a nozzle/tip. Icings (frostings), choux pastry (see page 44) and the decorative crosses on hot cross buns all require piping.

Preheat Bringing the oven to a specified temperature before baking. A properly preheated oven is essential for crusts to form and set, and breads and pastries to rise properly.

Prove The final rise of yeasted doughs before they are baked.

Resting After handling pastry, it is necessary to let it sit for a while, generally in the refrigerator. This 'resting' time allows any gluten that may have formed to relax. Gluten can develop when water is added to a dough, after rolling out dough or when dough is handled too much.

Rising This refers to the time during which a yeast-raised dough is initially left to increase to (generally) twice its size.

Rubbing in Using your fingertips to incorporate butter into dry ingredients. When it has been rubbed in successfully the mixture will resemble breadcrumbs (each recipe will specify fine or coarse breadcrumbs).

Smooth and elastic The feel and appearance of a properly kneaded bread dough. It should feel very smooth and soft and not at all sticky, unless a particular recipe states it should be slightly sticky. It should be very springy and should return to its original shape if you make an indentation in the surface.

Bread making techniques

Bread making is a simple procedure. If you are new to the act of kneading, follow our step-by-step guide and you'll have mastered it by the end of your first loaf. Rising and proving only require setting up — the dough itself will do the work — and knocking back requires little more than a 'punch' and brief knead.

Kneading

1 Place the dough on a lightly floured work surface and shape it into a round.

2 Hold one end down with one hand, and press firmly with the heel of your other hand to stretch it away from you.

3 Fold the dough back on itself, make a quarter turn and repeat the action. Continue to knead for about 10 minutes or until smooth and elastic. The dough is ready when you poke it with your finger and it springs back.

Rising

1 Shape the dough into a ball and put it in a lightly oiled bowl to prevent sticking, turning it to coat in the oil. Cover loosely with plastic wrap or a clean damp tea towel (dish towel). This helps retain moisture and stop a skin forming. Leave in a warm, draught-free place (around 30°C/86°F is ideal) to allow it to rise. Do not put the dough in a very hot environment in an attempt to speed up the rising process, as it will give an unpleasant flavour and may damage the yeast action.

2 When the dough is ready it should be doubled in size and won't spring back when poked with a finger. This will usually take about 1 hour, but each recipe will vary.

Knocking back

TIP After proving, enriched breads are often glazed with an egg wash or milk and sometimes, if sweet, sprinkled with sugar. Some savoury breads may be glazed and sprinkled with seeds, spices or dried herbs.

1 After proving, knock back the dough by punching it once with your fist to expel the air. Knead briefly for 1 minute or until smooth, to expel any air bubbles that have formed during rising and even out the texture of the finished bread.

2 Knead in any extra ingredients, such as dried fruits, if specified. Shape the dough — either free-form on a tray or placed in a prepared tin.

Proving

This is the final rise before a loaf is baked and is always carried out once the loaf is shaped. During this time the uncooked loaves or rolls nearly assume their final size, though they will rise more in the oven. This rise is generally not as long as the first, as the gluten strands are already quite stretched.

1 During proving, cover the dough with a damp tea towel (dish towel) or plastic wrap to prevent the surface drying out.

2 The dough is ready for baking if it springs about halfway back when you poke it and it feels very soft. Do not over-prove bread, or it will develop large holes during baking and the crust may collapse.

Using a bread maker

The recipes in this book have been developed to be made by hand. Bread-making machines vary in their capacity, depending on the brand, so these recipes may not be suitable for your machine. You can adapt a recipe so it will work in a bread maker by calculating the amount of flour your machine ideally requires, then calculating the correct ratios of the other ingredients accordingly. You'll also need to take into account that bread makers specify a strict order for adding ingredients, which may differ to the recipe you're converting, so the method may also require modification.

Nuts

Toasting nuts

Many dessert recipes using nuts require them to be toasted before using — it enhances their flavour and makes them slightly crunchier. Some nuts can be bought 'dry roasted', but it is easy to toast almonds, hazelnuts, macadamias, pecans, pistachios or pine nuts yourself.

1 Preheat the oven to 180°C (350°F/ Gas 4). Spread the raw nuts over a baking tray and cook for 6–10 minutes, shaking the tray occasionally to toast them evenly, until they are aromatic and lightly golden. Coconut can also be toasted this way.

Skinning hazelnuts

After toasting hazelnuts, you will need to remove their papery skins to make them more palatable.

1 Immediately wrap the warm hazelnuts, straight after they have been toasted, in a clean tea towel (dish towel). Rub with the palms of your hands to remove as much of the skin as possible. Open the tea towel and remove any remaining loosened skins with your fingernails.

Making nut meal

Almond meal and hazelnut meal can be bought ready-made, but it takes very little time to grind up a batch of nut meal at home.

1 Place raw or toasted nuts in the bowl of a food processor. If grinding a small quantity, it is best to use a small processor for efficiency. Use the pulse button to briefly process the nuts until they resemble fine, even breadcrumbs. Be careful not to overprocess — the natural oils in the nuts will be released during grinding and if processed for too long the nut meal will turn into a nut butter.

Chocolate decorations

Chocolate curls

1 Wrap a strip of non-stick baking paper around a block of chocolate as a barrier between your hands and the chocolate to help prevent it melting while you hold it.

2 Use a vegetable peeler to shave curls from the chocolate (the wider the blade, the larger the curls will be). Catch them on a plate or non-stick baking paper and refrigerate until required. Alternatively, do this directly over the dessert just before serving.

Chocolate scrolls and shards

1 Pour melted chocolate onto a flat, hard surface, such as a baking tray or marble benchtop, then use a palette knife to quickly spread it as evenly as possible until it is about the thickness of thick cardboard. If the chocolate is too thick, it won't roll. Leave the chocolate until almost set.

2 Holding a large sharp knife with both hands, blade facing away from you and on a 45 degree angle, gently and slowly push it along the chocolate to form thin scrolls. You can also use a metal pastry scraper. If the chocolate is warm and hasn't set enough, it will simply stick to the knife or scraper.

3 As the chocolate cools and hardens, shards will form instead of scrolls. If the chocolate hardens too much before you are finished, dip the knife in hot water and then dry it thoroughly before using.

Caramel

Caramel is used as the foundation of numerous desserts, from rich caramel sauces to brittle nut pralines and for dressing fruit in a crunchy, sweet coating. Follow our step-by-step recipe below for perfect results every time.

Making caramel

1 Combine sugar and water (usually in a 4:1 ratio) in a small saucepan and stir over medium heat until the sugar dissolves. Don't allow it to boil before the sugar is completely dissolved or it will crystallise.

2 Wash down the side of the pan with a pastry brush dipped in water. This will remove any sugar crystals that have formed there. If you leave them, they may cause the mixture to crystallise later.

3 Increase the heat slightly and bring to the boil. Boil the syrup without stirring, as stirring at this stage can also cause the mixture to crystallise.

4 Boil the mixture, washing down the side of the pan occasionally to prevent sugar crystals forming, until it starts to turn a caramel colour. Continue to cook, swirling the pan once or twice, until the caramel is evenly coloured.

5 Watch the syrup closely as it will change colour quickly at this stage. When it's ready it should be a rich caramel colour — the darker the colour, the more intense the caramel flavour will be.

6 When the caramel reaches the desired colour immediately remove the pan from the heat and place it in a sink or large bowl of cold water to stop the cooking process. Allow the bubbles on the surface to subside and then use immediately, as directed.

Making praline

Praline is usually made with the same quantity of nuts (such as almonds or hazelnuts) and sugar. Toasted nuts will give a better final flavour than raw nuts. Praline is usually ground to fine crumbs in a food processor, but it can also be used roughly chopped or broken into shards.

1 Brush a baking tray with a little oil to grease or line with non-stick baking paper. Place the nuts in a single layer on the tray, loosely together.

2 Make the caramel as directed on the opposite page. When the bubbles subside, pour the caramel over the nuts to cover. Set aside until the caramel cools and sets, then break the praline into small pieces.

3 Place the praline pieces in a food processor (working in small batches is best) and use the pulse button to process briefly until the mixture reaches the desired consistency. Use as directed.

Caramel-coated fruits

This is a simple, yet effective, way to dress up berries, cherries, grapes or sliced fruits, to use as a decoration for your desserts. They also make a lovely sweet treat for kids.

1 Make a light caramel as directed on the opposite page. Hold onto the stems of the fruits if possible (this works well for fruits such as grapes), or secure them to a skewer or a fork to make dipping easy. Dip the fruits, one at a time, in the caramel. Allow any excess caramel to drain off and then transfer to a lightly greased wire rack to cool and set.

TIP Take care when making caramel as the concentrated sugar mixture reaches very high temperatures and can cause intense burns. Handle the pan and its contents with care, and never leave the pan unattended or within reach of children.

Citrus

Making candied citrus zest

An attractive and tasty way to decorate desserts, candied citrus zest can be made using orange, lemon and lime zest. It takes just over an hour to make and all you need is zest, sugar and water.

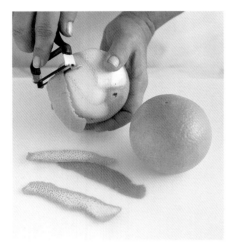

1 Wash the fruit well, then use a vegetable peeler to remove the zest in long strips.

2 Use a small sharp knife to remove any white pith from the zest.

3 The zest can be left in wide strips or shredded finely lengthways with the knife (try to keep the strips an even thickness).

4 Add the zest to a saucepan of simmering water and cook for 2 minutes — this will remove any residual bitterness. Remove using a slotted spoon and drain well.

5 Combine equal amounts of sugar and water in a small saucepan and stir over low heat until the sugar dissolves. Bring to a simmer, add the citrus zest and simmer for 10 minutes or until the mixture is syrupy and the zest is translucent.

6 Use a fork to remove the zest from the syrup and place on a wire rack. Set aside at room temperature for about 1 hour to drain and dry slightly. Use as desired. Candied citrus zest will keep in an airtight container in a cool, dry place for up to 2 days.

Segmenting citrus

Citrus fruits are sometimes segmented when used in fruit salads and citrus desserts. This is an easy technique to master, and the results are impressive.

1 Use a small sharp knife to remove the skin and pith from the fruit.

2 Cut down the side of a fruit segment, cutting as close to the membrane that divides the segments as possible.

3 Cut down the other side of the segment and remove it. Repeat with the remaining segments until they are all removed.

Removing zest from citrus fruit

Citrus zest can be removed in a number of ways, depending on how it is to be used in a recipe. Take care to only remove the very top layer of zest so you don't include any bitter white pith.

Fine-toothed perforations on box graters and Microplanes will produce very fine, almost powder-like, pieces. To prevent zest getting stuck between the holes, cover the grater with non-stick baking paper before grating.

Fine shredding perforations on box graters and Microplanes are usually used for hard cheeses but will effectively shred citrus zest.

A zesting tool will remove citrus zest in long thin strips, which make great decorations.

Preparing and storing stone fruit and berries

Peeling stone fruit is much like peeling tomatoes. Do not leave the fruit in the hot water for any longer than a minute, as it will begin to cook and soften. Plunging the fruit into iced water afterwards will prevent the flesh becoming soft and mushy, and will also help lift the skin from the fruit.

Peeling stone fruit

1 Firm, ripe fruit are the best for peeling. Use a small sharp knife to cut a shallow cross in the base of each piece of fruit and then place in a heatproof bowl.

2 Add enough boiling water to the bowl to cover the fruit, then stand for 1 minute.

3 Drain and place the fruit in a bowl of iced water for 1 minute. The skin will loosen as the fruit stands in the water.

4 Peel away the skin, from the cross towards the stem end.

TIP The terms 'clingstone' and 'freestone' are used to describe whether or not the stones cling to the fruit's flesh. Freestone varieties are the best choice when you would like to cut neat slices. If you are unsure, ask your greengrocer for advice on what is available.

Frosted fruits

Fruits such as blueberries, small strawberries, redcurrants and raspberries make great decorations for desserts when frosted or dipped in caramel (see page 51).

TIP Frosted fruits will keep in an airtight container in the refrigerator for up to 1 day.

1 Lightly whisk an egg white. Use a fork to dip the fruit, one at a time, in the egg white, then allow any excess to drain away.

2 Roll the fruit in a plate of caster (superfine) sugar to lightly coat and then transfer to a wire rack to dry.

Storing berries

All berries are highly perishable and are best eaten as soon as possible. If you need to store them however, this is the best way to do it.

1 Pick over the berries and discard any that have deteriorated. Place the remaining berries in a single layer on a tray or plate lined with a double layer of paper towels. Cover loosely with plastic wrap and keep in the refrigerator. Berries should not be washed before storing, as water will hasten their deterioration. If necessary, you can rinse them very briefly and then drain on paper towels just before using.

Freezing berries

Berries such as strawberries, raspberries, blackberries, blueberries, mulberries, red, black or white currants, boysenberries and logan berries all freeze well.

1 Spread the fresh berries in a single layer on a freezerproof tray and place in the freezer, uncovered, until frozen. Transfer to an airtight container or freezer bag and return to the freezer. The frozen berries will keep for up to 12 months. Use frozen, as directed, or thaw by spreading in a single layer on a tray lined with several layers of paper towel and refrigerating overnight or until thawed.

Biscuits,
Meringues
& Slices

Jumbo chocolate fudge cookies

The name says it all. These biscuits are big, decadent and totally irresistible. They'll be a surefire success at a kid's party, will win over guests at afternoon tea and are sure to satisfy sweet cravings. You can replace the white chocolate with roughly chopped walnuts or macadamia nuts if you like.

MAKES about 18 **PREPARATION TIME** 15 minutes (+ 10 minutes cooling) **COOKING TIME** 12 minutes

225 g (8 oz/1½ cups) plain
   (all-purpose) flour
80 g (2¾ oz/¾ cup) unsweetened
   cocoa powder
285 g (10¼ oz/1½ cups, lightly packed)
   light brown sugar
180 g (6¼ oz) unsalted butter, chopped
300 g (10½ oz) dark chocolate,
   chopped
3 eggs, at room temperature,
   lightly whisked
75 g (2¾ oz/½ cup) chopped
   white chocolate

1 Preheat the oven to 180°C (350°F/ Gas 4). Line 2 large baking trays with non-stick baking paper.

2 Sift the flour and cocoa into a large bowl. Stir in the sugar and make a well in the centre.

3 Put the butter and half the dark chocolate in a small heatproof bowl over a saucepan of simmering water (make sure the base of the bowl doesn't touch

the water). Stir over low heat until the mixture is melted and smooth *(pic 1)*. Remove from the heat and set aside for 10 minutes or until lukewarm.

4 Add the chocolate mixture and egg to the dry ingredients and use a wooden spoon to stir until evenly combined. Stir in the remaining dark and white chocolate *(pic 2)*.

5 Roll 2 tablespoons of mixture into a ball and place on a lined tray. Repeat with the remaining mixture, leaving about 7 cm (2¾ inches) between each ball to allow for spreading. Flatten the balls slightly with your fingertips *(pic 3)*.

6 Bake the biscuits for 12 minutes, swapping the trays around halfway through cooking. Leave the biscuits on the trays for 5 minutes before transferring to a wire rack to cool.

> **TIP** To make smaller biscuits, use 1 tablespoon of mixture per ball. Bake for 12 minutes as before.
> Keep in an airtight container for up to 1 week.

Gingernuts

These delicious biscuits, also called ginger snaps and ginger biscuits, are popular in a number of countries so there are many different versions of the recipe. This one produces crunchy biscuits with an intense ginger flavour that are perfect for dunking in tea or coffee.

MAKES about 35   **PREPARATION TIME** 15 minutes   **COOKING TIME** 15 minutes

300 g (10½ oz/2 cups) plain (all-purpose) flour
½ teaspoon bicarbonate of soda (baking soda)
1 tablespoon ground ginger
½ teaspoon mixed (pumpkin pie) spice
220 g (7¾ oz/1 cup, firmly packed) light brown sugar
125 g (4½ oz) chilled unsalted butter, chopped
60 ml (2 fl oz/¼ cup) boiling water
1 tablespoon golden syrup

1 Preheat the oven to 180°C (350°F/ Gas 4). Line 2 large baking trays with non-stick baking paper.

2 Sift the flour, bicarbonate of soda, ginger and mixed spice into a large bowl. Stir in the sugar. Add the butter and use your fingertips to rub it in until the mixture is fine and crumbly *(pic 1)*.

3 Combine the water and golden syrup and stir well. Add to the flour mixture and use a flat-bladed knife to mix to a soft dough *(pic 2)*.

4 Roll 2 teaspoons of mixture into a ball and place on a lined tray. Repeat with the remaining mixture, leaving about 5 cm (2 inches) between each ball to allow for spreading. Use the base of a glass to flatten them slightly *(pic 3)*.

5 Bake the gingernuts for 15 minutes, swapping the trays around halfway through cooking, or until golden and cooked through. Leave on the trays for 10 minutes before transferring to a wire rack to cool completely.

1

2

3

TIP These biscuits are lovely iced (frosted). Combine 60 g (2¼ oz/ ½ cup) sifted icing (confectioners') sugar, 10 g (¼ oz) melted butter and 2–3 teaspoons lemon juice and spread over the cooled biscuits.
Keep in an airtight container for up to 1 week.

Anzac biscuits

A great way to satisfy the troops, both past and present, these biscuits were designed to withstand the long journey to Australian and New Zealand soldiers who were stationed overseas in World War I. This durability, coupled with their slightly chewy texture and caramel taste, makes them a lunchbox favourite.

MAKES about 24   **PREPARATION TIME** 20 minutes   **COOKING TIME** 20 minutes

150 g (5½ oz/1 cup) plain
   (all-purpose) flour
165 g (5¾ oz/¾ cup) caster
   (superfine) sugar
100 g (3½ oz/1 cup) rolled
   (porridge) oats
90 g (3¼ oz/1 cup) desiccated coconut
125 g (4½ oz) unsalted butter
90 g (3¼ oz/¼ cup) golden syrup
½ teaspoon bicarbonate of soda
   (baking soda)
1 tablespoon boiling water

1 Preheat the oven to 180°C (350°F/ Gas 4). Line 2 large baking trays with non-stick baking paper.

2 Sift the flour into a large bowl. Stir in the sugar, oats and coconut, then make a well in the centre *(pic 1)*.

3 Combine the butter and golden syrup in a small saucepan. Stir over low heat until the butter has melted and the mixture is smooth. Remove from the heat. Dissolve the bicarbonate of soda in the boiling water and immediately add to the butter mixture, which will foam up instantly *(pic 2)*. Add to the dry ingredients and use a wooden spoon to stir until well combined.

4 Roll level tablespoons of mixture into balls and place on the prepared trays, leaving about 5 cm (2 inches) between each to allow for spreading. Flatten slightly with the base of a glass *(pic 3)*.

5 Bake for 20 minutes or until golden. Leave on the trays for 5 minutes before transferring to a wire rack to cool.

1

2

3

TIP Honey may be used instead of the golden syrup.
   For crisper biscuits, cook for a further 5 minutes and cool completely on the trays.
   Keep in an airtight container for up to 1 week.

Greek almond crescents

Rich and buttery, with flavourings of almond and cinnamon, these biscuits are traditionally made as crescents, but you can roll the dough into balls and flatten slightly before cooking if you prefer.

MAKES about 38　　**PREPARATION TIME** 20 minutes　　**COOKING TIME** 20 minutes

200 g (7 oz) butter, softened slightly
125 g (4½ oz/1 cup) icing
　　(confectioners') sugar, sifted,
　　plus extra, for dusting
1 teaspoon finely grated orange zest
1 egg, at room temperature
1 egg yolk
1 tablespoon brandy
375 g (13 oz/2½ cups) plain
　　(all-purpose) flour
1½ teaspoons baking powder
1 teaspoon ground cinnamon
155 g (5½ oz/1 cup) blanched almonds,
　　toasted (see tip) and finely chopped

1 Preheat the oven to 160°C (315°F/ Gas 2–3). Line 2 large baking trays with non-stick baking paper.

2 Use an electric mixer to beat the butter, sugar and orange zest in a small bowl until pale and creamy. Add the egg, egg yolk and brandy and continue to beat until well combined.

3 Transfer the mixture to a large bowl. Sift together the flour, baking powder and cinnamon, then stir in the almonds. Add to the butter mixture and use a wooden spoon to mix until well combined *(pic 1)*.

4 Shape level tablespoons of mixture into crescents and place on the trays, leaving about 3 cm (1¼ inches) between each to allow for spreading *(pic 2)*.

5 Bake for 15–20 minutes, swapping the trays around after 10 minutes, or until lightly golden and cooked through. Leave on the trays for 5 minutes before transferring to a wire rack. Dust heavily with icing sugar while still warm *(pic 3)*, then cool to room temperature.

1

2

3

TIP To toast almonds, spread on a baking tray and cook in a 180°C (350°F/Gas 4) oven for 8 minutes or until pale golden. Cool on the tray.
　　Dust the biscuits with icing sugar again before serving to freshen them up.
　　Keep in an airtight container for up to 1 week.

Monte creams

These biscuits are reminiscent of a well-known commercially made biscuit, but with that special home-made quality. You can experiment with the icing used to fill them — any of the buttercreams on page 22 will work, or you can create your own flavour combinations.

MAKES about 18   **PREPARATION TIME** 20 minutes (+ cooling)   **COOKING TIME** 18 minutes

125 g (4½ oz) unsalted butter, softened
110 g (3¾ oz/½ cup) caster
   (superfine) sugar
60 ml (2 fl oz/¼ cup) milk
225 g (8 oz/1½ cups) self-raising flour
35 g (1¼ oz/¼ cup) custard powder
   (instant vanilla pudding mix),
   plus extra, for dipping
30 g (1 oz/⅓ cup) desiccated coconut

FILLING
50 g (1¾ oz) unsalted butter, softened
60 g (2¼ oz/½ cup) icing
   (confectioners') sugar, sifted
2 teaspoons milk
115 g (4 oz/⅓ cup) raspberry jam

1 Preheat the oven to 180°C (350°F/ Gas 4). Line 2 large baking trays with non-stick baking paper.

2 Use an electric mixer to beat the butter and sugar in a medium bowl until pale and creamy. Add the milk and beat until combined.

3 Sift together the flour and custard powder, add to the butter mixture with the coconut *(pic 1)* and use a wooden spoon to mix to a soft dough.

4 Roll 2 teaspoons of mixture into a ball and place on a prepared tray. Repeat with the remaining mixture, leaving about 5 cm (2 inches) between each ball to allow for spreading. Dip a fork in the extra custard powder, then tap off any excess and use to flatten the balls to about 5 cm (2 inch) rounds *(pic 2)*. (You'll need to dip the fork in the custard powder occasionally to prevent it sticking to the dough.)

5 Bake the biscuits for 18 minutes, swapping the trays around halfway through cooking, or until lightly golden. Leave on the trays to cool.

6 Meanwhile, to make the filling, use an electric mixer to beat the butter and icing sugar in a small bowl until pale and creamy. Add the milk and beat until combined. Spread a biscuit with a heaped teaspoon of the icing and spread another biscuit with a teaspoon of jam, then sandwich them together *(pic 3)*. Repeat with the remaining biscuits, icing and jam.

1

2

3

TIP Keep in an airtight container in a cool place (but not in the refrigerator) for up to 2 days.

Almond biscotti

The word biscotti translates from Italian as 'twice-baked', and that's what gives these biscuits their characteristic crunch and makes them ideal for dunking in a hot drink. They've come a long way since their days as a long-life food for Roman soldiers and are now regular fixtures at cafes and restaurants.

MAKES about 60   **PREPARATION TIME** 20 minutes (+ 45 minutes cooling)   **COOKING TIME** 45 minutes

250 g (9 oz/1²⁄₃ cups) plain
(all-purpose) flour
¼ teaspoon bicarbonate of soda
(baking soda)
2 eggs, at room temperature
220 g (7¾ oz/1 cup) caster
(superfine) sugar
1 teaspoon natural vanilla extract
200 g (7 oz) blanched almonds

1 Preheat the oven to 180°C (350°F/ Gas 4). Line 2 large baking trays with non-stick baking paper.

2 Sift the flour and bicarbonate of soda together. Use an electric mixer to beat the eggs, sugar and vanilla on medium speed for 5–6 minutes or until thick and pale. Add the flour mixture and beat on low speed until just combined and a soft dough forms. Use a wooden spoon to stir in the almonds.

3 Turn the dough out onto a lightly floured work surface and divide into 4 equal portions. Use lightly floured hands to shape each portion into a log about 12 cm (4½ inches) long *(pic 1)*.

4 Transfer the logs to the lined baking trays, leaving about 7 cm (2¾ inches) between each. Use your hands to flatten the logs slightly so they are about 8 cm (3¼ inches) wide *(pic 2)*.

5 Bake for 25 minutes, swapping the trays around halfway through cooking, or until the logs are light golden and firm to touch. Leave on the trays for 45 minutes to cool.

6 Reduce the oven temperature to 130°C (250°F/Gas 1). Put the logs on a chopping board and use a sharp serrated knife to cut them diagonally into 8 mm (⅜ inch) thick slices *(pic 3)*. Return to the lined trays and bake for 20 minutes, swapping the trays around halfway through cooking, or until light golden. Leave on the trays for 5 minutes, then transfer to a wire rack to cool completely.

VARIATIONS

Pistachio and dried cranberry biscotti: Replace the almonds with 100 g (3½ oz/ ¾ cup) pistachios and 100 g (3½ oz) dried sweetened cranberries.

Coffee and hazelnut biscotti: Replace the vanilla with 2 teaspoons instant coffee granules combined with 1½ teaspoons boiling water (cool before adding). Replace the almonds with 200 g (7 oz) hazelnuts, roasted at 180°C (350°F/Gas 4) for 10 minutes and rubbed with a tea towel (dish towel) while hot to remove the skins (cool before adding).

1

2

3

TIP It is best to avoid using dark or non-stick baking trays for this recipe as they will add too much colour to the biscotti.
Keep in an airtight container for up to 3 weeks.

Vanilla biscuits

Every cook needs a recipe such as this — absolutely reliable, simple, quick and easy to adapt. You can customise it to suit your tastes, adding different ingredients to provide flavour or crunch. Try our variations, then let them inspire you to create your own combinations.

MAKES about 24 **PREPARATION TIME** 15 minutes **COOKING TIME** 18 minutes

125 g (4½ oz) butter, softened
110 g (3¾ oz/½ cup) caster
   (superfine) sugar
1 teaspoon natural vanilla extract
60 ml (2 fl oz/¼ cup) milk
150 g (5½ oz/1 cup) plain
   (all-purpose) flour
110 g (3¾ oz/¾ cup) self-raising flour

1 Preheat the oven to 180°C (350°F/ Gas 4). Line 2 baking trays with non-stick baking paper.

2 Use an electric mixer to beat the butter, sugar and vanilla in a medium bowl until pale and creamy. Add the milk and beat until combined.

3 Sift together the flours. Add to the butter mixture and mix on low speed until smooth and just combined (*pic 1*).

4 Roll level tablespoons of the mixture into balls (*pic 2*) and place on the prepared trays, leaving about 5 cm (2 inches) between each to allow for spreading. Flatten the balls slightly with your fingertips, then press with a fork in a criss-cross pattern (*pic 3*). The biscuits should be about 5 cm (2 inches) in diameter.

5 Bake the biscuits for 15–18 minutes, swapping the trays around after 10 minutes, or until lightly golden and cooked through. Leave on the trays for 3 minutes before transferring to a wire rack to cool completely.

VARIATIONS

Chocolate biscuits: Add 2 extra teaspoons of milk and replace 75 g (2¾ oz/½ cup) of the plain flour with 40 g (1½ oz/⅓ cup) unsweetened cocoa powder. Flatten the balls with your fingertips, but do not press with a fork. Dip the cooled, cooked biscuits into melted white chocolate melts to coat half of each biscuit and place on a tray lined with non-stick baking paper to set. Dip the biscuits in melted milk chocolate melts to cover a quarter of the coated side and a quarter of the plain side. Place on the lined tray to set.

Citrus biscuits: Replace the vanilla with 2 teaspoons finely grated orange or lemon zest. Flatten the balls with the base of a glass instead of your fingertips, but do not press with a fork. Put 250 g (9 oz/2 cups) pure icing (confectioners') sugar, 20 g (¾ oz) softened butter and 1 tablespoon lemon or orange juice in a small bowl and mix well. Spread the citrus icing (frosting) over the cooled biscuits and decorate with finely grated orange or lemon zest.

Nutty biscuits: Add 60 g (2¼ oz/ ½ cup) finely chopped walnuts or pecans to the butter mixture before adding the flours. Press a whole nut into the top of each biscuit instead of flattening with your fingertips and do not press with a fork.

Choc chip biscuits: Mix in 100 g (3½ oz/ ⅔ cup) chopped dark chocolate with the flours. Flatten the balls with your fingertips; don't press with a fork.

1

2

3

TIP Keep in an airtight container for up to 2 weeks.

FROM TOP: Vanilla biscuits, Nutty biscuits, Citrus biscuits, Chocolate biscuits (left) and Choc chip biscuits (right)

Decorative finishes

Cakes aren't the only baked goods that can be dressed up with a luscious topping or filling. Try these simple ideas to elevate your biscuits to the sublime.

Icing sugar

The easiest way to decorate basic biscuits is to dust them with sifted icing (confectioners') sugar. Use a fine sieve and dust the cooled, cooked biscuits heavily or lightly, depending on the effect you wish to achieve. A light dusting of icing sugar is also effective on iced (frosted) biscuits.

Chocolate coating

Place chopped dark, milk or white chocolate in a small heatproof bowl over a saucepan of simmering water (making sure the base of the bowl doesn't touch the water) and stir until it is melted and smooth. Dip half a cooled, cooked biscuit in the chocolate. Alternatively, dip half the biscuit in one type of chocolate and the other half in another. If dipping the whole biscuit, use two forks (see page 82). Tap the fork holding the biscuit on the side of the bowl after dipping to remove any excess chocolate. Use the other fork to push the biscuit onto a baking tray lined with non-stick baking paper and leave in a cool place to set.

Chocolate drizzle

Melt chocolate in a small bowl as above. Cool slightly and transfer to a piping (icing) bag with a small plain nozzle or a snap-lock bag. If using a snap-lock bag, cut a very small hole in the corner. Pipe or drizzle the chocolate over the cooled, cooked biscuits in a pattern. You can also fill one bag with dark chocolate and another with white chocolate, and then pipe or drizzle alternating rows onto the biscuits.

Icing

Icing (frosting) comes in various thicknesses, textures and flavours. The glacé icings on page 22 are perfect for decorating biscuits. Use a flat-bladed or palette knife to spread the icing over the cooled, cooked biscuits. Alternatively, use a piping (icing) bag fitted with a small plain or star nozzle (or a snap-lock bag with a small hole cut into the corner) to drizzle the icing over. Sprinkle with a topping such as whole or chopped nuts, candied zest (see below), finely grated zest or desiccated, flaked or shredded coconut, if desired.

Candied citrus zest

Serve iced (frosted) biscuits sprinkled with candied zest (see page 52). Use orange, lemon or lime zest, or a mixture, and colour the icing with a few drops of food colouring to complement the colour of the zest, if you like.

Fillings

Make up the filling of your choice, then spread half the cooled, cooked biscuits with the filling and cover with the remaining biscuits. You can use just one filling, such as a buttercream, or two, such as an icing (frosting) and jam. If using two fillings, spread one on each biscuit, then sandwich the biscuits together.

Coconut macaroons

These coconut macaroons will become firm favourites thanks to their crisp and chewy texture, and toasty coconut flavour. Other points in their favour are that they're gluten free, require few ingredients and one batch makes a large quantity. We've included a variation for traditional almond macaroons, too.

MAKES about 35   **PREPARATION TIME** 15 minutes   **COOKING TIME** 22 minutes

3 egg whites, at room temperature
275 g (9¾ oz/1¼ cups) caster
  (superfine) sugar
2 teaspoons finely grated lemon zest
2 tablespoons cornflour
  (cornstarch), sifted
270 g (9½ oz/3 cups) desiccated
  coconut

1 Preheat the oven to 160°C (315°F/ Gas 2–3). Brush 2 large baking trays with melted butter or oil, then line with non-stick baking paper.

2 Put the egg whites in a clean, dry, medium mixing bowl. Use an electric mixer with a whisk attachment to whisk on medium speed until firm peaks form. Gradually add the sugar, 1 tablespoon at a time, whisking well after each addition. Continue whisking until the mixture is thick and glossy and all the sugar has dissolved. Add the lemon zest and whisk until just combined.

3 Use a large metal spoon or spatula to fold in the cornflour and coconut, in 2 batches, until just combined *(pic 1)*.

4 Drop heaped tablespoons of mixture onto the prepared trays, leaving about 3 cm (1¼ inches) between each *(pic 2)*. Bake the macaroons for 20–22 minutes, until pale golden. Leave on the trays for 5 minutes before transferring to a wire rack to cool *(pic 3)*.

VARIATION

Almond macaroons: Whisk 120 g (4¼ oz) almond meal with 220 g (7¾ oz/1 cup) caster (superfine) sugar and 2 egg whites for 5 minutes. Add 1 tablespoon plain (all-purpose) flour and 2 teaspoons natural vanilla extract and whisk until smooth. Add 2 teaspoons finely grated orange or lemon zest, if desired. Cook as directed above. Makes about 15.

1

2

3

TIP You can drizzle the cooled macaroons with melted chocolate to decorate, if desired.
  Keep in an airtight container for up to 1 week.

Gingerbread people

This recipe is a great one to involve kids in — they can tint the icing different colours and use their imaginations to 'dress' their little people. They can even add small lollies for decorations.

MAKES about 10   **PREPARATION TIME** 40 minutes (+ 2 hours chilling/cooling/setting)   **COOKING TIME** 12 minutes

125 g (4½ oz) unsalted butter,
   softened slightly
75 g (2¾ oz/⅓ cup, firmly packed)
   dark brown or light brown sugar
115 g (4 oz/⅓ cup) golden syrup
1 egg, at room temperature,
   lightly whisked
375 g (13 oz/2½ cups) plain
   (all-purpose) flour
50 g (1¾ oz/⅓ cup) self-raising flour
1 tablespoon ground ginger
1 teaspoon bicarbonate of soda
   (baking soda)

ICING
1 egg white, at room temperature
½ teaspoon lemon juice
125 g (4½ oz/1 cup) pure icing
   (confectioners') sugar, sifted
Assorted food colourings of your choice

1 Preheat the oven to 180°C (350°F/ Gas 4). Line 2 large baking trays with non-stick baking paper.

2 Use an electric mixer to beat the butter, sugar and golden syrup in a medium bowl until pale and creamy. Add the egg and beat well.

3 Sift the flours, ginger and bicarbonate of soda over the butter mixture and use a flat-bladed knife to mix until just combined. Use a well-floured hand to combine the dough thoroughly. Turn onto a floured work surface and knead lightly for 1 minute or until smooth.

4 Divide the dough into 2 portions and shape each into a disc. Wrap each disc in plastic wrap and refrigerate for 20–30 minutes or until the dough has firmed slightly.

5 Evenly roll out one disc between 2 sheets of non-stick baking paper to a thickness of 5 mm (¼ inch) *(pic 1)*. Transfer to a tray and repeat with the remaining disc. Refrigerate for 15 minutes or until firm enough to cut.

6 Use gingerbread people cutters to cut the dough into shapes *(pic 2)* and place on the lined trays, leaving about 3 cm (1¼ inches) between each to allow for spreading. Re-roll and cut out any scraps. Bake for 12 minutes or until the biscuits are lightly browned and cooked through. Cool completely on the trays.

7 To make the icing (frosting), put the egg white in a small dry bowl. Use an electric mixer with a whisk attachment to whisk the egg white until foamy. Add the lemon juice and then gradually whisk in the icing sugar, whisking well after each addition, until thick and creamy. Divide the icing among several bowls, depending on how many colours you want. Tint each bowl of icing with food colouring. Spoon into small paper piping (icing) bags or snap-lock bags and seal the open ends. Snip the tips off the bags, then pipe faces and clothing onto the cooled biscuits *(pic 3)*. Set aside for 1 hour or until the icing sets.

TIP Keep in an airtight container for up to 1 week.

Scottish shortbread

MAKES 16 pieces   **PREPARATION TIME** 15 minutes (+ 20 minutes chilling)   **COOKING TIME** 35 minutes

250 g (9 oz) butter, softened slightly
110 g (3¾ oz/½ cup) caster
  (superfine) sugar
335 g (11¾ oz/2¼ cups) plain
  (all-purpose) flour
45 g (1¾ oz/¼ cup) rice flour
1 tablespoon sugar, to sprinkle

1 Preheat the oven to 160°C (315°F/ Gas 2–3). Trace around a round 20 cm (8 inch) cake tin to mark a circle on each of 2 sheets of non-stick baking paper *(pic 1)*, then turn them over.

2 Use an electric mixer to beat the butter and sugar until pale and creamy. Sift together the flours. Add to the butter mixture and use a flat-bladed knife to mix to a soft dough. Gather together with your fingertips, then divide into 2 equal portions. Shape each portion into a disc and wrap in plastic wrap. Refrigerate for 20 minutes.

3 Use a lightly floured rolling pin to roll out a portion of dough on each sheet of baking paper to fit the marked circles. Neaten the edges, then use your thumb and index finger to pinch to create a decorative edge *(pic 2)*.

Place each round, still on the baking paper, on a baking tray. Use a sharp knife to mark each round into eight wedges. Prick the surface with a fork *(pic 3)* and sprinkle with sugar.

4 Bake the shortbread for 35 minutes, swapping the trays around halfway through cooking, or until pale golden and cooked through. Leave on the trays to cool. Cut into wedges to serve.

VARIATION

Shortbread fingers: Roll the dough out between 2 sheets of non-stick baking paper to a rectangle 1 cm (½ inch) thick. Using a ruler as a guide, cut the dough into 2 x 7 cm (¾ x 2¾ inch) fingers. Place on baking trays lined with non-stick baking paper, leaving about 2 cm (¾ inch) between each. Prick the surface of each biscuit with a fork and sprinkle with the sugar. Bake for 20–25 minutes, until lightly golden and cooked through. Leave on the trays for 5 minutes before transferring to a wire rack to cool.

1

2

3

TIP Keep in an airtight container for up to 1 week.

Digestive biscuits

Also known as wheatmeal biscuits, these are made with a pastry-like dough using wholemeal flour and unprocessed bran. Despite their name, they do not have any special 'digestive' properties. They can be eaten plain, served with blue cheese and honey, or spread or drizzled with melted chocolate.

MAKES about 25   **PREPARATION TIME** 35 minutes (+ 1 hour 20 minutes chilling)   **COOKING TIME** 15 minutes

125 g (4½ oz) butter, softened
60 g (2¼ oz/⅓ cup, lightly packed)
   light brown sugar
1 tablespoon malt extract
1 egg, at room temperature,
   lightly whisked
150 g (4½ oz/1 cup) plain
   (all-purpose) flour
150 g (5½ oz/1 cup) plain (all-purpose)
   wholemeal (whole-wheat) flour
1 teaspoon baking powder
35 g (1¼ oz/½ cup) unprocessed bran

1 Use an electric mixer to beat the butter, sugar and malt extract in a medium bowl until pale and creamy. Add the egg and beat well.

2 Sift the flours and baking powder into a bowl, returning the husks to the bowl *(pic 1)*. Add to the butter mixture with the bran and use a wooden spoon and then your hands to mix until evenly combined and a dough forms. Gather together and shape into a disc, then wrap in plastic wrap and refrigerate for 1 hour or until firm enough to roll.

3 Preheat the oven to 180°C (350°F/ Gas 4). Line 2 baking trays with non-stick baking paper.

4 Roll out half the dough between 2 sheets of baking paper to 4 mm (¼ inch) thick *(pic 2)*. Use a 7 cm (2¾ inch) cutter to cut out the biscuits and place them on the lined trays *(pic 3)*. Prick the surface of each once with a fork. Repeat with the remaining dough, re-rolling any scraps. Refrigerate for 20 minutes to firm.

5 Bake the biscuits for 15 minutes, swapping the trays around halfway through cooking, or until golden brown and cooked through. Leave on the trays for 5 minutes before transferring to a wire rack to cool completely.

TIP Keep in an airtight container for up to 2 weeks.

Hazelnut creams

MAKES about 12   **PREPARATION TIME** 40 minutes (+ 35 minutes chilling and 1–2 hours standing)   **COOKING TIME** 12 minutes

90 g (3¼ oz) unsalted butter, softened
40 g (1½ oz/⅓ cup) icing
   (confectioners') sugar, sifted
1 egg, at room temperature
185 g (6½ oz/1¼ cups) plain
   (all-purpose) flour
1 tablespoon unsweetened cocoa
   powder, plus extra, for cutting
35 g (1¼ oz/⅓ cup) hazelnut meal

CHOCOLATE CREAM FILLING
70 g (2½ oz) unsalted butter, softened
40 g (1½ oz/⅓ cup) icing
   (confectioners') sugar, sifted
1 tablespoon unsweetened cocoa
   powder, sifted
2 teaspoons milk
1 tablespoon chocolate hazelnut spread

CHOCOLATE COATING
300 g (10½ oz) milk chocolate
30 g (1 oz) Copha (white vegetable
   shortening)

1 Preheat the oven to 180°C (350°F/ Gas 4). Line 2 large baking trays with non-stick baking paper.

2 Use an electric mixer to beat the butter and icing sugar in a small bowl until pale and creamy. Add the egg and beat until well combined. Transfer to a large bowl. Sift together the flour and cocoa. Add to the butter mixture with the hazelnut meal and use a wooden spoon and then your hands to mix to a dough. Shape into a disc, wrap in plastic wrap and refrigerate for 15–20 minutes or until firm enough to roll.

3 Divide the dough into two portions. Roll each portion out between 2 sheets of non-stick baking paper to 4 mm (⅛ inch) thick. Use a sharp knife or biscuit cutter dipped in extra cocoa

powder to cut the dough into 6–7 cm (2½–2¾ inch) squares, then cut each square in half *(pic 1)*. Press any scraps of dough together, roll again and cut out more squares. Place on the prepared trays, leaving about 3 cm (1¼ inches) between each to allow for spreading.

4 Bake for 12 minutes or until the biscuits are just cooked through and are slightly paler in colour. Leave on the trays for 5 minutes before transferring to a wire rack to cool. Line the trays with fresh non-stick baking paper.

5 To make the chocolate cream filling, use an electric mixer to beat the butter and icing sugar in a small bowl until pale and creamy. Add the cocoa and milk and beat until light and fluffy. Beat in the hazelnut spread until combined.

6 Spread the filling over the base of half the biscuits *(pic 2)*. Sandwich with the remaining biscuits. Refrigerate on trays for 15 minutes or until the filling is firm.

7 To make the chocolate coating, put the chocolate and shortening in a heatproof bowl over a saucepan of simmering water (make sure the base of the bowl doesn't touch the water). Stir until smooth, then remove from the heat. Sit a biscuit on a fork and dip in the coating to cover completely. Gently tap the fork on the side of the bowl to drain the excess chocolate *(pic 3)*. Use another fork to push the biscuit onto a lined tray. Repeat with the remaining biscuits. Leave in a cool place to set, then repeat the dipping process. Leave in a cool place for 1–2 hours or until set.

TIP Keep in an airtight container, layered with non-stick baking paper, in a cool place for up to 3 days.

Florentines

Although their name sounds Italian in origin, Austrian bakers are the ones credited with creating this heavenly combination of nuts, dried fruit, honey, butter and spice, finished with a chocolate coating. They're chewy and more-ish, and can be made any size you like (simply adjust the cooking time to suit).

MAKES about 25   **PREPARATION TIME** 20 minutes (+ cooling and setting)   **COOKING TIME** 20 minutes

190 g (6¾ oz/2 cups) flaked almonds
260 g (9¼ oz) dried sweetened
    cranberries or glacé cherries
150 g (5½ oz/1 cup) mixed peel
    (mixed candied citrus peel)
75 g (2¾ oz/½ cup) plain
    (all-purpose) flour, sifted
½ teaspoon ground nutmeg
Finely grated zest of 1 orange
260 g (9¼ oz/¾ cup) honey
165 g (5¾ oz/¾ cup) caster
    (superfine) sugar
30 g (1 oz) unsalted butter, chopped
330 g (11½ oz) dark couverture
    chocolate (70% cocoa solids),
    finely chopped

1 Preheat the oven to 190°C (375°F/ Gas 5). Line 2 large baking trays with non-stick baking paper.

2 Put the flaked almonds, dried cranberries, mixed peel, flour, nutmeg and orange zest in a large bowl and mix to combine.

3 Put the honey, sugar and butter in a small saucepan over low heat and stir occasionally until melted and combined. Increase the heat to medium and simmer until the mixture reaches

115°C/239°F (soft ball stage) on a sugar thermometer *(pic 1)*. Pour over the dry ingredients and use a wooden spoon to mix until well combined.

4 Place heaped tablespoons of the mixture on the lined trays, leaving about 7 cm (2¾ inches) between each. (You will need to bake the biscuits in two batches.) Use the back of a teaspoon, dipped in hot water as often as needed to prevent sticking, to flatten each ball into a round about 7.5 cm (3 inches) in diameter *(pic 2)*. Bake for 8–10 minutes or until the almonds are golden and the mixture has bubbled slightly. Cool completely on the trays.

5 Put the chocolate in a heatproof bowl over a saucepan of simmering water (make sure the base of the bowl doesn't touch the water). Stir occasionally until melted and smooth. Set aside to cool slightly. Turn the florentines over so the flat side is facing up and spread 2 teaspoons of melted chocolate over each. Set aside to firm a little, then use a fork to make a wavy pattern in the chocolate, if desired *(pic 3)*. Place in the refrigerator to set.

1

2

3

TIP Keep in airtight containers, layered with non-stick baking paper, in the refrigerator for up to 1 week. Stand at room temperature for 15 minutes before serving.

Sweet hearts

These pretty biscuits make lovely gifts. The strawberry essence gives a subtle fruity flavour, and you can vary the shape by using any shaped cutter you wish, provided it comes in two sizes.

MAKES about 15   **PREPARATION TIME** 25 minutes   **COOKING TIME** 15 minutes

125 g (4½ oz) butter, softened
85 g (3 oz/⅔ cup) icing
    (confectioners') sugar
1 egg, at room temperature
Red food colouring
Natural strawberry essence (optional)
    (see tip)
½ teaspoon natural vanilla extract
335 g (11¾ oz/2¼ cups) plain
    (all-purpose) flour

1 Preheat the oven to 180°C (350°F/ Gas 4). Line 2 baking trays with non-stick baking paper.

2 Use an electric mixer to beat the butter and icing sugar in a medium bowl until pale and creamy. Add the egg and beat until the mixture is well combined.

3 Transfer half the mixture to another bowl. Add a few drops each of red food colouring and strawberry essence to the first bowl, enough to achieve your desired colour and flavour, and beat well. Add the vanilla to the second bowl and beat well. Divide the flour evenly between the bowls and use a flat-bladed knife and then your hands to mix each until well combined. You should now have 2 portions of soft dough.

4 Roll out each portion of dough between 2 sheets of non-stick baking paper to 4 mm (¼ inch) thick *(pic 1)*. Use a 7 cm (2¾ inch) heart-shaped cutter to cut out shapes from each portion of dough and place on the prepared trays, leaving about 3 cm (1¼ inches) between each to allow for spreading. Use a smaller heart-shaped cutter (about 3.5 cm/1⅓ inches) to cut hearts from the centre of the larger shapes *(pic 2)*. Use a palette or flat-bladed knife to carefully swap the inner shapes, making two-tone biscuits *(pic 3)*.

5 Bake the biscuits for 12–15 minutes, swapping the trays around after 8 minutes, until they are lightly golden and cooked through. Leave on the trays for 5 minutes before transferring to a wire rack to cool.

1

2

3

TIP Strawberry essence is available from most supermarkets. You can substitute rosewater or extra vanilla extract if you prefer.
    Keep in an airtight container for up to 1 week.

Parmesan biscuits

There are many versions of cheese biscuits and these ones are crisp and buttery with a piquant flavour courtesy of the parmesan cheese. They make an excellent accompaniment to a glass of wine and are also a popular choice for a gift.

MAKES about 26 **PREPARATION TIME** 20 minutes **COOKING TIME** 12 minutes

150 g (5½ oz) unsalted butter, softened

100 g (3½ oz/1 cup) finely grated parmesan cheese

35 g (1¼ oz/⅓ cup, loosely packed) finely shredded cheddar cheese

185 g (6½ oz/1¼ cups) plain (all-purpose) flour

25 g (1 oz/¼ cup) finely grated parmesan cheese, extra

½ teaspoon sweet paprika (optional)

2 teaspoons sesame seeds (optional)

1 Preheat the oven to 180°C (350°F/ Gas 4). Line 2 large baking trays with non-stick baking paper.

2 Use an electric mixer to beat the butter in a medium bowl until pale and creamy. Add the cheeses and beat until combined. Add the flour and use a flat-bladed knife in a cutting action to mix to a rough dough *(pic 1)*. Turn out onto a lightly floured work surface and press together until smooth.

3 Use a rolling pin to roll the dough between 2 sheets of non-stick baking paper to 5 mm (¼ inch) thick *(pic 2)*. Use a lightly floured 4 cm (1½ inch) round cutter to cut out biscuits and place them on the prepared trays, leaving about 5 cm (2 inches) between each to allow for spreading. Re-roll and cut any remaining dough. Sprinkle with the extra parmesan combined with a little paprika and/or sesame seeds *(pic 3)*, if desired.

4 Bake the biscuits for 12 minutes, swapping the trays around halfway through cooking, or until golden and cooked through. Leave on the trays to cool completely.

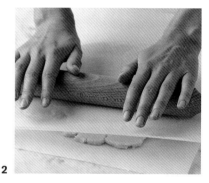

1

2

3

TIP Keep in an airtight container for up to 1 week.

Melting moments

These enormously popular biscuits have a sublime melt-in-the-mouth texture teamed with a smooth buttercream filling. Experiment with different flavoured buttercreams (see page 22) to suit your tastes. You can make regular shaped biscuits by using a plain nozzle in the piping bag.

MAKES about 20   **PREPARATION TIME** 30 minutes (+ cooling)   **COOKING TIME** 12 minutes

150 g (5½ oz/1 cup) plain
   (all-purpose) flour
40 g (1½ oz/⅓ cup) cornflour
   (cornstarch)
180 g (6¼ oz) unsalted butter,
   softened slightly
40 g (1½ oz/⅓ cup) icing
   (confectioners') sugar
1 teaspoon natural vanilla extract
1 quantity citrus buttercream
   (see page 22), made using pure icing
   sugar and orange zest, chilled

1 Preheat the oven to 180°C (350°F/ Gas 4). Line 2 large baking trays with non-stick baking paper.

2 Sift both the flours together. Use an electric mixer to beat the butter, icing sugar and vanilla in a medium bowl until pale and creamy. Add the sifted flours and beat on low speed until just combined, scraping down the side of the bowl when necessary.

3 Spoon the mixture into a piping (icing) bag fitted with a 1 cm (½ inch) fluted nozzle. Hold the nozzle 1 cm (½ inch) above a lined tray and pipe the mixture in rosettes, 4 cm (1½ inches) in diameter, leaving about 5 cm (2 inches) between each *(pic 1)*.

4 Bake the biscuits for 12 minutes, swapping the trays around halfway through cooking, or until pale golden and cooked through. Leave on the trays for 5 minutes before transferring to a wire rack to cool *(pic 2)*.

5 Spread a cooled biscuit with the citrus buttercream and then sandwich with another biscuit *(pic 3)*. Repeat with the remaining biscuits and buttercream.

1

2

3

TIP Keep these biscuits in an airtight container at room temperature for up to 3 days.

Tuiles

The curved shape of these delicate biscuits was thought to resemble a tile (*tuile* in French). For perfect tuiles, you need to ensure the mixture is spread into rounds of even thickness, and the biscuits must be removed from the trays and shaped quickly. For this reason, it's wise to cook only a few at a time.

MAKES 20–25   **PREPARATION TIME** 25 minutes (+ 1 hour chilling)   **COOKING TIME** 7–8 minutes per batch

110 g (3¾ oz) butter
125 g (4½ oz/1 cup) icing
    (confectioners') sugar, sifted
3 egg whites, at room temperature
110 g (3¾ oz/¾ cup) plain
    (all-purpose) flour, sifted
½ teaspoon natural vanilla extract
Nuts (such as flaked almonds or
    finely chopped pecans, walnuts or
    macadamias) and/or finely chopped
    dark chocolate (optional)

1 Heat the butter in a small saucepan over low heat until just melted. Remove from the heat and set aside for 5 minutes to cool slightly.

2 Put the icing sugar in a food processor. Add the egg whites and process until well combined. Add the flour and vanilla and process briefly, until smooth *(pic 1)*. Add the melted butter and pulse until just combined. Transfer to a small bowl, cover and refrigerate for 1 hour or until chilled.

3 Preheat the oven to 170°C (325°F/ Gas 3). Line a baking tray with non-stick baking paper or a silpat mat.

4 Use a small palette knife to spread teaspoons of the mixture into four 9 cm (3½ inch) diameter circles or 5 x 12 cm (2 x 4½ inch) rectangles/ovals using the back of a teaspoon *(pic 2)*. They need to be quite thin and even or the end product won't be crisp. Lightly sprinkle with nuts and/or chocolate, if using.

5 Bake the tuiles, in batches, for 7–8 minutes or until golden. Have 2 rolling pins ready. Immediately use a palette knife to transfer the tuiles to the rolling pins and set aside to cool *(pic 3)*. Repeat with the remaining mixture.

1

2

3

TIP The uncooked mixture will keep, covered, in the refrigerator for up to 1 week so you can make tuiles as you need them.
    The cooked biscuits will keep in an airtight container for up to 3 days.

Secrets to a successful meringue

Here are the 10 commandments that will ensure your meringues are crisp, light and snowy white every time.

1 Moisture is meringue's greatest enemy. Cool, dry days are best for making meringues, not humid and/or rainy ones. Moisture in the air will prevent them drying completely and can make them 'weep' during or after cooking.

2 Egg whites at room temperature are best for making meringue as they are able to hold more air than cold ones. However, eggs are easier to separate if cold so it is a good idea to separate them straight from the refrigerator, then leave them at room temperature for 30 minutes or so before using.

3 Separate eggs one at a time into a small ramekin and then transfer to the mixing bowl. This way, if a yolk breaks into the white you only lose that one egg, rather than ruining all the whites you've already separated.

4 Always ensure your equipment is totally clean and dry when whisking egg whites. Even a speck of fat, such as egg yolk, or a drop of moisture in the bowl or on the whisk attachment will inhibit the ability of the egg whites to hold air and therefore produce good volume.

5 A pinch of salt or cream of tartar added to the egg whites before beginning to whisk will help stabilise them.

6 When starting to whisk the egg whites, do it slowly on low or medium speed until soft peaks form.

7 Add the sugar a spoonful at a time and then whisk until combined. The sugar should be added gradually, but there is no need to whisk for an extended amount of time after each addition. It doesn't need to be completely dissolved before the next spoonful is added.

8 Once all the sugar has been added, increase the speed to high and whisk for 2–3 minutes, until all the sugar has dissolved and the mixture is very thick and glossy. A long trailing peak will form when the whisk is lifted. The best way to test if the sugar has dissolved is to rub a little of the mixture between your thumb and finger.

9 Don't overwork the mixture. Once the sugar has dissolved and the mixture is thick and glossy, stop whisking. If the mixture is whisked too much, the meringue will collapse during cooking and beads of sugar will form on the surface.

10 Often the oven is preheated at a slightly higher temperature and then reduced once the meringue goes in. The initial higher temperature will set the outside of the meringue and then the lower temperature will dry the mixture out without colouring it.

Vanilla meringues

MAKES about 14   **PREPARATION TIME** 15 minutes   **COOKING TIME** 1 hour 10 minutes

2 egg whites (see tip)
1 vanilla bean, split lengthways and
    seeds scraped (see tip)
110 g (3¾ oz/½ cup) caster
    (superfine) sugar
1 teaspoon cornflour (cornstarch)

1 Preheat the oven to 120°C (235°F/
Gas ½). Line 2 baking trays with
non-stick baking paper.

2 Put the egg whites and vanilla seeds
in a clean, dry medium bowl. Use an
electric mixer with a whisk attachment
to whisk on medium speed until soft
peaks form. Gradually add the sugar,
1 tablespoon at a time *(pic 1)*, whisking
well after each addition. Continue
whisking until the sugar has dissolved
and the meringue is thick and glossy.
Whisk in the cornflour.

3 Drop heaped tablespoons of the
meringue onto the prepared trays,
leaving about 3 cm (1¼ inches)
between each *(pic 2)*. Reduce the oven
temperature to 100°C (200°F/Gas ½)

and bake the meringues for 1 hour
10 minutes or until they are crisp and
sound hollow when tapped *(pic 3)*. Turn
off the oven and leave the meringues to
cool in the oven with the door ajar.

VARIATIONS

Rosewater and pistachio meringues:
Omit the vanilla bean. Whisk
3 teaspoons rosewater into the meringue
mixture after the sugar. Sprinkle the
meringues with 2 tablespoons finely
chopped unsalted pistachio nuts
before baking.

Orange and almond meringues: Omit
the vanilla bean. Beat in 1 teaspoon
finely grated orange zest with the sugar.
Fold 2 tablespoons toasted slivered
almonds into the meringue mixture
after whisking in the sugar. Sprinkle the
meringues with 2 tablespoons slivered
almonds before baking.

1

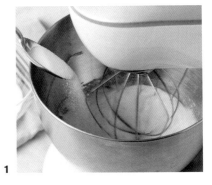

2

3

> **TIP** To ensure egg whites whisk
> to their greatest potential volume,
> use eggs that are at room
> temperature and a clean, dry
> mixing bowl.
>   You can replace the vanilla bean
> seeds with 1 teaspoon natural
> vanilla extract or ½ teaspoon
> vanilla bean paste, if you prefer.
>   Keep in an airtight container for
> up to 1 week.

Espresso meringue kisses

Light and crisp coffee-flavoured meringues with a delectable chocolate ganache filling, these sweet treats are perfect little bites to have with an afternoon coffee or to serve guests after dinner.

MAKES 28   **PREPARATION TIME** 20 minutes (+ cooling and 30 minutes chilling)   **COOKING TIME** 30 minutes

2 teaspoons instant coffee granules
1 tablespoon boiling water
2 egg whites, at room temperature
110 g (3¾ oz/½ cup) caster
    (superfine) sugar
2 teaspoons cornflour (cornstarch)

CHOCOLATE GANACHE
100 g (3½ oz) dark chocolate, chopped
60 ml (2 fl oz/¼ cup) pouring
    (whipping) cream

1 Preheat the oven to 150°C (300°F/ Gas 2). Brush 2 large baking trays with melted butter or oil, then line with non-stick baking paper.

2 Dissolve the coffee in the boiling water and set aside to cool.

3 Put the egg whites in a clean, dry medium bowl. Use an electric mixer with a whisk attachment to whisk on medium speed until soft peaks form. Gradually add the sugar, 1 tablespoon at a time, whisking well after each addition. Continue whisking until the sugar has dissolved and the meringue is thick and glossy. Whisk in the cornflour and cooled coffee mixture until just combined *(pic 1)*.

4 Spoon the meringue into a piping (icing) bag fitted with a 1 cm (½ inch) plain nozzle. Holding the nozzle about 1 cm above the lined trays, pipe small swirls to make 2 cm (¾ inch) meringues, leaving about 3 cm (1¼ inches) between each *(pic 2)*.

5 Bake the meringues for 30 minutes, swapping the trays around halfway through cooking, or until dry to touch. Turn off the oven and leave the meringues to cool in the oven with the door ajar.

6 Meanwhile, make the chocolate ganache. Put the chocolate and cream in a small saucepan over low heat and stir until the chocolate has melted and the mixture is smooth. Transfer to a small bowl. Refrigerate for 30 minutes, stirring occasionally, or until thickened to a spreadable consistency.

7 Spread the base of a cooled meringue with a little ganache and sandwich with another meringue. Repeat with the remaining meringues and ganache.

1

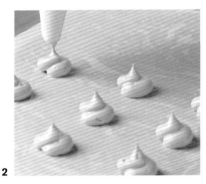

2

3

TIP Keep in an airtight container in a cool, dry place for up to 3 days.

Macarons

MAKES 24   **PREPARATION TIME** 35 minutes (+ 25 minutes standing, 30 minutes chilling, and cooling)
COOKING TIME 36–45 minutes

125 g (4½ oz/1¼ cups) almond meal
215 g (7½ oz/1¾ cups) icing
   (confectioners') sugar
3 egg whites, at room temperature
55 g (2 oz/¼ cup) caster
   (superfine) sugar
1 quantity buttercream (see page 22),
   or ganache filling (see below)

1 Grease 3 large baking trays, then line with non-stick baking paper.

2 Process the almond meal and icing sugar in a food processor until well combined. Put the egg whites and sugar in a clean, dry medium bowl and use an electric mixer with a whisk attachment to whisk on medium speed until thick and glossy.

3 Sift the almond meal mixture over the egg whites and use a spatula or large metal spoon to fold together until combined. As you continue to fold the mixture will start to loosen up. The texture you need is when it falls slowly off the spatula *(pic 1)*.

4 Transfer the mixture to a piping (icing) bag fitted with a 1 cm (½ inch) plain nozzle. Hold the nozzle about 1 cm above the tray and pipe straight down to make 4 cm (1½ inch) rounds, leaving 3 cm (1¼ inches) between each *(pic 2)*. The macarons should soften slightly once piped, spreading to about 4.5 cm (1¾ inches). The peak should also soften, leaving a smooth top. If not, gently flatten the peak with a wet finger.

5 Set aside at room temperature for 25 minutes or until a skin forms. After 10 minutes, preheat the oven to 140°C (275°F/Gas 1). Gently touch a macaron to check a light skin has formed *(pic 3)* and they are ready to bake. On humid days this may take longer.

6 Bake the macarons, one tray at a time, for 12–15 minutes, until they have a firm outer shell. Leave on the tray for 2 minutes, then remove a macaron and check the base is cooked. If it is slightly sticky, return them to the oven for 2–3 minutes and then check again. Cool completely on the trays.

7 Match up similar-sized pairs of macarons. Make the buttercream (see tip). Transfer to a piping (icing) bag with a 1 cm (½ inch) plain nozzle, then pipe onto the base of half the macarons and top each with its pair. Chill for 30 minutes. Before serving the macarons, remove them from the refrigerator and stand at room temperature for 10 minutes.

GANACHE FILLING

Dark chocolate ganache: Stir 100 g (3½ oz) dark chocolate (70% cocoa solids), chopped, and 125 ml (4 fl oz/ ½ cup) pouring (whipping) cream over low heat until melted and smooth. Transfer to a bowl and cool to room temperature, stirring occasionally. Chill for 20–30 minutes, stirring occasionally, until thick enough to pipe. Use a piping bag with a 7 mm (⅜ inch) plain nozzle to fill the macarons with the ganache.

1

2

3

TIP If the weather is warm, you may need to chill the buttercream for 15–30 minutes before using.
   To make chocolate macaron shells, process 1½ tablespoons sifted good-quality unsweetened cocoa powder with the icing sugar and almond meal.
   Keep the macarons in an airtight container in the refrigerator for up to 4 days. Serve at room temperature.

CLOCKWISE, FROM TOP LEFT: Orange buttercream macarons, Chocolate ganache macarons, Raspberry jam buttercream macarons

Brownies

Slightly more cakey than fudgy, this brownie is rich and decadent. Serve it with a cuppa or warm with ice cream and chocolate sauce for a fuss-free dessert. Good-quality dark chocolate, with 50–70% cocoa solids, will give the best result. Try our variations for a twist on this traditional recipe.

MAKES about 15 pieces **PREPARATION TIME** 15 minutes **COOKING TIME** 30–35 minutes

220 g (7¾ oz) dark chocolate, chopped
90 g (3¼ oz) unsalted butter, chopped
4 eggs, at room temperature
165 g (5¾ oz/¾ cup) caster
    (superfine) sugar
60 g (2¼ oz/¼ cup, firmly packed)
    light brown sugar
1 teaspoon natural vanilla extract
50 g (1¾ oz/⅓ cup) plain
    (all-purpose) flour
2 tablespoons unsweetened cocoa
    powder, plus extra, for dusting

1 Preheat the oven to 170°C (325°F/ Gas 3). Brush the base and sides of a shallow 18 x 28 cm (7 x 11¼ inch) tin with melted butter or oil, then line the base and 2 long sides with a piece of non-stick baking paper, extending over the sides.

2 Put the chocolate and butter in a heatproof bowl over a saucepan of simmering water (make sure the base of the bowl doesn't touch the water). Stir often until melted and smooth *(pic 1)*. Remove from the heat and set aside.

3 Use an electric mixer to beat the eggs, sugars and vanilla for 2 minutes or until pale and starting to thicken. Use a balloon whisk to whisk in the warm chocolate mixture *(pic 2)*. Sift the flour and cocoa together over the top *(pic 3)* and whisk until just combined.

4 Pour the mixture into the prepared tin and smooth the surface with the back of a spoon. Bake for 25–30 minutes or until a skewer inserted into the centre comes out clean. Transfer to a wire rack and allow to cool in the tin.

5 Dust with the extra cocoa and cut into squares or fingers to serve.

VARIATIONS

Raspberry brownies: Spoon half the brownie mixture into the prepared tin and spread evenly. Sprinkle with 100 g (3½ oz) fresh or frozen raspberries, then spoon over the remaining mixture and smooth the top. Dust with icing (confectioners') sugar to serve.

Malt and chocolate chunk brownies: Beat 55 g (2 oz/½ cup) malted milk powder with the eggs, sugars and vanilla. Fold 100 g (3½ oz) good-quality milk chocolate, cut into 1 cm (½ inch) chunks, through the brownie mixture before pouring into the tin. Dust with extra malted milk powder to serve.

1

2

3

TIP Keep in an airtight container, layered with non-stick baking paper, for up to 5 days.

Chocolate caramel slice

A combination of crisp biscuit, sweet caramel and rich dark chocolate make this slice a firm favourite with all ages. It's popular, simple to make and keeps well, so it's a great recipe to add to your baking repertoire. Serve it for morning or afternoon tea or as an indulgent after-dinner treat.

MAKES about 24 pieces **PREPARATION TIME** 15 minutes (+ cooling and setting) **COOKING TIME** 45 minutes

50 g (1¾ oz/⅓ cup) plain
  (all-purpose) flour
50 g (1¾ oz/⅓ cup) self-raising flour
60 g (2¼ oz/⅔ cup) desiccated
  coconut
75 g (2¾ oz/⅓ cup, firmly packed)
  light brown sugar
65 g (2¼ oz) butter, melted and cooled

FILLING
2 x 395 g (14 oz) tins condensed milk
115 g (4 oz/⅓ cup) golden syrup
60 g (2¼ oz) butter, chopped

TOPPING
125 g (4½ oz) dark chocolate, chopped
30 g (1 oz) butter

1 Preheat the oven to 180°C (350°F/ Gas 4). Line the base and sides of a shallow 18 x 28 cm (7 x 11¼ inch) tin with a piece of non-stick baking paper, cutting into the corners to fit (see page 123) and allowing the paper to extend about 5 cm (2 inches) above the sides.

2 Sift the flours together into a medium mixing bowl. Stir in the coconut and sugar and make a well in the centre. Add the butter and use a wooden spoon to stir until well combined. Use the back of a spoon to press the mixture firmly over the base of the lined tin *(pic 1)*. Bake for 12–15 minutes or until lightly coloured. Set aside.

3 To make the filling, combine the condensed milk, golden syrup and butter in a small saucepan. Use a wooden spoon to stir constantly over low heat for about 10 minutes, until the mixture boils and darkens in colour slightly *(pic 2)*. Immediately pour over the pastry base. Bake for 15 minutes or until golden brown. Transfer to a wire rack and allow to cool in the tin.

4 To make the topping, combine the chocolate and butter in a heatproof bowl over a saucepan of simmering water (make sure the base of the bowl doesn't touch the water). Stir with a metal spoon until the chocolate has melted and the mixture is smooth. Remove from the heat and cool slightly.

5 Remove the slice from the tin. Spread the topping over the cooled filling *(pic 3)*. Set aside at room temperature until the chocolate sets (see tip). Cut into squares or fingers to serve.

TIP On a warm day you may need to put the slice in the refrigerator to help the chocolate set.
  This slice will keep in an airtight container, layered with non-stick baking paper, in a cool place for up to 5 days. Refrigerate the slice if the weather is warm.

Hazelnut meringue and chocolate fingers

MAKES 24 fingers **PREPARATION TIME** 30 minutes (+ cooling and 2 hours chilling) **COOKING TIME** 25 minutes

220 g (7¾ oz/2 cups) hazelnut meal
85 g (3 oz/⅔ cup) icing (confectioners')
   sugar, plus extra, to dust
2 tablespoons good-quality
   unsweetened cocoa powder,
   plus extra, to dust
30 g (1 oz/¼ cup) cornflour (cornstarch)
6 egg whites, at room temperature
⅛ teaspoon cream of tartar
220 g (7¾ oz/1 cup) caster
   (superfine) sugar

GANACHE
330 g (11½ oz) dark couverture
   chocolate (70% cocoa solids),
   finely chopped
300 ml (10½ fl oz) pouring
   (whipping) cream
75 g (2¾ oz) unsalted butter, diced,
   at room temperature

1 Preheat the oven to 130°C (250°F/Gas 1). Lightly grease 3 baking trays. Cut a piece of non-stick baking paper to fit each tray. Use a pencil to draw a 24 x 28 cm (9½ x 11¼ inch) rectangle on each, then turn over and press onto the trays. Lightly brush with melted butter and dust lightly with extra cocoa.

2 Sift the hazelnut meal, icing sugar, cocoa and cornflour into a bowl.

3 Put the egg whites and cream of tartar in a separate clean, dry large bowl and use an electric mixer with a whisk attachment to whisk on medium speed until foamy. Add the sugar, 1 tablespoon at a time, whisking well after each addition. Continue whisking until the sugar has dissolved and the mixture is thick and glossy. Use a spatula or large metal spoon to fold in the cocoa mixture, in 3 batches, until just incorporated.

4 Divide the mixture evenly among the marked rectangles and use a palette knife or spatula to carefully spread it to the edge of each rectangle *(pic 1)*. Bake for 10 minutes, then rotate and swap the trays around in the oven to ensure even cooking. Bake for 5 minutes longer or until the meringue on the top tray is starting to colour a little at the edges and look set, but is still soft. Remove the top tray from the oven. Bake the remaining meringues for 6 more minutes, swapping the trays around after 3 minutes. Cool on the trays, then refrigerate (still on the trays) to chill.

5 To make the ganache, put the chocolate in a heatproof bowl. Bring the cream to the boil over medium heat, pour over the chocolate and stir with a whisk until smooth. Set aside for 15 minutes, stirring occasionally, to cool slightly. Add the butter and stir until melted and combined *(pic 2)*. Set aside at room temperature to thicken to a spreadable consistency.

6 Place a piece of non-stick baking paper on a large, flat baking tray. Flip a meringue layer onto the new piece of paper. Peel off the top paper *(pic 3)*. Spread half the ganache over the meringue. Repeat to flip another meringue layer on top and spread with the remaining ganache. Place the final meringue layer on top of the ganache (don't flip this layer over). Put a fresh piece of non-stick baking paper on top and gently place a baking tray on it. Apply gentle pressure to the tray to ensure the layers are even.

7 Refrigerate for 2 hours or until the ganache has set. Use a large sharp knife to trim the edges, then cut into 24 fingers. Serve dusted with icing sugar.

1

2

3

TIP Store these fingers in an airtight container, separated by pieces of non-stick baking paper, in the refrigerator for up to 2 days.

Choc-coconut slice

Coconut and cocoa is always a winning combination and this old-fashioned slice is no exception. A classic melt-and-mix recipe using cocoa rather than chocolate, it's a great option for cake stalls, fetes and fundraisers as it's easy to make and doesn't require any costly ingredients.

MAKES about 20 pieces   **PREPARATION TIME** 20 minutes   **COOKING TIME** 20 minutes

150 g (5½ oz/1 cup) plain
   (all-purpose) flour
40 g (1½ oz/⅓ cup) unsweetened
   cocoa powder
295 g (10½ oz/1⅓ cups) caster
   (superfine) sugar
135 g (4¾ oz/1½ cups) desiccated
   coconut
200 g (7 oz) butter, melted and cooled
½ teaspoon natural vanilla extract
2 eggs, at room temperature,
   lightly whisked
2 tablespoons desiccated coconut,
   extra, to decorate

ICING
155 g (5½ oz/1¼ cups) icing
   (confectioners') sugar
2 tablespoons unsweetened
   cocoa powder
30 g (1 oz) butter, softened
1 tablespoon hot water

1 Preheat the oven to 180°C (350°F/ Gas 4). Brush the base and sides of a shallow 18 x 28 cm (7 x 11¼ inch) tin with melted butter or oil, then line the base and 2 long sides with a piece of non-stick baking paper, extending over the sides.

2 Sift the flour and cocoa together into a medium bowl. Stir in the sugar and coconut and make a well in the centre. Add the melted butter, vanilla and egg and use a wooden spoon to stir until well combined *(pic 1)*.

3 Spoon the mixture into the prepared tin and use the back of the spoon to press evenly over the base *(pic 2)*. Bake for 20 minutes or until a skewer inserted into the centre comes out clean. Transfer to a wire rack and allow to cool in the tin.

4 To make the icing (frosting), sift the icing sugar and cocoa together into a small bowl. Add the butter and hot water and stir until smooth.

5 Use the paper to lift the slice from the tin. Use a palette knife to spread the icing over the surface and then sprinkle with the extra coconut. Set aside at room temperature until the icing sets. Cut into squares or fingers to serve.

1

2

3

TIP Keep this slice in an airtight container for up to 5 days.

Coconut jam slice

This more-ish slice is as simple as they come. Pop a piece in the kids' lunchboxes or serve it for morning or afternoon tea, or warm with cream for dessert. Use your favourite jam — mixed berry, blackberry and apricot will all work well, and even orange marmalade can be used.

MAKES about 12 pieces   **PREPARATION TIME** 20 minutes (+ 10 minutes chilling, and cooling)   **COOKING TIME** 35 minutes

150 g (5½ oz/1 cup) plain
   (all-purpose) flour
75 g (2¾ oz/½ cup) self-raising flour
60 g (2¼ oz/½ cup) icing
   (confectioners') sugar
150 g (5½ oz) chilled butter, chopped
1 egg yolk
165 g (5¾ oz/½ cup) strawberry or
   raspberry jam

TOPPING
110 g (3¾ oz/½ cup) caster
   (superfine) sugar
3 eggs, at room temperature
270 g (9½ oz/3 cups) desiccated
   coconut, toasted

1 Preheat the oven to 180°C (350°F/ Gas 4). Brush the base and sides of a shallow 18 x 28 cm (7 x 11¼ inch) tin with melted butter or oil. Line the base and 2 long sides with a piece of non-stick baking paper, cutting into the corners to fit (see page 123) and allowing the paper to extend above the sides.

2 Put the flours, icing sugar, butter and egg yolk in a food processor. Using the pulse button, process until the mixture starts to come together *(pic 1)*. Turn the dough out onto a lightly floured work surface and press together until smooth. Use your fingertips to press the dough evenly into the prepared tin *(pic 2)*. Refrigerate for 10 minutes. Bake for 15 minutes, or until golden brown and cooked through. Transfer to a wire rack and allow to cool in the tin.

3 Spread the jam evenly over the cooled slice base in the tin.

4 To make the topping, put the sugar and eggs in a medium bowl and use a balloon whisk to whisk until combined. Stir in the coconut. Spread the topping evenly over the jam, pressing down with the back of a spoon *(pic 3)*. Bake for 20 minutes or until the topping is light golden. Transfer to a wire rack and allow to cool in the tin. Cut into squares or fingers to serve.

1

2

3

TIP This slice will keep in an airtight container for up to 5 days.

Date crumble slice

With a delicious caramel flavour teamed with dates and oats, this slice is warming and comforting. It's ideal for lunchboxes and to take on picnics, as it travels well.

MAKES about 20 pieces   **PREPARATION TIME** 20 minutes   **COOKING TIME** 50–55 minutes

300 g (10½ oz) pitted dried
   dates, chopped
250 ml (9 fl oz/1 cup) water
200 g (7 oz) butter, softened
220 g (7¾ oz/1 cup, firmly packed)
   light brown sugar
260 g (9¼ oz/1¾ cups) plain
   (all-purpose) flour
½ teaspoon bicarbonate of soda
   (baking soda)
150 g (5½ oz/1½ cups) rolled
   (porridge) oats

1 Preheat the oven to 180°C (350°F/ Gas 4). Brush the base and sides of a shallow 18 x 28 cm (7 x 11¼ inch) tin with melted butter or oil, then line the base and 2 long sides with a piece of non-stick baking paper, extending over the sides.

2 Put the dates and water in a small saucepan over medium–low heat and cook, stirring occasionally, for 15 minutes, until the water has been absorbed *(pic 1)*. Remove from the heat and cool to room temperature.

3 Use an electric mixer to beat the butter and sugar in a small bowl until pale and creamy. Transfer to a large bowl. Sift together the flour and bicarbonate of soda. Add to the butter mixture with the oats and use a wooden spoon to mix until combined *(pic 2)*.

4 Spoon half the crumble mixture into the prepared tin and use the back of the spoon to press evenly over the base. Spread evenly with the date mixture. Spoon the remaining crumble mixture over the top and use the back of the spoon to press down lightly to cover the date mixture *(pic 3)*. Bake for 35–40 minutes or until cooked and golden brown. Transfer to a wire rack and allow to cool in the tin. Cut into squares or fingers to serve.

1

2

3

Cutting a slice

When cutting a slice always follow the recipe instructions as to whether you should do this while it's warm or when it's cooled. If you remove it from the tin too early, it may break or crumble. Remove the whole slice from the tin to cut it up and use a ruler as a guide to ensure even squares or fingers.

A long, sharp knife is easier to use and steadier than a small knife. Wipe the knife of crumbs or other mixture in between cuts so that it will cut cleanly and not drag the slice. Diamond shapes are easy: first make parallel cuts lengthways, then cut diagonally across the pan.

TIP Keep this slice in an airtight container for up to 5 days.

Cakes

Simple chocolate cake

SERVES 12   **PREPARATION TIME** 20 minutes (+ cooling)   **COOKING TIME** 50–55 minutes (+ 15 minutes chilling)

185 g (6½ oz) unsalted butter, softened
330 g (11½ oz/1½ cups) caster
    (superfine) sugar
1 teaspoon natural vanilla extract
3 eggs, at room temperature
260 g (9¼ oz/1¾ cups) self-raising
    flour
55 g (2 oz/½ cup) unsweetened
    cocoa powder
180 ml (6 fl oz/¾ cup) milk

CHOCOLATE CURLS

200 g (7 oz) block couverture milk
    chocolate (see tip), at room
    temperature

CHOCOLATE FROSTING

125 g (4½ oz) dark chocolate, chopped
40 g (1½ oz) butter, chopped
165 g (5¾ oz/1⅓ cups) icing
    (confectioners') sugar, sifted
2 tablespoons milk

1 Preheat the oven to 180°C (350°F/ Gas 4). Grease a round 22 cm (8½ inch) cake tin and line the base with non-stick baking paper.

2 Use an electric mixer to beat the butter, sugar and vanilla in a medium bowl until pale and creamy. Add the eggs one at a time, beating well after each addition. Transfer to a large bowl.

3 Sift together the flour and cocoa. Use a spatula or large metal spoon to fold in the flour mixture alternately with the milk, in two separate batches each. Stir until just combined and almost smooth.

4 Spoon the mixture into the prepared tin and smooth the surface with the back of the spoon. Bake the cake for 45–50 minutes or until a skewer inserted into the centre comes out clean. Leave in the tin for 10 minutes before turning out onto a wire rack to cool.

5 Meanwhile, to make the chocolate curls, use a vegetable peeler (see tip) to shave curls from the chocolate block *(pic 1)*. Use small strips of non-stick baking paper as a barrier between your hands and the chocolate to help prevent it melting while you hold it. Catch the curls on a plate or a piece of non-stick baking paper and refrigerate until required. (You can do them directly over the frosted cake if you prefer.)

6 To make the chocolate frosting, put the chocolate and butter in a small heatproof bowl over a saucepan of simmering water (make sure the water doesn't touch the base of the bowl). Stir until melted and smooth. Remove the bowl from the heat and gradually stir in the icing sugar *(pic 2)* and milk until the frosting is thick and smooth. Refrigerate, stirring occasionally, for 15 minutes or until the frosting is a thick, spreadable consistency.

7 Spread the top and sides of the cooled cake with the frosting *(pic 3)* and decorate with the chocolate curls.

2

3

1

TIP Milk chocolate has a higher content of fat solids and is less brittle than dark chocolate, so is better suited to making curls. Dark chocolate tends to flake. The wider the blade on your vegetable peeler, the larger the curls will be.
  You can replace the frosting with 1 quantity of chocolate buttercream (see page 22).
  Keep in an airtight container for up to 4 days.

Classic sponge

The trick to making a perfect sponge is to use a light touch, avoid overworking the cake batter and ensure it is well aerated. A good sponge should have a light texture and yet be solid enough to support the layer of jam and whipped cream.

SERVES 8   **PREPARATION TIME** 40 minutes (+ cooling)   **COOKING TIME** 15 minutes

100 g (3½ oz/⅔ cup) self-raising flour,
    plus extra, for dusting
2 tablespoons cornflour (cornstarch)
4 eggs, at room temperature, separated
110 g (3¾ oz/½ cup) caster
    (superfine) sugar
185 ml (6 fl oz/¾ cup) thickened
    (whipping) cream
1 tablespoon icing (confectioners')
    sugar, plus extra, to dust
110 g (3¾ oz/⅓ cup) good-quality
    strawberry jam

1 Preheat the oven to 180°C (350°F/ Gas 4). Grease 2 shallow, round 20 cm (8 inch) cake tins with butter, line the bases with non-stick baking paper and dust with a little of the extra flour to lightly coat, shaking off any excess.

2 Sift the flour and cornflour twice onto a sheet of non-stick baking paper.

3 Use an electric mixer with a whisk attachment to whisk the egg yolks and 2 tablespoons of the caster sugar in a medium bowl for about 4 minutes or until very thick and pale and tripled in volume. Transfer to a large bowl. Clean the whisk attachment and dry it thoroughly.

4 Use the electric mixer with the cleaned whisk attachment to whisk the egg whites in a large bowl until soft peaks form. Add the remaining sugar and whisk until thick and glossy. Add to the egg yolk mixture, sift the combined flours evenly over and use a large metal spoon or spatula to gently fold together until just combined *(pic 1)*.

5 Divide the mixture evenly between the prepared tins *(pic 2)* and gently smooth the surfaces with the back of the spatula or spoon. Bake in the centre of the oven for 15 minutes or until the cakes are lightly golden, slightly coming away from the sides of the tins, and a skewer inserted into the centre of each cake comes out clean. Set aside in the tins for 5 minutes before turning out onto wire racks, top side up, to cool.

6 Use an electric mixer with a whisk attachment to whisk the cream and icing sugar in a medium bowl until firm peaks just form. Spread jam and then cream over the top of one cake *(pic 3)*. Place the remaining sponge cake on top and dust with extra icing sugar to serve.

VARIATIONS

Mascarpone and fig sponge: Replace the strawberry jam with fig jam and replace the cream mixture with 250 g (9 oz) softened mascarpone (soften it by stirring gently until it loosens slightly and becomes spreadable).

Lemon curd and strawberry sponge: Omit the strawberry jam and icing sugar. Stir 160 g (5¾ oz/½ cup) of good-quality ready-made or home-made lemon curd through the whipped cream. Spread the bottom sponge layer with curd mixture, top with 150 g (5½ oz) hulled and thinly sliced strawberries and then the remaining sponge cake.

TIP An easy way to divide the mixture between the tins is to use a set of scales and weigh the mixture as you put it in the tins.
    This cake is best eaten on the day it is baked.

Vanilla buttercake

This is a really handy, reliable, basic cake recipe that can be easily adapted to create different flavours. Try our variations, and decorate with your choice of flavoured buttercream or glacé icing (see page 22).

SERVES 12   **PREPARATION TIME** 25 minutes (+ cooling)   **COOKING TIME** 1 hour

200 g (7 oz) unsalted butter,
  softened slightly
220 g (7¾ oz/1 cup) caster
  (superfine) sugar
1 teaspoon natural vanilla extract
3 eggs, at room temperature
300 g (10½ oz/2 cups) self-raising
  flour, sifted
(5¼ fl oz/⅔ cup) milk
1 quantity buttercream of your choice
  (see page 26, citrus buttercream
  pictured)

1 Preheat the oven to 170°C (325°F/ Gas 3). Grease a square 20 cm (8 inch) cake tin and line the base with non-stick baking paper.

2 Use an electric mixer to beat the butter, sugar and vanilla in a medium bowl until pale and creamy. Add the eggs one at a time, beating well after each addition *(pic 1)*. Use a large metal spoon or spatula to fold in the flour and milk until combined.

3 Spoon the mixture into the prepared tin and smooth the surface with the back of the spoon *(pic 2)*. Bake for 1 hour or until a skewer inserted into the centre of the cake comes out clean *(pic 3)*. Leave the cake in the tin for 5 minutes before turning out onto a wire rack to cool completely.

4 Spread the buttercream evenly over the top and sides of the cooled cake.

VARIATIONS

Lemon buttercake: Replace the vanilla extract with 1 teaspoon finely grated lemon zest and replace 2 tablespoons of the milk with 2 tablespoons of lemon juice.

Coffee buttercake: Omit the vanilla extract and replace 125 ml (4 fl oz/ ½ cup) of the milk with freshly brewed strong coffee. Sprinkle the cake with 35 g (1¼ oz/¼ cup) slivered almonds before baking.

1

2

3

TIP This cake can be baked in a round 22 cm (8½ inch) cake tin. Keep the cake, iced or un-iced, in an airtight container for up to 3 days.

Preparing cake tins

Greasing, lining and dusting with flour

The best way to grease a tin is by using a pastry brush to apply melted butter or oil evenly, and not too thickly, over the base and sides. Vegetable oil sprays can also be used.

Non-stick baking paper is excellent for lining cake tins and doesn't need to be greased before you add the cake batter.

Patty pan and muffin tins can be lined with paper cases, which will prevent the mixture sticking while also providing a convenient and attractive case.

Sometimes a recipe asks for a cake tin to be dusted lightly with flour after greasing, instead of lining with paper. To do this, add a spoonful of flour to the tin and then carefully tilt the tin until the flour evenly coats the base and sides, then tap out any excess. Bundt and kugelhopf tins need to be greased and sometimes lightly floured as they can't, for obvious reasons, be lined with baking paper.

Always follow the instructions for each recipe as to how the tin (or tins) needs to be prepared.

Buttercakes and chocolate cakes

You can usually get away with greasing the tin and lining just the base, but it's better to line both the base and sides.

Sponge cakes

Grease the tin, line the base with non-stick baking paper and then dust the whole tin with flour.

Rich fruit cakes

When baking rich fruit cakes, the tins need to have the base and side/s lined with a double thickness of paper and they also need a collar to give extra protection during the long cooking.

1 To make the collar, cut a double strip of baking paper long enough to fit around the outside of the tin and wide enough to extend at least 5 cm (2 inches) above the top.

2 For added protection from the heat, wrap layers of newspaper around the outside of the tin, and then sit the tin on layers of newspaper or an old magazine on a baking tray. The oven temperature when cooking rich fruit cakes is low enough to make this safe.

Lining round tins

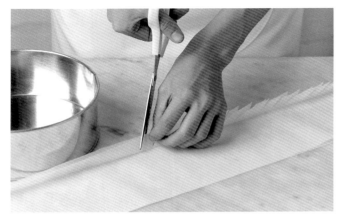

1 Put the tin on non-stick baking paper, draw around it and cut out as marked. Cut a strip of baking paper the same length as the tin's circumference and about 5 cm (2 inches) wider than the height. Fold down a cuff, about 2 cm (³/₄ inch), along one edge and cut it diagonally at 2 cm intervals.

2 Grease the tin. Place the baking paper strip in the tin with the cuff on the base. The diagonal cuts on the cuff will act like pleats and sit neatly on the base. Press the paper onto the base and side, then place the round of baking paper on the base over the pleats.

Lining square tins

Lining a square cake tin is similar to lining a round tin, but simpler. Put the tin on non-stick baking paper, draw around it, then cut out as marked. Cut a strip of baking paper the same length as the circumference of the tin and about 3 cm (1¼ inches) wider than the height. Grease the tin. Place the square of paper in the base and press the strip onto the sides.

Lining Swiss roll (jelly roll) tins

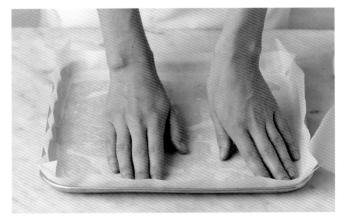

1 Put the tin on non-stick baking paper and draw around it. Measure the tin's depth, add 2 cm (³/₄ inch), then cut out at that distance from the drawn lines all around. Crease the paper along the lines, then cut from each corner to the drawn corner.

2 Lightly grease the tin. Press the paper into the tin, fitting it neatly into the corners. This method can also be used for lining a slice tin.

Rich fruit cake

MAKES 22 cm (8½ inch) cake   **PREPARATION TIME** 30 minutes (+ overnight soaking and cooling)
COOKING TIME 2 hours 15 minutes

160 g (5¾ oz) sultanas (golden raisins)

125 g (4½ oz) glacé apricots (see tip), finely chopped

100 g (3½ oz) glacé orange (see tip), finely chopped

100 g (3½ oz) pitted prunes, finely chopped

100 g (3½ oz) dried figs, finely chopped

100 g (3½ oz) glacé cherries, quartered

100 g (3½ oz) pitted dried dates, finely chopped

80 g (2¾ oz) currants

125 ml (4 fl oz/½ cup) rum or brandy

200 g (7 oz) unsalted butter, softened

150 g (5½ oz/⅔ cup, firmly packed) dark brown sugar

2 teaspoons finely grated orange zest

4 eggs, at room temperature

185 g (6½ oz/1¼ cups) plain (all-purpose) flour, sifted

110 g (6½ oz/¾ cup) self-raising flour, sifted

1 teaspoon mixed spice

125 g (4½ oz) whole mixed nuts of your choice (such as blanched almonds, pecan halves and/or hazelnuts)

1 Combine all the fruit and the rum or brandy in a large bowl. Cover and set aside overnight to soak *(pic 1)*.

2 Preheat the oven to 150°C (300°F/ Gas 2). Grease a round 22 cm (8½ inch) cake tin. Line with 2 layers of non-stick baking paper *(pic 2)* (see page 122).

3 Use an electric mixer to beat the butter, sugar and orange zest in a medium bowl until just combined. Add the eggs one at a time, beating well after each addition. Use a spatula or large metal spoon to stir the butter mixture into the fruit mixture. Stir in the sifted flours and mixed spice until combined. Spread the mixture evenly into the tin and tap the tin on the bench to remove any large air pockets. Smooth the surface with the back of a spoon. Decorate the top of the cake with nuts.

4 Bake the cake in the centre of the oven for 2¼ hours or until a skewer inserted into the centre of the cake comes out clean. Check the cake after 1¾ hours and if it is browning too much on top, cover loosely with a piece of foil. Remove from the oven, cover the top with non-stick baking paper, wrap firmly in foil to seal, then wrap the cake and tin in a clean tea towel (dish towel) *(pic 3)* and leave to cool. (This will help the cake remain moist.) Unwrap and remove from the tin when cooled.

TIP Glacé orange and apricots can be found at health food stores. You can replace them with mixed peel (mixed candied citrus peel) and dried apricots, respectively, if you prefer.
Keep this cake wrapped in foil and stored in an airtight container in a cool place for up to 6 weeks.

Passionfruit genoise

SERVES 8–10   **PREPARATION TIME** 1 hour (+ cooling)   **COOKING TIME** 35 minutes

165 g (5¾ oz) plain (all-purpose) flour

6 eggs, at room temperature

165 g (5¾ oz/¾ cup) caster
(superfine) sugar

30 g (1 oz) butter, melted and cooled

125 ml (4 fl oz/½ cup) thickened
(whipping) cream

1 teaspoon icing (confectioners') sugar

100 g (3½ oz) flaked almonds, toasted,
to decorate

Icing (confectioners') sugar, to dust

ORANGE LIQUEUR SYRUP

55 g (2 oz/¼ cup) caster
(superfine) sugar

1 tablespoon orange liqueur
(such as Cointreau)

PASSIONFRUIT CREAM

185 ml (6 fl oz/¾ cup) thickened
(whipping) cream

1 tablespoon icing (confectioners')
sugar

120 g (4¼ oz/½ cup) fresh
passionfruit pulp (see tip)

1 Preheat the oven to 160°C (315°F/
Gas 2–3). Grease a deep, round 20 cm
(8 inch) cake tin with butter and dust
with flour, shaking off any excess.

2 Sift the flour twice onto baking
paper. Use hand-held electric beaters
with a whisk attachment to whisk the
eggs and caster sugar in a large heatproof
bowl until combined. Put the bowl over
a saucepan of simmering water (make
sure the base doesn't touch the water)
and whisk on high speed for 10 minutes
or until very thick and pale and a ribbon
trail forms when the beaters are lifted
(pic 1). Remove the bowl from the pan.

3 Working quickly and lightly, drizzle
the butter evenly over the egg mixture.
Add half the flour, sprinkling it from

the paper as evenly as possible *(pic 2)*.
Use a spatula or large metal spoon to
fold in the butter and flour quickly and
lightly until just combined. Repeat with
the remaining flour until just combined.

4 Pour into the prepared tin and use
the back of a spatula or spoon to smooth
the surface. Bake for 35 minutes or until
lightly golden, slightly coming away
from the side of the tin, and a skewer
inserted into the centre comes out clean.
Cool for 5 minutes in the tin, then turn
out onto a wire rack to cool completely.

5 To make the orange liqueur syrup,
stir the sugar and 80 ml (2½ fl oz/⅓ cup)
water in a saucepan over low heat until
the sugar dissolves. Bring to the boil,
then remove from the heat and cool to
room temperature. Stir in the liqueur.

6 To make the passionfruit cream,
use an electric mixer with a whisk
attachment to whisk the cream and
icing sugar in a medium bowl until
firm peaks form. Gently fold in the
passionfruit pulp.

7 Use a serrated knife to cut the cake
evenly into 3 layers (see page 131). Use
a pastry brush to brush the bottom
layer with half the syrup. Spread with
half the passionfruit cream. Place the
middle layer on top and brush with the
remaining syrup *(pic 3)*. Spread with the
remaining passionfruit cream and cover
with the top layer.

8 Use an electric mixer with a whisk
attachment to whisk the cream and
icing sugar until firm peaks form. Use
a palette knife to spread over the side of
the cake. Press the flaked almonds onto
the cream around the side to decorate.
Dust the top with icing sugar.

1

2

3

TIP You will need between
6 to 8 average-sized passionfruit
to produce the required amount of
passionfruit pulp.
  This cake is best eaten on the
day it is baked and assembled.

Pound cake

Traditionally, a pound cake is made using equal weights of flour, butter, sugar and eggs, which is a great help for those who need to make a cake by memory. This version has slightly different proportions, resulting in a buttery, moist cake that keeps well.

SERVES 8   **PREPARATION TIME** 25 minutes   **COOKING TIME** 50 minutes

185 g (6½ oz) unsalted butter, softened slightly
165 g (5½ oz/¾ cup) caster (superfine) sugar
1 teaspoon natural vanilla extract
3 eggs, at room temperature
100 g (3½ oz/⅔ cup) plain (all-purpose) flour
75 g (2¾ oz/½ cup) self-raising flour
60 ml (2 fl oz/¼ cup) milk
Icing (confectioners') sugar, to dust

1 Preheat oven to 180°C (350°F/Gas 4). Grease an 8 x 19 cm (3¼ x 7½ inch) loaf (bar) tin with melted butter or oil and line the base and 2 long sides with a piece of non-stick baking paper, extending over the sides *(pic 1)*.

2 Use an electric mixer to beat the butter, sugar and vanilla in a mixing bowl until pale and creamy *(pic 2)*. Add the eggs one at a time, beating well after each addition. Transfer to a large bowl. Sift together the flours. Use a large metal spoon to fold in the sifted flours alternately with the milk, in two separate batches each, until just combined and smooth *(pic 3)*.

3 Spoon the mixture into the prepared tin and smooth the surface with the back of the spoon. Bake the cake for 45–50 minutes or until a skewer inserted into the centre comes out clean. Leave the cake in the tin for 10 minutes, then turn out onto a wire rack to cool. Serve lightly dusted with icing sugar.

VARIATION

Marble cake: At the end of step 2, divide the cake batter evenly among 3 bowls. Mix a few drops of pink food colouring into the first bowl and 1 tablespoon sifted unsweetened cocoa powder into the second bowl. Leave the third bowl plain. Drop spoonfuls of each mixture alternately into the prepared tin. Use a palette knife to lightly swirl the mixtures together. Bake as directed above. Dust the cooled cake with icing sugar or spread with 1 quantity of chocolate buttercream (see page 22) to serve.

1

2

3

TIP Keep this cake in an airtight container for up to 4 days.

Handling cakes

Removing cakes from tins

Some cakes, such as angel food cakes, are left to cool in the tin completely so they don't shrink or collapse. Rich fruit cakes are also left to cool in the tin to keep them moist. However, most cakes are only left in the tin for a few minutes after removing from the oven to allow them to settle and pull away from the sides of the tin a little. They then need to be turned out (or unclipped if using a spring-form tin) to allow the steam to escape while they cool, preventing them from becoming soggy. Whisked cakes, such as sponges, are a little more delicate than creamed cakes, such as buttercakes or pound cakes, so they require a little more care when being turned out of the tin.

1 First, run a small palette or flat-bladed knife around the outside of the cake, as close to the tin as possible so you don't cut into the side of the cake.

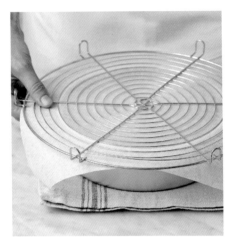

2 Place a wire rack, covered with a tea towel (dish towel) or non-stick baking paper to prevent it marking the cake, on top of the tin.

3 Invert the cake onto the rack and remove any paper stuck to the base of the cake so that the steam can escape and the bottom of the cake won't become soggy.

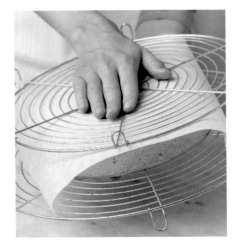

4 Use a second wire rack to invert the cake the right way up and cool to room temperature before decorating or cutting.

TIP Delicate cakes, such as those made without flour or cheesecakes, that are too fragile to turn upside down when removing from the tin are best made in a spring-form tin. To remove cakes from spring-form tins, leave the cake in the tin for 5–10 minutes after removing from the oven, then run a small palette or flat-bladed knife around the outside of the cake, as close to the tin as possible. Release the clip on the side of the tin and remove the side. Use 2 egg flips or large palette knives to transfer the cake from the base of the tin to a wire rack to cool. If the cake is very delicate, it is best to allow it to cool on the base of the tin, standing on a wire rack.

Cutting cakes into even layers

Cutting cakes into horizontal layers can be a challenge, but a little forward planning will give you a good success rate. You'll need a ruler, some toothpicks and a long serrated knife.

1 Using a ruler as a guide, insert toothpicks around the outside of the cake to indicate where the cake is to be cut, making sure the layers are an even thickness. The height of the cake will usually determine how many layers it can be cut into. Layers less than 2 cm (¾ inch) high will be hard to cut evenly.

2 Place your hand lightly on top of the cake to hold it steady and use a long serrated knife (if it's longer than the diameter of the cake it will be easier to use) to cut the top layer from the cake, using the toothpicks as a guide.

3 Use the base of a tart (flan) tin, a large spatula or an egg flip to carefully lift the top layer from the cake and set it aside. Repeat to cut any remaining layers.

Rolling a Swiss roll (jelly roll)

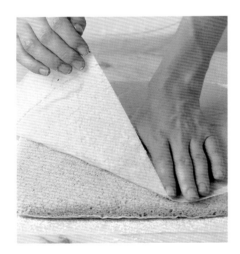  

1 Sprinkle a sheet of non-stick baking paper slightly larger than the cake with sugar, icing (confectioners') sugar or cocoa, depending on the recipe. This will coat the outside of the roll and prevent it sticking to the paper. Turn the cake out onto the paper and remove the paper that was lining the tin.

2 Use the paper underneath the cake to help you roll up the cake. Depending on the type of cake, recipes will direct you to either leave the cake rolled up, unroll and re-roll it several times, or unroll it and leave it to cool covered with a slightly damp tea towel (dish towel) to keep it moist.

3 If the cake is cooled while rolled up, unroll it, still on the paper. Use a palette knife to spread the cake with filling. Then, using the paper as a guide, roll it up as tightly as possible. Wrap the paper around it to hold its shape and place on a tray, seam side down. Chill before serving, if directed.

Flourless chocolate cake

This is quite a modern flourless chocolate cake, using only a small amount of hazelnut meal to give body, resulting in a mousse-like texture. As eggs are the main ingredient, this cake rises up during cooking and then collapses and cracks a little on standing. Serve it chilled with fresh berries.

SERVES 8–10   **PREPARATION TIME** 10 minutes (+ 3 hours chilling)   **COOKING TIME** 1 hour 10 minutes

300 g (10½ oz) dark chocolate
 (50% cocoa solids), chopped
150 g (5½ oz) unsalted butter, chopped
5 eggs, at room temperature, separated
55 g (2 oz/¼ cup) caster (superfine)
 sugar, plus 75 g (2¾ oz/⅓ cup), extra
60 ml (2 fl oz/¼ cup) milk
110 g (3¾ oz/1 cup) hazelnut meal
Unsweetened cocoa powder, to dust
125 g (4½ oz/1 cup) raspberries,
 to serve
Cream, to serve (optional)

1 Preheat the oven to 150°C (300°F/ Gas 2). Grease a round 20 cm (8 inch) spring-form cake tin and line with non-stick baking paper, extending 5 cm (2 inches) above the side *(pic 1)*. (The collar will support the cake as it rises during cooking and then fall as it cools.)

2 Put the chocolate and butter in a heatproof bowl over a saucepan of simmering water (make sure the base of the bowl doesn't touch the water). Stir occasionally until melted and smooth. Remove the bowl from the pan and set aside.

3 Use an electric mixer with a whisk attachment to whisk the egg whites and sugar in a clean, dry medium bowl until stiff peaks form. Set aside.

4 Put the eggs yolks and the extra sugar in a medium mixing bowl and use a balloon whisk to whisk until thick and pale *(pic 2)*. Whisk in the milk. Add the chocolate mixture and hazelnut meal and whisk to combine. Use a spatula or large metal spoon to fold in one-third of the egg whites until just combined *(pic 3)*. Fold in the remaining egg whites in two more batches. Spoon into the prepared tin and smooth the surface.

5 Bake for 45 minutes without opening the oven door. Turn the cake tin around to ensure even cooking and bake for a further 20 minutes or until the top of the cake feels set. Transfer to a wire rack and cool in the tin. Refrigerate for 3 hours or until well chilled.

6 Cut away the excess paper from around the side of the tin. Invert the cake onto a plate and remove the baking paper. Gently place a serving plate on top and turn the cake the right way up. Use a fine sieve to dust with cocoa powder. Use a sharp knife, dipped in very hot water and then dried, to cut the cake into slices. Serve accompanied by raspberries and cream, if desired.

TIP This cake will keep in an airtight container in the refrigerator for up to 4 days.

White chocolate mud cake

SERVES 16–20   **PREPARATION TIME** 20 minutes (+ cooling and 4 hours chilling)   **COOKING TIME** 1 hour 15 minutes

250 g (9 oz) white chocolate, chopped

200 g (7 oz) butter, chopped

330 g (11½ oz/1½ cups) caster
(superfine) sugar

2 eggs, at room temperature

1 teaspoon natural vanilla extract

150 g (5½ oz/1 cup) plain
(all-purpose) flour

150 g (5½ oz/1 cup) self-raising flour

1 quantity white chocolate buttercream
(see page 22)

1 Preheat the oven to 160°C (315°F/
Gas 2–3). Grease a deep, square 20 cm
(8 inch) cake tin and line the base and
sides with non-stick baking paper.

2 Put the chocolate, butter and 200 ml
(7 fl oz) water in a medium saucepan.
Stir over low heat until melted and
well combined. Transfer to a large bowl,
stir in the sugar and set aside until the
mixture is lukewarm.

3 Add the eggs and vanilla to the
chocolate mixture and use a balloon
whisk to whisk until just combined.
Sift the flours together over the
chocolate mixture and stir with the
whisk until smooth *(pic 1)*. Pour into
the prepared tin and tap gently on the
bench to settle the mixture.

4 Bake for 1 hour 10 minutes, turning
the tin around halfway through cooking
to ensure even cooking, or until a
skewer inserted into the centre of the
cake comes out clean. (The top of the
cake might crack slightly as it nears the
end of the cooking time.) Cool the cake
in the tin placed on a wire rack for
15 minutes, then turn it out onto the
wire rack and cool completely. Remove
the cake from the tin, wrap in plastic
wrap and place in the refrigerator for
4 hours or until well chilled. This will
make icing (frosting) the cake easier.

5 Use a sharp serrated knife to trim
the top of the cake if you wish *(pic 2)*.
Use a pastry brush to brush away any
crumbs. Place the cake upside-down
on a serving plate or cake stand. Use
a palette knife to spread the white
chocolate buttercream over the top
and sides of the cake *(pic 3)*.

1

2

3

TIP This cake can be served
straight after it has been iced
or you can place it in an airtight
container and refrigerate for up
to 4 days. Remove it up to 1 hour
before serving to bring it back to
room temperature.
　　Don't use a non-stick pan for
this cake, as the crust will become
too dark due to the extended
cooking time.

Honey spice Swiss roll

The key to a good Swiss roll (jelly roll) is not overcooking the cake. To avoid cracking, make sure the work surface you turn the sponge cake out onto isn't cold and work quickly so the cake is still warm when you roll it up the first time.

SERVES 8 **PREPARATION TIME** 40 minutes (+ cooling) **COOKING TIME** 8–10 minutes

110 g (3¾ oz/¾ cup) self-raising flour
1 teaspoon mixed (pumpkin pie) spice
3 eggs, at room temperature, separated
110 g (3¾ oz/½ cup) caster
 (superfine) sugar
2 tablespoons hot milk
30 g (1 oz/¼ cup) icing (confectioners')
 sugar, plus extra, to serve

HONEY CREAM
185 ml (6 fl oz/¾ cup) thickened
 (whipping) cream
2 tablespoons honey

1 Preheat the oven to 200°C (400°F/Gas 6). Lightly grease a 25 x 31 cm (10 x 12½ inch) (base measurement) Swiss roll (jelly roll) tin and line with a piece of non-stick baking paper, cutting into the corners to fit (see page 135) and extending 5 cm (2 inches) over the sides.

2 Sift the flour and mixed spice together twice. Use an electric mixer with a whisk attachment to whisk the egg whites in a clean, dry large bowl until soft peaks form. Gradually add the caster sugar, 1 tablespoon at a time, whisking well after each addition, until thick and glossy. Add the egg yolks one at a time, whisking until combined. Whisk for 5 minutes or until the mixture is thick and pale.

3 Pour the hot milk down the side of the bowl and sift the flour mixture over the top. Use a spatula or large metal spoon to fold together until just combined. Gently spread the mixture into the prepared tin and use the back of the spatula or spoon to smooth the surface.

4 Bake for 8–10 minutes or until the cake is light golden and springy to touch, and a skewer inserted into the centre comes out clean.

5 Place a piece of non-stick baking paper a little larger than the cake on a work surface. Sift the icing sugar evenly over the paper *(pic 1)*. Turn the cooked cake out onto the sugar. Peel away the paper that was lining the tin. Carefully roll up the cake, using the paper as a guide, starting at a short side *(pic 2)*. Set aside on a wire rack to cool completely.

6 To make the honey cream, use a balloon whisk or an electric mixer with a whisk attachment to whisk the cream in a medium bowl until soft peaks form. Add the honey and whisk until firm peaks form. Unroll the cake, spread evenly with the honey cream and then re-roll, using the paper as a guide *(pic 3)*. Serve sprinkled with extra icing sugar and cut into slices.

1

2

3

> **TIP** This cake is best eaten on the day it is baked.

Coffee and walnut cake

Coffee and walnuts are a gorgeous combination, and this cake is good proof. It's a straightforward melt-and-mix cake, so there's no beating, no whisking and no special equipment required, and it takes very little preparation to get it into the oven.

SERVES 8–10   **PREPARATION TIME** 10 minutes (+ cooling)   **COOKING TIME** 45 minutes

125 ml (4 fl oz/½ cup) milk

75 g (2¾ oz) butter, chopped

1 tablespoon instant coffee granules

110 g (3¾ oz/½ cup) caster
   (superfine) sugar

60 g (2¼ oz/½ cup) coarsely chopped
   walnuts, plus walnut halves, extra,
   to decorate

1 egg, at room temperature,
   lightly whisked

150 g (5½ oz/1 cup) self-raising
   flour, sifted

⅔ quantity coffee buttercream
   (see page 22)

1 Preheat the oven to 160°C (315°F/ Gas 2–3). Grease an 8 x 19 cm (3¼ x 7½ inch) loaf (bar) tin and line the base and 2 long sides with one piece of non-stick baking paper, extending over the sides.

2 Put the milk, butter and coffee in a large saucepan over medium–high heat. Stir for 2 minutes or until the butter melts and the coffee dissolves *(pic 1)*. Remove from the heat. Use a wooden spoon to stir in the sugar and walnuts. Stir in the egg until combined. Stir in the flour until just combined *(pic 2)*.

3 Pour the mixture into the prepared tin and smooth the surface with the back of a spoon. Bake for 40 minutes or until a skewer inserted into the centre of the cake comes out clean. Cool in the tin for 5 minutes, then turn onto a wire rack to cool completely.

4 Spread the top of the cake with coffee buttercream *(pic 3)* and decorate with extra walnut halves.

1

2

3

TIP Keep this cake in an airtight container for up to 3 days.

Angel food cake

Originating in North America, this heavenly cake is based on a meringue-like mixture, with no egg yolks and no butter. It is snowy white inside and has an exceptionally light and airy texture due to the high proportion of beaten egg whites. Unlike other cakes, it is left upside down in the cake tin to cool.

SERVES 12   **PREPARATION TIME** 30 minutes (+ cooling)   **COOKING TIME** 40 minutes

150 g (5½ oz/1 cup) self-raising flour
12 egg whites, at room temperature
1½ teaspoons cream of tartar
¼ teaspoon salt
220 g (7¾ oz/1 cup) caster
    (superfine) sugar
1½ teaspoons natural vanilla extract
Icing (confectioners') sugar, to dust
Thick (double/heavy) or whipped
    cream and hulled and quartered
    strawberries, to serve

1 Preheat the oven to 180°C (350°F/ Gas 4). Have an ungreased angel food cake tin ready. Sift the flour three times onto non-stick baking paper.

2 Use an electric mixer with a whisk attachment to whisk the egg whites, cream of tartar and salt in a clean, dry large bowl until soft peaks form. Gradually whisk in the caster sugar, 2 tablespoons at a time, until thick and glossy. Whisk in the vanilla.

3 Use a spatula or large metal spoon to gently fold in a quarter of the flour until just combined *(pic 1)*. Repeat with the remaining flour in 3 more batches.

4 Spoon the mixture into the angel food cake tin and smooth the surface *(pic 2)*. Bake for 40 minutes or until puffed and golden and a skewer inserted into the centre of the cake comes out clean. Turn upside down onto a wire rack, without removing the tin, and set aside to cool *(pic 3)*. Pass a small flat-bladed knife around the edge of the cooled cake to dislodge it from the tin. Gently shake the tin over a serving plate to remove the cake.

5 Dust with the icing sugar and serve with the cream and strawberries.

1

2

3

TIP It is important not to grease the tin or the cake will fall away from the side of it and collapse. Keep in an airtight container for up to 2 days.

Cupcakes

There are two great things about cupcakes: they're single portions and therefore ready to serve, and they are open to myriad flavouring and decorating options. This simple recipe is the perfect starting point for a foray into cupcakes, complete with variations in flavour and decorating ideas for inspiration.

MAKES 12 **PREPARATION TIME** 15 minutes **COOKING TIME** 18–20 minutes

225 g (8 oz/1½ cups) plain
   (all-purpose) flour
1½ teaspoons baking powder
150 g (5½ oz/⅔ cup) caster
   (superfine) sugar
125 g (4½ oz) unsalted butter, softened
60 ml (2 fl oz/¼ cup) milk
3 eggs, at room temperature
1 teaspoon natural vanilla extract
Icing (frosting) and decorations of your
   choice (see suggestions below)

1 Preheat the oven to 170°C (325°F/ Gas 3). Line twelve 80 ml (2½ fl oz/ ⅓ cup) muffin tin holes with paper cases.

2 Sift the flour and baking powder into a mixing bowl. Add the sugar, butter, milk, eggs and vanilla (*pic 1*). Use an electric mixer to beat on low speed until combined. Increase speed to medium and beat for 3 minutes or until well combined and the mixture is paler in colour (*pic 2*). Divide the mixture evenly among the cases.

3 Bake for 18–20 minutes or until golden and a skewer inserted into the centre of the cakes comes out clean. Cool for 5 minutes in the tin, then transfer to a wire rack to cool completely (*pic 3*).

4 Spread the cupcakes with icing and finish with decorations of your choice.

DECORATING IDEAS

Lemon daisy cupcakes: Ice 12 cupcakes with 1 quantity citrus glacé icing (frosting) (see page 22). Cut 15 white marshmallows in half crossways, then in half lengthways. Arrange the marshmallow quarters, cut side up, on the cakes to make flower shapes. Place a yellow jelly bean in the centre of each marshmallow flower.

Vanilla sparkle cupcakes: Put 1 quantity vanilla buttercream (see page 22) in a piping (icing) bag fitted with a 1 cm (½ inch) star nozzle. Pipe a large circle in the centre of a cupcake. Then, starting near the outside edge of the cupcake, generously pipe a swirl around and over the circle. Sprinkle with silver cachous or sprinkles of your choice. Repeat with the remaining buttercream, sprinkles and cupcakes.

Strawberries and cream cupcakes: Spread 12 cupcakes with 1 quantity vanilla buttercream (see page 22). Hull 12 medium strawberries and thinly slice lengthways. Arrange the strawberry slices, overlapping slightly, on each cupcake. Melt 2 tablespoons strawberry jam and 1 tablespoon water in a small saucepan and use a pastry brush to brush over the strawberries.

1

2

3

TIP These cupcakes can be served immediately or refrigerated in an airtight container for up to 2 days. Remove from the refrigerator 15–30 minutes before serving to bring the cupcakes to room temperature.

CLOCKWISE, FROM TOP RIGHT: Strawberries and cream cupcake, Lemon daisy cupcake, Vanilla sparkle cupcake

Blueberry and almond friands

Friands are small cakes made with almond meal and whisked egg white that are based on the French *financier* (interestingly, a French *friand* is a sausage roll). They're a breeze to make, as all the ingredients are simply folded into the whisked egg whites and then baked.

MAKES 12   **PREPARATION TIME** 15 minutes   **COOKING TIME** 20 minutes

6 egg whites, at room temperature
160 g (5¾ oz) butter, melted and cooled
250 g (9 oz/2 cups) icing
  (confectioners') sugar
125 g (4½ oz/1¼ cups) almond meal
100 g (3½ oz/⅔ cup) plain
  (all-purpose) flour
150 g (5½ oz) frozen blueberries
20 g (¾ oz/¼ cup) flaked almonds

1 Preheat the oven to 200°C (400°F/ Gas 6). Lightly grease a 12-hole friand tin with melted butter.

2 Use a balloon whisk to whisk the egg whites in a medium bowl until frothy but not firm *(pic 1)*. Use a wooden spoon to stir in the butter, icing sugar, almond meal and flour until just combined. Quickly stir through the frozen blueberries *(pic 2)*.

3 Divide the mixture evenly among the greased friand holes and sprinkle with flaked almonds *(pic 3)*.

4 Bake for 20 minutes or until a skewer inserted into the centre of a friand comes out clean. Cool in the tin for 5 minutes, then turn out onto a wire rack to cool.

VARIATIONS

Raspberry and pistachio friands: Replace the blueberries with frozen raspberries and the flaked almonds with roughly chopped pistachios.

Cherry and hazelnut friands: Replace the almond meal with ground hazelnuts and the blueberries with frozen cherries. Omit the flaked almonds.

1

2

3

TIP Friand tins are available from large supermarkets and kitchenware stores.
  You can also use a 12-hole 80 ml (2½ fl oz/⅓ cup) muffin tin.
  Keep in an airtight container for up to 4 days.

Double ginger cake with lime frosting

This cake has a double hit of ginger, both fresh and crystallised, which produces a strong flavour that becomes surprisingly addictive when teamed with the creamy lime frosting.

SERVES 8–10   **PREPARATION TIME** 30 minutes (+ cooling)   **COOKING TIME** 1 hour 5 minutes – 1 hour 15 minutes

250 g (9 oz) butter, chopped
110 g (3¾ oz/½ cup, firmly packed) light brown sugar
175 g (6 oz/½ cup) golden syrup
1 tablespoon finely grated fresh ginger
150 g (5½ oz/1 cup) plain (all-purpose) flour
150 g (5½ oz/1 cup) self-raising flour
½ teaspoon bicarbonate of soda (baking soda)
185 ml (6 fl oz/¾ cup) milk
2 eggs, lightly whisked, at room temperature
2 tablespoons finely chopped crystallised ginger, plus extra, sliced, to serve

LIME FROSTING
250 g (9 oz) cream cheese, at room temperature
60 g (2¼ oz) butter, softened
185 g (6½ oz/1½ cups) icing (confectioners') sugar
2 teaspoons finely grated lime zest, plus extra, to serve
1 tablespoon lime juice

1 Preheat the oven to 180°C (350°F/ Gas 4). Grease a round 20 cm (8 inch) cake tin with melted butter, then line with non-stick baking paper.

2 Combine the butter, sugar and golden syrup in a small heavy-based saucepan and stir over medium heat until the butter melts and the sugar dissolves. Stir in the grated ginger.

3 Sift together the flours and bicarbonate of soda into a large bowl. Add the butter mixture, milk, egg and crystallised ginger and use a large metal spoon or spatula to mix until just combined. Pour into the prepared tin. Bake for 1 hour–1 hour 10 minutes or until firm to touch and a skewer comes out clean when inserted into the centre. Cool in the tin for 10 minutes, then turn out onto a plate and invert, right way up, onto a wire rack to cool.

4 To make the lime frosting, use an electric mixer to beat the cream cheese, butter and icing sugar in a medium bowl until smooth and well combined. Add the lime zest and juice and beat until combined *(pic 1)*.

5 Insert toothpicks into the cooled cake as a guide for where to cut to produce 3 even cake layers. Use a long serrated knife to cut the cake horizontally into the 3 layers *(pic 2)*. Place the bottom layer on a serving plate and spread with one-third of the lime frosting *(pic 3)*. Repeat the layering process with the remaining cake layers and frosting, finishing with frosting. Top with extra lime zest and sliced crystallised ginger, and serve cut into wedges.

1

2

3

> **TIP** This cake will keep in an airtight container in the refrigerator for up to 4 days. Serve at room temperature.

Nectarine and almond cake

This is one of those fabulously no-fuss cakes you will come back to time and again. Mixing the cake batter with a food processor makes it quick and easy, then all you have to do is layer it with the fruit and nuts in the tin. For a quick dessert, serve it warm with pouring (whipping) cream or ice cream.

SERVES 8   **PREPARATION TIME** 15 minutes   **COOKING TIME** 50 minutes

150 g (5½ oz/1 cup) plain
   (all-purpose) flour
110 g (3¾ oz/½ cup) caster
   (superfine) sugar
1 teaspoon baking powder
2 teaspoons finely grated lemon zest
125 g (4½ oz) chilled unsalted
   butter, cubed
2 eggs, at room temperature
35 g (1¼ oz/⅓ cup) flaked almonds
4 yellow nectarines, about 450 g (1 lb),
   each cut into 12 wedges
Icing (confectioners') sugar (optional),
   to dust
Pouring (whipping) cream or vanilla
   ice cream (optional), to serve

1 Preheat the oven to 180°C (350°F/ Gas 4). Grease a round 20 cm (8 inch) spring-form cake tin well with butter.

2 Put the flour, caster sugar, baking powder and lemon zest in a food processor and process until well combined. Add the butter and process until the mixture resembles fine

breadcrumbs *(pic 1)*. With the motor running, add the eggs and process using the pulse button until the mixture is just combined.

3 Spread half the mixture evenly into the greased tin. Sprinkle with half the almonds and top with half the nectarines *(pic 2)*. Cover with the remaining batter, smoothing the surface with the spatula *(pic 3)*. Arrange the remaining nectarines on top and sprinkle with the remaining almonds. Bake for 50 minutes or until golden and a skewer inserted into the centre of the cake comes out clean. Leave in the tin for 5 minutes, then remove and transfer the cake to a wire rack to cool.

4 Serve either warm or at room temperature, dusted with icing sugar and accompanied by cream or ice cream, if desired.

TIP You can vary the fruit and nuts depending on the season. In autumn, try apple and pine nuts or pear and almonds.
   Keep in an airtight container for up to 3 days.

Chocolate and hazelnut praline roll

SERVES 8   **PREPARATION TIME** 30 minutes (+ cooling and 2 hours chilling)   **COOKING TIME** 30–35 minutes

200 g (7 oz) dark chocolate
(70% cocoa solids), chopped
6 eggs, separated, at room temperature
110 g (3¾ oz/½ cup) caster
(superfine) sugar
250 ml (9 fl oz/1 cup) thickened
(whipping) cream
1 tablespoon unsweetened cocoa
powder

HAZELNUT PRALINE
75 g (2¾ oz/⅓ cup) caster
(superfine) sugar
75 g (2¾ oz/½ cup) roasted and
skinned hazelnuts (see page 48)
10 g (¼ oz) butter

1 To make the hazelnut praline, line a baking tray with non-stick baking paper. Put the sugar and 2 tablespoons water in a small saucepan. Stir over low heat until the sugar dissolves. Increase the heat to high and bring to the boil, brushing down the side of the pan with a pastry brush dipped in water. Boil, without stirring, for 4–5 minutes or until caramel in colour. Remove from the heat and stir in the hazelnuts and butter. Spoon onto the lined tray *(pic 1)* and set aside until cool.

2 Preheat the oven to 180°C (350°F/ Gas 4). Grease a 24 x 30 cm (9½ x 12 inch) Swiss roll (jelly roll) tin and line with one piece of non-stick baking paper, cutting into the corners to fit.

3 Place the chocolate in a small saucepan with 60 ml (2 fl oz/¼ cup) water. Stir over low heat until the chocolate melts and the mixture is smooth. Set aside to cool slightly.

4 Use an electric mixer with a whisk attachment to whisk the egg yolks and sugar in a large bowl until thick and pale. Whisk in the chocolate mixture.

5 Clean and dry the whisk attachment. Whisk the egg whites in a large bowl until soft peaks form. Use a large metal spoon or spatula to fold one-third of the egg whites into the chocolate mixture. Gently fold in the remaining egg whites until just combined. Pour into the prepared tin and smooth the surface.

6 Bake for 18–20 minutes or until a skewer inserted into the centre comes out clean. Remove from the oven and immediately cover with non-stick baking paper and a tea towel (dish towel). Set aside to cool completely.

7 Meanwhile, coarsely chop the hazelnut praline. Put half the praline in a small food processor and process until finely ground. Use an electric mixer with a whisk attachment to whisk the cream until firm peaks just form. Fold in the finely ground praline.

8 Cut a piece of non-stick baking paper slightly larger than the cake and place on a work surface, with a short end towards you. Sprinkle the furthest third of the paper with half the coarsely chopped praline, then sprinkle all the paper with cocoa *(pic 2)*. Remove the tea towel and paper from the cake. Turn the cake onto the coated paper. Spread with the cream mixture *(pic 3)*. Starting at the side closest to you and using the paper as a guide, roll the sponge up tightly to enclose the filling. Wrap the paper around the roll to retain its shape and place, seam side down, on a tray. Refrigerate for 2 hours, until firm.

9 Serve sprinkled with the reserved coarsely chopped praline.

1

2

3

Caramel apple cake

If you're looking for a cake that's simple to make, yet has an extra-special flavour, this will fit the bill nicely. The caramel apple topping has just the right balance of tartness and sweetness.

SERVES 8   **PREPARATION TIME** 30 minutes (+ 10 minutes standing)   **COOKING TIME** 1 hour 20 minutes

75 g (2¾ oz/⅓ cup, firmly packed)
   light brown sugar
3 small granny smith apples, peeled,
   cored and thickly sliced (see tip)
1 tablespoon lemon juice
125 g (4½ oz) butter, softened
220 g (7¾ oz/1 cup) caster
   (superfine) sugar
1 teaspoon ground cinnamon
1 teaspoon natural vanilla extract
3 eggs, at room temperature
150 g (5½ oz/1 cup) self-raising flour
35 g (1¼ oz/¼ cup) plain
   (all-purpose) flour
60 ml (2 fl oz/¼ cup) milk
Thick (double/heavy) cream, to serve

1 Preheat the oven to 180°C (350°F/ Gas 4). Grease a round 20 cm (8 inch) cake tin and line with non-stick baking paper. Sprinkle the brown sugar over the base. Put the apples in a bowl and toss with the lemon juice. Arrange the apples over the brown sugar *(pic 1)* and drizzle over any remaining lemon juice.

2 Use an electric mixer to beat the butter, caster sugar and cinnamon until creamy. Add the vanilla and eggs and beat until well combined. Sift together the self-raising and plain flours. Use a large metal spoon or spatula to gently stir in the flours and milk in 2 separate batches each *(pic 2)*. Spoon the mixture over the apples and use the back of a spoon to smooth the surface.

3 Bake for 1 hour 20 minutes or until golden and cooked when tested with a skewer. Stand in the tin for 10 minutes, then place a serving plate over the cake tin and invert to turn out the cake *(pic 3)*. Serve the cake warm or at room temperature with the cream.

1

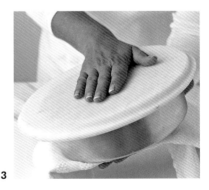

2

3

TIP Golden delicious and pink lady apples are also suitable to use in this cake.

Lemon macaroon and strawberry mousse cake

This delicate dessert cake is light, yet decadent. It's a good choice for a celebration cake as it can be made ahead, looks beautiful and has a wonderful combination of flavours.

SERVES 8   **PREPARATION TIME** 40 minutes (+ 30 minutes cooling and 3 hours chilling)   **COOKING TIME** 30 minutes

4 egg whites, at room temperature
165 g (5¾ oz/¾ cup) caster
    (superfine) sugar
1 teaspoon natural vanilla extract
135 g (4¾ oz/1⅓ cups) almond meal
35 g (1¼ oz/¼ cup) plain
    (all-purpose) flour
1 teaspoon finely grated lemon zest
2 tablespoons strawberry jam
125 ml (4 fl oz/½ cup) thickened
    (whipping) cream, whisked to
    firm peaks
95 g (3¼ oz/1 cup) flaked almonds,
    toasted and lightly crushed
Strawberries and icing (confectioners')
    sugar, to garnish

STRAWBERRY MOUSSE
600 ml (21 fl oz) thickened
    (whipping) cream
180 g (6¼ oz) white chocolate,
    finely chopped
250 g (9 oz) strawberries, hulled
2 tablespoons strawberry jam
1 tablespoon powdered gelatine

1 Preheat the oven to 180°C (350°F/ Gas 4). Grease two 22 cm (8½ inch) spring-form cake tins and line each tin with non-stick baking paper.

2 Put the egg whites in a clean, dry bowl and use an electric mixer with a whisk attachment to whisk until soft peaks form. Gradually add the sugar, whisking well after each addition, until thick and glossy. Whisk in the vanilla.

3 Combine the almond meal, flour and zest. Add to the meringue mixture and use a large metal spoon to fold until just combined. Divide between the tins and smooth the surface. Bake for 18 minutes, until lightly browned. Cool in the tins.

4 To make the strawberry mousse, bring 125 ml (4 fl oz/½ cup) of the cream almost to the boil in a small saucepan. Remove from heat, add the chocolate and set aside for 30 seconds. Stir until melted. Set aside for 30 minutes to cool.

5 Meanwhile, process the strawberries and jam until smooth. Push through a sieve set over a bowl. Discard the seeds.

6 Sprinkle the gelatine over 60 ml (2 fl oz/¼ cup) warm water in a small heatproof jug. Set aside for 5 minutes to soften. Stand the jug in a small saucepan of simmering water and heat gently until the gelatine dissolves (pic 1).

7 Use an electric mixer with a whisk attachment to whisk the remaining cream until firm peaks form. Fold in the strawberry purée, chocolate mixture and gelatine until just combined (pic 2).

8 Remove a macaroon from the tin. Spread the other macaroon, still in the tin, with the jam. Spread the strawberry mousse (pic 3) over the jam, then top with the remaining macaroon. Cover and refrigerate for 3 hours or overnight.

9 Remove the cake from the tin. Spread cream over the side, then press almonds onto the cream. Top with strawberries, dust with icing sugar and serve.

1

2

3

Muffins, Scones & Quick Breads

Banana muffins

This is a good, reliable recipe from which to build your muffin repertoire. Once you've mastered this recipe, try our variations and let them inspire you to create other flavour combinations.

MAKES 12 **PREPARATION TIME** 15 minutes **COOKING TIME** 20–25 minutes

300 g (10½ oz/2 cups) self-raising flour
½ teaspoon ground cinnamon
    or nutmeg
110 g (3¾ oz/½ cup, firmly packed)
    light brown sugar
125 ml (4 fl oz/½ cup) milk
2 eggs, at room temperature,
    lightly whisked
1 teaspoon natural vanilla extract
300 g (10½ oz/1¼ cups) mashed
    very ripe banana (see tip)
125 g (4½ oz) butter, melted and cooled
60 g (2¼ oz/½ cup) pecan or walnut
    halves, coarsely chopped, to sprinkle

1 Preheat the oven to 180°C (350°F/ Gas 4). Lightly brush twelve 80 ml (2½ fl oz/⅓ cup) muffin holes with melted butter to grease.

2 Sift the flour and cinnamon or nutmeg together into a large bowl. Stir in the sugar, then make a well in the centre.

3 Whisk the milk, egg and vanilla together in a jug *(pic 1)*, then pour into the well. Add the mashed banana and melted butter. Use a large metal spoon to fold together until just combined but not smooth *(pic 2)*. (Do not overmix or the muffins will be tough — the batter should still be a little lumpy.)

4 Divide the mixture evenly among the muffin holes and sprinkle with the nuts. Bake for 20–25 minutes, or until the muffins are golden and a skewer inserted into the centre comes out clean. Leave in the tin for 3 minutes, then use a palette knife to release each muffin from the tin and lift out *(pic 3)*. Cool on a wire rack and serve at room temperature.

VARIATIONS

Chocolate muffins: Omit the spice, banana and nuts. Replace 75 g (2¾ oz/ ½ cup) of the flour with 55 g (2 oz/ ½ cup) unsweetened cocoa powder and increase the milk to 185 ml (6 fl oz/¾ cup).

Orange muffins: Omit the spice, banana and nuts. Replace the brown sugar with 110 g (3¾ oz/½ cup) caster (superfine) sugar. Replace the milk with 185 ml (6 fl oz/¾ cup) buttermilk. Replace the vanilla with 1 tablespoon finely grated orange zest.

1

2

3

TIP You'll need 3 medium-sized, very ripe bananas for this recipe.
    Store in an airtight container for up to 2 days. To freeze, wrap individually in plastic wrap, then put in a freezer bag or airtight container. Seal, label, date and freeze for up to 3 months. Thaw at room temperature.

White chocolate and blackberry muffins

Berries are a terrific addition to muffin batters, and when chocolate is also put in the mix the results are heavenly. If you can't find blackberries, use blueberries or raspberries, and if you are using frozen berries, don't thaw them or they will streak the batter. Dark chocolate works just as well as white.

MAKES 12　**PREPARATION TIME** 20 minutes　**COOKING TIME** 25–30 minutes

375 g (13 oz/2½ cups) self-raising flour
200 g (7 oz) white chocolate, chopped
125 g (4½ oz) butter
110 g (3¾ oz/½ cup, firmly packed) light brown sugar
125 ml (4 fl oz/½ cup) milk
3 eggs, at room temperature
300 g (10½ oz/2⅓ cups) fresh or frozen blackberries
2 tablespoons sugar, to sprinkle

1 Preheat the oven to 180°C (350°F/ Gas 4). Lightly brush twelve 80 ml (2½ fl oz/⅓ cup) muffin holes with oil or melted butter to grease.

2 Sift the flour into a bowl and stir in 125 g (4½ oz) of the chocolate. Make a well in the centre.

3 Place the remaining chocolate and the butter in a medium heatproof bowl over a saucepan of simmering water (make sure the base of the bowl doesn't touch the water). Stir until melted and combined *(pic 1)*. Remove the bowl from the pan, add the brown sugar and milk and stir with a balloon whisk until well combined. Whisk in the eggs.

4 Add the butter mixture to the flour mixture and use a spatula or large metal spoon to gently fold together until just combined but not smooth. Gently stir in the blackberries *(pic 2)*. (Do not overmix or the muffins will be tough — the batter should still be a little lumpy.)

5 Divide the mixture evenly among the muffin holes *(pic 3)*. Sprinkle with the sugar. Bake for 20–25 minutes or until the muffins are risen, golden and come away slightly from the side of the tin. Leave in the tin for 3 minutes, then use a palette knife to release each muffin from the tin and lift out. Cool on a wire rack and serve at room temperature.

1

2

3

TIP Store in an airtight container for up to 2 days. To freeze, wrap individually in plastic wrap, then put in a freezer bag or airtight container. Seal, label, date and freeze for up to 3 months. Thaw the muffins at room temperature.

Spinach and feta muffins

Savoury muffins make a great snack for lunchboxes or to take on picnics, or you can serve them with a warming bowl of soup. They are also delicious served warm with lashings of butter. You can replace the feta in this recipe with haloumi, cut into small pieces, if you prefer.

MAKES 12   **PREPARATION TIME** 20 minutes   **COOKING TIME** 25 minutes

250 g (9 oz) frozen spinach, thawed
335 g (11¾ oz/2¼ cups) self-raising flour
200 g (7 oz) feta cheese, crumbled
100 g (3½ oz/1¼ cups) finely shredded parmesan cheese
250 ml (9 fl oz/1 cup) milk
2 eggs, at room temperature
125 g (4½ oz) butter, melted and cooled

1 Preheat the oven to 190°C (375°F/ Gas 5). Lightly brush twelve 80 ml (2½ fl oz/⅓ cup) muffin holes with oil or melted butter.

2 Use your hands to squeeze as much moisture as you can from the spinach *(pic 1)*, then finely chop it.

3 Sift the flour into a bowl and season well with freshly ground black pepper. Stir in half each of the feta and parmesan, then make a well in the centre. Whisk the milk and eggs together in a jug, then pour into the well. Add the melted butter *(pic 2)*. Use a spatula or large metal spoon to gently fold together until just combined but not smooth. Stir in the spinach. (Do not overmix or the muffins will be tough — the batter should still be a little lumpy.)

4 Fill each muffin hole three-quarters full. Mix together the remaining cheeses and sprinkle over each muffin *(pic 3)*. Bake for 25 minutes, or until golden and a skewer inserted into the centre of a muffin comes out clean. As soon as you remove them from the oven, use a palette knife to release each muffin from the tin and transfer to a wire rack. Serve the muffins warm.

1

2

3

TIP Store in an airtight container for up to 2 days. To freeze, wrap individually in plastic wrap, then put in a freezer bag or airtight container. Seal, label, date and freeze for up to 3 months. Thaw the muffins at room temperature.

Toppings

Sweet muffins, and their cupcake cousins, are the perfect contenders for this tempting array of toppings. They are all quick and easy to make, but the results are impressive and give them a touch of decadence. Each recipe is enough for twelve 80 ml (2½ fl oz/⅓ cup) muffins or 24 small cupcakes.

Butterfly

Use a small sharp knife to cut a cone shape from the top of the cupcake or muffin, removing a scoop about 1.5 cm (⅝ inch) deep. Place a teaspoon of jam (strawberry, raspberry, mixed berry and blackberry are all good) into the hole and top with thick (double/heavy) or whipped cream. Cut the cone shape in half and stand in the cream to resemble wings. Dust lightly with icing (confectioners') sugar. These are perfect for kids' parties.

Hazelnut caramel spread

Put 150 g (5½ oz) ready-made hard caramels and 100 ml (3½ fl oz) pouring (whipping) cream in a small saucepan and stir over low heat until the caramels have melted and blended with the cream to form a paste. Remove from the heat and stir in 15 g (½ oz) chopped roasted and skinned hazelnuts. Set aside at room temperature until cooled to a spreadable consistency. Spread over the top of muffins or cupcakes and sprinkle with extra chopped roasted and skinned hazelnuts.

Glacé icing

Make 1 quantity glacé icing (frosting) (see page 22). The icing should be just flowing, but not too thin and runny (add a little icing/confectioners' sugar if it is too thin, or a little more water if it is too thick). Use food colouring to tint the icing to your desired colour or leave it plain. Put the muffins or cupcakes on a wire rack and spoon the icing over, allowing it to drizzle down the sides. Decorate with sugar flowers or sprinkles, as desired. Leave to set before serving.

Cream cheese frosting

Use an electric mixer to beat 250 g (9 oz) cream cheese, at room temperature; 60 g (2¼ oz/½ cup) icing (confectioners') sugar; and 1½ tablespoons lemon juice until pale and creamy. Use a palette knife to spread over the cupcakes or muffins, then sprinkle with shredded or flaked coconut or chopped nuts. This topping is particularly good with the banana muffins (see page 158), but don't sprinkle them with the nuts before baking.

Chocolate ganache

Put 200 g (7 oz) dark chocolate, 80 ml (2½ fl oz/⅓ cup) pouring (whipping) cream and 40 g (1½ oz) butter in a small heatproof bowl over a saucepan of hot water (make sure the base of the bowl doesn't touch the water) and stir occasionally until melted and smooth. Refrigerate, stirring occasionally, until the mixture reaches a spreadable consistency. Use a palette knife to spread the ganache over the cupcakes or muffins. Sprinkle with chocolate curls (see page 49), if desired.

Hot chocolate sauce

Place 185 ml (6 fl oz/¾ cup) pouring (whipping) cream, 125 g (4½ oz) chopped dark chocolate and 1 teaspoon natural vanilla extract in a small saucepan and stir over low heat until the chocolate melts and the mixture is well combined. Serve warm, drizzled over hot plain, chocolate or berry cupcakes or muffins straight from the oven. Add a scoop of vanilla ice cream to make a quick, decadent dessert.

CLOCKWISE FROM
BOTTOM RIGHT:
Butterfly, Hazelnut caramel
spread, Glacé icing, Cream
cheese frosting

Plain scones

Scones are the cornerstone of all good baking repertoires. The techniques of rubbing in and mixing with a flat-bladed knife are both required, and if done with a light touch will produce light, fluffy scones. This recipe will have you whipping up a perfect batch of scones in just under half an hour.

MAKES about 9   **PREPARATION TIME** 15 minutes   **COOKING TIME** 10–12 minutes

375 g (13 oz/2½ cups) self-raising flour,
   plus extra, for dusting (optional)
1 teaspoon baking powder
Pinch of salt
60 g (2¼ oz) chilled butter, chopped
250 ml (9 fl oz/1 cup) milk,
   plus extra, to glaze
Butter and jam, to serve

1 Preheat the oven to 220°C (425°F/ Gas 7). Lightly grease a baking tray or line with non-stick baking paper.

2 Sift the flour, baking powder and salt into a medium mixing bowl. With your palms facing upwards, use your fingertips to rub in the butter *(pic 1)* until the mixture resembles fine breadcrumbs. Make a well in the centre.

3 Add almost all the milk and mix with a flat-bladed knife, using a cutting action, until the dough comes together in clumps *(pic 2)*. Mix to a soft dough, adding the remaining milk if necessary.

4 Use lightly floured hands to gently gather the dough, lift it onto a lightly floured work surface and knead very lightly and briefly to bring it together into a smooth ball. Pat the dough out to 2.5 cm (1 inch) thick. Use a floured round 6–7 cm (2½–2¾ inch) cutter to cut out scones, pressing straight down on the cutter and not twisting it (see tip). Gather the dough trimmings together and, without handling them

too much, press out again to a 2.5 cm (1 inch) thickness and cut out more rounds. Place the scones close together on the prepared tray. Brush lightly with the extra milk *(pic 3)* and dust lightly with extra flour, if desired.

5 Bake the scones for 10–12 minutes, or until they are well risen, golden brown on top and sound hollow when tapped on the base. Serve warm or at room temperature, with butter and jam.

VARIATIONS

Sultana scones: Stir 85 g (3 oz/½ cup) sultanas (golden raisins) into the flour mixture before adding the milk.

Date scones: Stir 150 g (5½ oz) fresh dates, pitted and chopped, into the flour mixture before adding the milk.

Buttermilk scones: Use buttermilk instead of the milk.

Cheese scones: Stir 50 g (1¾ oz/½ cup, loosely packed) coarsely grated cheddar and 25 g (1¼ oz/¼ cup) finely grated parmesan cheese into the flour mixture before adding the milk. Sprinkle the scones with 25 g (1 oz/¼ cup, loosely packed) coarsely grated cheddar cheese after brushing with the extra milk.

1

2

3

TIP If you twist the cutter when cutting out the scones, the scones will rise unevenly.
  To keep the scones warm, wrap in a clean tea towel (dish towel).
  These scones are best eaten on the day they are baked.

Rich scones

These scones are enriched by the addition of an egg and cream instead of milk, making their texture wonderfully tender and light. They are delicious served simply with good-quality butter or teamed with cream and berry jam, honey or even golden syrup.

MAKES about 10 **PREPARATION TIME** 15 minutes **COOKING TIME** 10–12 minutes

300 g (10½ oz/2 cups) self-raising flour
1 teaspoon baking powder
Pinch of salt
40 g (1½ oz) chilled butter, chopped
55 g (2 oz/¼ cup) caster
  (superfine) sugar
1 egg, at room temperature
185 ml (6 fl oz/¾ cup) pouring
  (whipping) cream
½ teaspoon natural vanilla extract
1 egg, lightly whisked, to glaze
Jam and whipped cream, to serve
  (optional)

1 Preheat the oven to 220°C (425°F/ Gas 7). Lightly grease a baking tray or line with non-stick baking paper.

2 Sift the flour, baking powder and salt into a bowl. With your palms facing upwards, use your fingertips to rub in the butter until the mixture resembles fine breadcrumbs. Stir in the sugar and make a well in the centre *(pic 1)*.

3 Whisk the egg, cream and vanilla together with a fork. Add to the dry ingredients and mix with a flat-bladed knife, using a cutting action, until the dough comes together in clumps. Use lightly floured hands to gently gather the dough together, lift it onto a lightly floured work surface and knead very lightly and briefly to bring it together into a smooth ball *(pic 2)*.

4 Pat the dough out to 2.5 cm (1 inch) thick. Use a floured round 6–7 cm (2½–2¾ inch) cutter to cut out rounds *(pic 3)*. Gather the dough trimmings together and, without handling them too much, press out again to a 2.5 cm (1 inch) thickness and cut out more rounds. Place the scones close together on the prepared tray and brush lightly with the whisked egg.

5 Bake the scones for 10–12 minutes or until they are risen, golden brown on top and sound hollow when tapped on the base. Serve warm with jam and cream, if desired.

1

2

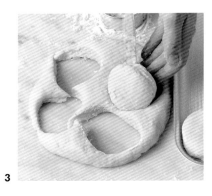

3

TIP These scones are best eaten on the day they are baked.

Strawberry shortcakes

This American classic is comprised of a scone or biscuit-like pastry that is split in half and filled with cream and berries. The pastry has the addition of a shortening, in this case butter, to make it tender and this is where the name 'shortcake' comes from. Serve it for afternoon tea or as a dessert.

MAKES 16 **PREPARATION TIME** 30 minutes (+ cooling) **COOKING TIME** 20 minutes

600 g (1 lb 5 oz/4 cups) self-raising flour
110 g (3¾ oz/½ cup) caster (superfine) sugar
1½ teaspoons salt
175 g (6 oz) chilled butter, chopped
160 ml (5¼ fl oz/⅔ cup) milk
600 ml (21 fl oz) pouring (whipping) cream, chilled
2 tablespoons icing (confectioners') sugar, plus extra, for dusting
1 teaspoon natural vanilla extract
500 g (1 lb 2 oz) ripe strawberries, hulled and sliced

1 Preheat the oven to 180°C (350°F/Gas 4). Line a baking tray with non-stick baking paper.

2 Put the flour, caster sugar and salt in a large bowl and stir to combine well. With your palms facing upwards, use your fingertips to rub in the butter until the mixture resembles fine breadcrumbs.

3 Combine the milk and 250 ml (9 fl oz/1 cup) of the cream and add to the flour mixture. Use a flat-bladed knife to mix, using a cutting action, until a rough dough forms *(pic 1)*.

4 Turn out onto a lightly floured work surface and use lightly floured hands to knead the dough lightly and briefly until almost smooth. Pat the dough into a square, about 20 cm (8 inches). Use a large, lightly floured knife to cut it into 16 even squares and place on the lined tray, about 2 cm (¾ inch) apart *(pic 2)*. Brush lightly with a little of the remaining cream.

5 Bake the shortcakes for 20 minutes or until they are golden, cooked through and sound hollow when tapped on the base. Leave on the tray for 5 minutes, then transfer to a wire rack and allow to cool completely.

6 Combine the remaining cream with the icing sugar and vanilla in a medium bowl and use an electric mixer with a whisk attachment or a balloon whisk to whisk until soft peaks form.

7 Split the cooled shortcakes in half horizontally *(pic 3)*. Put the bases on serving plates, top with the strawberries and whipped cream and then cover with the shortcake tops. Dust with icing sugar. Serve immediately with any remaining cream passed separately.

TIP Shortcakes are best eaten on the day they are made.
    This recipe can easily be halved to make 8 shortcakes.

Raspberry-filled scones

These scones have a clever twist. They're baked with a pocket of jam inside, so if you want to transport them all you need to take is some thick cream for dipping. Kids will be happy with just the jam, so they make a lovely, not-too-naughty addition to their lunchbox.

MAKES about 10   **PREPARATION TIME** 20 minutes   **COOKING TIME** 12 minutes

300 g (10½ oz/2 cups) self-raising flour
Pinch of salt
2 tablespoons caster (superfine) sugar
30 g (1 oz) chilled butter, chopped
200 ml (7 fl oz) milk, plus extra, to glaze
2½ tablespoons raspberry jam
Icing (confectioners') sugar, to dust
Thick (double/heavy) cream, to serve

1 Preheat the oven to 220°C (425°F/ Gas 7). Lightly grease a baking tray or line with non-stick baking paper.

2 Sift the flour and salt into a bowl and stir in the sugar. With your palms facing upwards, use your fingertips to rub in the butter until the mixture resembles fine breadcrumbs. Make a well in the centre.

3 Add almost all the milk and mix with a flat-bladed knife, using a cutting action, until the dough comes together in clumps. Mix to a soft dough, adding the remaining milk if necessary. Use lightly floured hands to gently gather the dough together, lift it onto a lightly floured work surface and knead very lightly and briefly to bring it together into a smooth ball.

4 Use a lightly floured rolling pin to roll the dough out to 1 cm (½ inch) thick. Use a lightly floured round 8 cm (3¼ inch) cutter to cut out scones. Use your fingertips to make an indentation on one side of each round *(pic 1)*, and place a little jam in each indentation *(pic 2)*. Brush the edges of the dough lightly with the extra milk, then fold the dough in half to make a semi-circle, covering the jam, then pinch the edges together *(pic 3)*. Place on the prepared tray, about 3 cm (1¼ inches) apart, and brush lightly with a little more milk.

5 Bake the scones for 12 minutes, or until they are well risen, lightly golden and sound hollow when tapped on the base. Serve warm, dusted with icing (confectioners') sugar and accompanied by thick cream.

1

2

3

TIP These scones are best eaten on the day they are baked.

Seeded rye damper

This easy quick bread is great for lunchtime and makes a tasty accompaniment for soups and stews. The caraway seeds add another dimension, but you could substitute cumin seeds for a different flavour if you like. The use of rye flour gives the damper an earthy flavour.

SERVES 8   **PREPARATION TIME** 15 minutes   **COOKING TIME** 20 minutes

225 g (8 oz/1½ cups) self-raising
   flour
120 g (4¼ oz/1 cup) rye flour
2 teaspoons baking powder
Pinch of salt
30 g (1 oz) chilled butter, chopped
1½ teaspoons poppy seeds
1½ teaspoons caraway seeds
250 ml (9 fl oz/1 cup) milk,
   plus extra, for glazing
Butter, to serve

1 Preheat the oven to 220°C (425°F/ Gas 7). Lightly grease a baking tray or line with non-stick baking paper.

2 Sift the flours, baking powder and salt into a bowl *(pic 1)*. With your palms facing upwards, use your fingertips to rub in the butter until the mixture resembles fine breadcrumbs. Combine the seeds, reserve 2 teaspoons of the mixture and add the rest to the flour. Make a well in the centre.

3 Add almost all the milk and mix with a flat-bladed knife, using a cutting action, until the dough comes together in clumps *(pic 2)*. Mix to a soft dough, adding the remaining milk if necessary.

4 Use lightly floured hands to gently gather the dough together, lift it onto a lightly floured work surface and knead very lightly and briefly to bring it together into a smooth ball. Pat the dough out to a round, 2.5 cm (1 inch) thick, and place on the prepared tray. Use a lightly floured large, sharp knife to deeply score the round of dough into 8 wedges, without cutting all the way through *(pic 3)*. Brush lightly with the extra milk and then sprinkle with the reserved seed mixture.

5 Bake the damper for 20 minutes, or until it is risen, golden brown on top and sounds hollow when tapped on the base. Serve warm or at room temperature with butter.

1

2

3

TIP This damper is best eaten on the day it is baked.

Cornbread

Before wheat replaced corn as a dominant crop in America, cornbread was a staple food that was served with just about everything. It's still popular as a comfort and convenience food, and is delicious served with soups, casseroles and barbecued meats.

SERVES 8–10   **PREPARATION TIME** 20 minutes   **COOKING TIME** 20 minutes

150 g (5½ oz/1 cup) plain
   (all-purpose) flour
2 teaspoons baking powder
190 g (6¾ oz/1 cup) polenta
2 tablespoons caster (superfine) sugar
1½ teaspoons salt
80 g (2¾ oz) unsalted butter, chopped
125 g (4½ oz) cheddar cheese, diced
1 large red chilli, chopped
1 egg, at room temperature,
   lightly whisked
250 ml (9 fl oz/1 cup) buttermilk
Butter, to serve (optional)

1 Preheat the oven to 200°C (400°F/ Gas 6). Brush a square 20 cm (8 inch) cake tin with melted butter to grease and lightly dust with flour.

2 Sift the flour and baking powder into a large bowl. Stir in the polenta, sugar and salt. With your palms facing upwards, use your fingertips to rub in the butter until the mixture resembles fine breadcrumbs. Stir through the cheese and chilli *(pic 1)*.

3 Whisk together the egg and buttermilk. Add to the flour mixture and use a large metal spoon to stir until just combined *(pic 2)*. Spoon the mixture into the prepared tin and use the back of the spoon to smooth the surface.

4 Bake the cornbread for 20 minutes or until light golden and a skewer inserted into the centre of the bread comes out clean *(pic 3)*. Leave in the tin for 5 minutes before turning out onto a wire rack. Serve warm or at room temperature, plain or spread with butter.

1

2

3

TIP Cornbread is best eaten on the day it is baked.

Corn tortillas

Masa harina (see tip, below) is used in the cooking of Mexico and Central and South America to make tortillas and tamales or to thicken sauces. You may need to search for it, but there is no substitute — cornmeal and cornflour are produced and processed very differently and plain flour will not work either.

MAKES 10   **PREPARATION TIME** 15 minutes   **COOKING TIME** 20–25 minutes

270 g (9½ oz/2 cups) masa harina (instant corn masa flour) (see tip), plus extra, for dusting
¼ teaspoon salt
330 ml (11¼ fl oz/1⅓ cups) lukewarm water

1 Put the masa harina and salt in a large bowl, add the lukewarm water and use your hands to mix together until well combined.

2 Sprinkle your work surface lightly with a little extra masa harina. Turn out the dough and knead for 3–5 minutes, until smooth and moist *(pic 1)*. If the dough seems a little dry, add a little water and if it seems too wet, add a little more masa harina.

3 Divide the dough into 10 equal portions and roll each into a ball. Cover with a slightly damp tea towel (dish towel). Cut up a medium to large snap-lock bag to make 2 squares that will cover the surface area of a 19 cm (7½ inch) diameter tortilla press (the corners can hang over the side).

4 Working with one ball of dough at a time, place a square of plastic on the base of the tortilla press and put the ball in the centre *(pic 2)*. Cover with the other square of plastic and close the press to flatten the dough. The tortilla should be about 16 cm (6¼ inches) in diameter. (Alternatively, if you don't have a tortilla press, you could flatten the balls, between the plastic, using the base of a heavy casserole dish or pan. Use a rolling pin to roll the flattened dough into 16 cm/6¼ inch rounds.)

5 Preheat a heavy-based frying pan (cast-iron is best for delivering consistent intense heat) over medium–high heat. Cook the tortilla for 30 seconds, then turn and cook for 1 minute *(pic 3)*. The tortilla should be very slightly puffed. Turn and cook for a final 30 seconds. The tortilla will be slightly charred.

6 Transfer the cooked tortilla to a tea towel and fold to enclose and keep warm. Repeat with the remaining balls of dough, pressing each tortilla as the previous one is cooking.

1

2

3

TIP Masa harina is flour made from corn that is dried, cooked, ground and dried again. Both masa harina and tortilla presses are available from speciality food stores and off the internet.
Tortillas are best eaten on the day they are made.

Skillet bread

Skillet bread was created out of necessity, by travellers with only a campfire for cooking. This recipe follows the tradition of cooking the bread in a frying pan, though it is baked for a more even cooking result. It would make a great accompaniment to Mexican-inspired meals, such as chilli con carne.

SERVES 8   **PREPARATION TIME** 20 minutes   **COOKING TIME** 30 minutes

190 g (6¾ oz/1 cup) polenta
150 g (5½ oz/1 cup) self-raising flour
2 teaspoons sea salt
2 eggs, lightly whisked
375 ml (13 fl oz/1½ cups) buttermilk
100 g (3½ oz) butter, softened

1 Preheat the oven to 200°C (400°F/ Gas 6). Place a 6 cm (2½ inch) deep, 26 cm (10½ inch) (top diameter) and 20 cm (8 inch) (base diameter) frying pan with a heatproof handle in the oven.

2 Meanwhile, combine the polenta, sifted flour and salt in a large bowl. Make a well in the centre *(pic 1)*. Slowly pour in the combined egg and buttermilk while mixing with a fork to gradually incorporate the dry ingredients *(pic 2)*, mixing until smooth. Take care not to overmix the batter, it doesn't matter if there are a few lumps.

3 Remove the hot pan from the oven. Add the butter and swirl it around to coat the base and side of the pan *(pic 3)*. Pour the excess butter into the batter and stir to combine. Pour the batter into the pan and bake for 30 minutes or until golden and a skewer inserted into the centre comes out clean. Turn out onto a wire rack. Serve warm.

1

2

3

TIP For cheesy skillet bread, mix 100 g (3½ oz/1 cup) coarsely grated sharp cheddar cheese and 2 tablespoons chopped oregano into the polenta, flour and salt.

Irish soda bread

As the name suggests, this bread uses bicarbonate of soda (and baking powder) to leaven it, rather than yeast. It will fast become a favourite, as it's quick to make and tastes so delicious. If you would prefer to use plain flour only, or wholemeal flour only, you may need to adjust the liquid slightly.

MAKES 20 cm (8 inch) diameter loaf   **PREPARATION TIME** 15 minutes   **COOKING TIME** 45–50 minutes

200 g (7 oz/1⅓ cups) plain
   (all-purpose) flour
200 g (7 oz/1⅓ cups) plain
   (all-purpose) wholemeal
   (whole-wheat) flour
1 teaspoon baking powder
1 teaspoon bicarbonate of soda
   (baking soda)
2 teaspoons salt
60 g (2¼ oz) chilled unsalted
   butter, chopped
300 ml (10½ fl oz) buttermilk

1 Preheat the oven to 180°C (350°F/ Gas 4). Grease and flour a baking tray.

2 Sift the flours, baking powder, bicarbonate of soda and salt into a large bowl, returning the husks from the wholemeal flour to the bowl. Use your fingertips to rub in the butter until the mixture resembles coarse breadcrumbs. Add the buttermilk and mix with a flat-bladed knife, using a cutting action, until a dough forms.

3 Turn the dough out onto a floured work surface and knead briefly until smooth *(pic 1)*. Shape the dough into a ball about 18 cm (7 inches) in diameter *(pic 2)* and place on the prepared tray. Use a large sharp knife to cut a deep cross into the surface *(pic 3)*.

4 Bake for 45–50 minutes or until the loaf is golden and sounds hollow when tapped on the base. Transfer to a wire rack to cool.

VARIATIONS

Raisin and rosemary soda bread:
Add 255 g (9¼ oz/1½ cups) raisins, 1 tablespoon chopped rosemary and 55 g (2 oz/¼ cup) caster (superfine) sugar after rubbing in the butter.

Cheddar and walnut soda bread:
Add 90 g (3¼ oz/¾ cup) chopped toasted walnuts and 150 g (5½ oz/ 1½ cups, loosely packed) coarsely grated tasty cheddar cheese after rubbing in the butter.

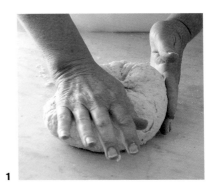

1

2

3

TIP This bread will keep, wrapped in plastic wrap or stored in an airtight container, for up to 3 days. It can be frozen, in a sealed freezer bag, for up to 6 weeks.

Yorkshire puddings

To many people, a meal of roast beef is incomplete without these small puffs. Originally, the fat from the roast would be used to grease the tins, however olive oil also works well. The secret to making perfect Yorkshire puddings is to work quickly and ensure both the oven and muffin tin are very hot.

MAKES 12   **PREPARATION TIME** 10 minutes   **COOKING TIME** 20 minutes

60 ml (2 fl oz/¼ cup) olive oil
250 ml (9 fl oz/1 cup) milk
2 eggs, lightly whisked
150 g (5½ oz/1 cup) plain
   (all-purpose) flour
1 teaspoon sea salt

1 Preheat the oven to 200°C (400°F/ Gas 6). Divide the oil among twelve 80 ml (2½ fl oz/⅓ cup) muffin tin holes *(pic 1)*. Place the tin in the oven and heat for 10 minutes.

2 Meanwhile, use a whisk to combine the milk, egg, flour and salt in a jug *(pic 2)*. Working quickly, remove the muffin tin from the oven and pour the batter evenly into the holes *(pic 3)*. Bake for 20 minutes or until golden and puffed. Serve immediately.

VARIATION

Herbed Yorkshire puddings: Add 2½ tablespoons chopped chives or parsley, or 2¼ teaspoons thyme leaves, when whisking the batter to combine.

1

2

3

Welsh cakes

These simple scone-like cakes are cooked directly on a heated flat surface, such as a cast-iron pan or griddle, rather than being baked in the oven. They are traditionally served with icing sugar or butter.

MAKES 10 **PREPARATION TIME** 20 minutes **COOKING TIME** 8 minutes

260 g (9¼ oz/1¾ cups) self-raising
   flour
75 g (2¾ oz/⅓ cup) caster
   (superfine) sugar
120 g (4¼ oz) chilled butter, chopped
1 egg, lightly whisked
80 ml (2½ fl oz/⅓ cup) milk,
   approximately
75 g (2¾ oz/½ cup) currants
20 g (¾ oz) butter, extra
Icing (confectioners') sugar or
   butter, to serve

1 Sift the flour into a medium bowl and stir in the caster sugar. With your palms facing upwards, use your fingertips to rub in the butter, lifting the flour mixture up as you rub to aerate it, until the mixture resembles fine breadcrumbs. Make a well in the centre. Add the egg and milk and mix with a flat-bladed knife, using a cutting action, until the dough comes together in clumps.

2 Use your hands to continue mixing until a soft dough forms, adding a little extra milk if necessary *(pic 1)*. Mix in the currants. Use lightly floured hands to gently gather the dough together, lift it onto a lightly floured work surface and knead very lightly and briefly to bring it together into a smooth ball.

3 Use a lightly floured rolling pin to roll the dough out to 1 cm (½ inch) thick *(pic 2)*. Use a lightly floured round 8 cm (3¼ inch) cutter to stamp out rounds of dough.

4 Melt half the extra butter in a large frying pan over medium–high heat. Cook half the rounds of dough for 2 minutes each side or until lightly browned and slightly puffed *(pic 3)*. Transfer to a plate and keep warm. Wipe out the pan with paper towels, add the remaining butter and cook the remaining rounds of dough as before. Serve warm, sprinkled with icing sugar or spread with butter, if desired.

1

2

3

TIP Welsh cakes are best eaten on the day they are made, but they can be frozen, in sealed freezer bags, for up to 6 weeks.

Crumpets

Crumpets are soft, spongy English griddle cakes that are served for afternoon tea or breakfast, most commonly with butter and jam. Bicarbonate of soda is added to the mixture shortly before cooking and this creates the characteristic holes on the crumpets' surface.

MAKES about 12   **PREPARATION TIME** 25 minutes (+ 1 hour proving)   **COOKING TIME** 44–56 minutes

250 ml (9 fl oz/1 cup) warm milk
2½ teaspoons caster (superfine) sugar
375 ml (13 fl oz/1½ cups) lukewarm
    water
10 g (¼ oz/3 teaspoons) dried yeast
450 g (1 lb/3 cups) plain
    (all-purpose) flour
1 teaspoon salt
½ teaspoon bicarbonate of soda
    (baking soda)
20 g (¾ oz) butter
Butter and berry jam, to serve

1 Combine the warm milk, sugar and 250 ml (9 fl oz/1 cup) of the lukewarm water in a large bowl or the bowl of a stand mixer. Sprinkle over the yeast, then set aside for 7–8 minutes or until foamy.

2 Add the flour and salt and use a wooden spoon or the stand mixer's paddle attachment to beat for 3–4 minutes or until smooth and elastic. Cover the bowl with plastic wrap and set aside in a warm, draught-free place for 1 hour or until the mixture is well risen and bubbly.

3 Stir the bicarbonate of soda into the remaining lukewarm water, then stir the mixture into the batter. Cover and set aside for 10 minutes *(pic 1)*.

4 Preheat the oven to 120°C (235°F/ Gas ½). Heat the butter in a large non-stick frying pan over low heat and place 3–4 greased 10 cm (4 inch) egg rings in the pan (this will depend on the size of your pan). Spoon about 80 ml (2½ fl oz/⅓ cup) crumpet batter into each ring *(pic 2)*. Cook the crumpets for 8–10 minutes or until they have risen, the bases are deep golden and the tops are dry to touch, with a few small holes *(pic 3)*.

5 Remove the rings, turn the crumpets and cook for a further 3–4 minutes or until the tops are light golden. Transfer to a plate, cover loosely with foil and keep warm in the preheated oven while cooking the remaining crumpets. Wash, dry and grease the rings before cooking each batch. Serve the crumpets warm, with butter and jam, if desired.

1

2

3

TIP Crumpets can be kept for up to 3 days in an airtight container in the refrigerator. They can also be frozen, in a sealed freezer bag, for up to 6 weeks. Toast them in a toaster before serving.

Apple popovers

Popovers are so named as the batter 'pops' or bursts over the top of the tin during baking, much like Yorkshire puddings. Savoury versions are flavoured with spices, herbs or cheese. A properly preheated oven will give the best result, and serve them promptly, as they will deflate and toughen on standing.

MAKES 6   **PREPARATION TIME** 25 minutes   **COOKING TIME** 18–25 minutes

75 g (2¾ oz) unsalted butter, melted, plus extra, to grease

75 g (2¾ oz/⅓ cup) caster (superfine) sugar

3 large granny smith apples (about 425 g/15 oz), peeled and cored, cut into 1 cm (½ inch) pieces

1 teaspoon ground cinnamon

185 ml (6 fl oz/¾ cup) milk

4 eggs

110 g (3¾ oz/¾ cup) plain (all-purpose) flour

Icing (confectioners') sugar and honey, to serve

1 Preheat the oven to 220°C (425°F/ Gas 7). Place a 6-hole, 250 ml (9 fl oz/ 1 cup) non-stick muffin tin in the oven to heat. Combine half each of the melted butter and caster sugar in a heavy-based frying pan over medium heat, then add the apples and cook, tossing often, for 8–10 minutes or until softened and light golden *(pic 1)*. Stir in the cinnamon.

2 Meanwhile, put the remaining butter and caster sugar, the milk, eggs and flour in a food processor and process until a smooth batter forms *(pic 2)*, scraping down the side of the bowl as necessary. Working quickly, remove the hot muffin tin from the oven and grease the holes with the extra melted butter. Divide the apple mixture among the holes, then pour over the batter *(pic 3)*.

3 Bake for 10–15 minutes, without opening the oven door as this can cause the popovers to deflate, or until puffed and deep golden. Turn out immediately and serve sprinkled with icing sugar and with honey passed separately.

1

2

3

Banana bread

Once you start making this cafe-style banana bread, you'll find it hard to stop. It ticks every box: simple to make (it's a melt-and-mix recipe), perfect for any time of day, and wonderfully flavoursome, with just the right balance of banana, nut and brown sugar.

SERVES 8–10   **PREPARATION TIME** 20 minutes   **COOKING TIME** 50 minutes

335 g (11¾ oz/2¼ cups) plain
   (all-purpose) flour
1 teaspoon baking powder
¼ teaspoon bicarbonate of soda
   (baking soda)
3 large (about 200 g/7 oz each) ripe
   bananas, mashed (see tip) (*pic 1*)
2 eggs, at room temperature,
   lightly whisked
125 ml (4 fl oz/½ cup) vegetable oil
220 g (7¾ oz/1 cup, firmly packed)
   brown sugar
2 teaspoons natural vanilla extract
100 g (3½ oz) pecan or walnut halves,
   coarsely chopped

1 Preheat the oven to 180°C (350°F/ Gas 4). Lightly grease and flour a 10 x 20 cm (4 x 8 inch) loaf (bar) tin.

2 Sift together the flour, baking powder and bicarbonate of soda into a large bowl.

3 Put the mashed bananas, egg, oil, sugar and vanilla in a separate bowl and stir with a fork to combine well (*pic 2*). Add the banana mixture to the flour mixture and stir with a large metal spoon until just combined. Stir in the pecans. Pour into the prepared tin (*pic 3*) and smooth the surface with the back of a spoon.

4 Bake for 50 minutes or until a skewer inserted into the centre of the loaf comes out clean. Cool in the tin for 10 minutes, then turn out onto a wire rack to cool completely.

VARIATION

Chocolate and raisin banana bread: Replace 50 g (1¾ oz/⅓ cup) of the flour with 40 g (1½ oz/⅓ cup) unsweetened cocoa powder. Replace the brown sugar with 220 g (7¾ oz/1 cup) caster (superfine) sugar. Replace the pecans with 170 g (5¾ oz/1 cup) raisins and add 100 g (3½ oz/⅔ cup) chopped dark chocolate. Cook for 55–65 minutes.

TIP You will need about 360 g (12¾ oz/1½ cups) mashed banana for this recipe.
   Keep in an airtight container for up to 3 days. To freeze, wrap well in plastic wrap, put in an airtight container or sealed freezer bag and freeze for up to 6 weeks.

Breads & Rich Yeast Breads

Basic white bread

This simple loaf is a great introduction to bread making. You can halve the quantities to make one loaf if you prefer, though making two loaves is more time-efficient as you can freeze one for later.

MAKES 2 x 17.5 cm (6¾ inch) loaves **PREPARATION TIME** 35 minutes (+ 2 hours 15 minutes proving)
COOKING TIME 40 minutes

310 ml (10¾ fl oz/1¼ cups)
   lukewarm water
Large pinch of caster (superfine) sugar
9 g (¼ oz/2½ teaspoons) dried yeast
60 g (2¼ oz) butter, melted
250 ml (9 fl oz/1 cup) milk, warmed
900 g (2 lb/6 cups) plain
   (all-purpose) flour
2 teaspoons salt

1 Combine 125 ml (4 fl oz/½ cup) of the water and the sugar in a large bowl. Sprinkle over the yeast and set aside for 5–6 minutes or until foamy *(pic 1)*.

2 Add the butter, milk, remaining water, half the flour and the salt and use a wooden spoon to mix well. Add the remaining flour, 150 g (5½ oz/ 1 cup) at a time, stirring until a coarse dough forms *(pic 2)*. Turn the dough out onto a lightly floured work surface and knead for 8–10 minutes or until it feels smooth, elastic and fairly soft, adding a little extra flour if it is too sticky.

3 Put the dough in a lightly oiled large bowl, turning to coat in the oil. Cover the bowl with plastic wrap and set aside in a warm, draught-free place for 1½ hours or until the dough has doubled in size *(pic 3)*.

4 Preheat the oven to 200°C (400°F/ Gas 6). Lightly grease two 8 x 17.5 cm (3¼ x 6¾ inch) loaf (bar) tins.

5 Knock back the dough with just one punch to expel the air. Turn out onto a lightly floured work surface and use a large sharp knife to cut in half. Working with one portion at a time, use your hands to pat the dough out into a rough rectangle, about 1.5 cm (⅝ inch) thick. Roll each rectangle up, like a Swiss roll (jelly roll), and place in the greased tins, seam side down, pushing them in to fit. Cover with a damp tea towel (dish towel) and set aside in a warm, draught-free place for 45 minutes or until the dough has risen just above the edge of each tin.

6 Use a sharp serrated knife or razor blade (see tip) to make 3–4 diagonal slashes in the top of each loaf, taking care not to deflate the dough. Bake for 10 minutes, then reduce the heat to 180°C (350°F/Gas 4) and bake for 30 minutes more or until the loaves are deep golden and sound hollow when tapped on the base. Turn out onto a wire rack to cool.

VARIATIONS

Wholemeal bread: Use 450 g (1 lb/ 3 cups) plain (all-purpose) flour and 450 g (1 lb/3 cups) plain (all-purpose) wholemeal (whole-wheat) flour.

1

2

3

TIP Razor blades are so sharp they can slash the dough cleanly and without deflating it.
   This bread can be frozen, in a sealed freezer bag, for up to 6 weeks.

Four-seed bread

The amount of time required to prove dough depends entirely on the ambient room temperature. Yeast loves warmth and humidity, so proving times are shorter during warm weather. In cool or dry weather, put the bowl of dough in a plastic bag and tie it to seal as this helps create a warm, humid environment.

MAKES 20 cm (8 inch) diameter loaf   **PREPARATION TIME** 40 minutes (+ 1–1½ hours proving)   **COOKING TIME** 25 minutes

500 g (1 lb 2 oz/3⅓ cups) plain
    (all-purpose) wholemeal
    (whole-wheat) flour
1½ teaspoons salt
350 ml (12 fl oz) lukewarm water
7 g (⅛ oz/2 teaspoons) dried yeast
1 tablespoon honey
1 tablespoon olive oil
1½ tablespoons poppy seeds
1½ tablespoons linseeds (flax seeds)
2 tablespoons sunflower seeds
40 g (1½ oz/¼ cup) sesame seeds

1 Sift the flour and salt into a large bowl. Place 50 ml (1½ fl oz) of the lukewarm water in a small bowl, add the yeast and stir to dissolve. Set aside for 5–6 minutes or until foamy.

2 Add the yeast mixture to the flour with the honey, oil and remaining lukewarm water and use a wooden spoon to mix until a rough dough forms *(pic 1)*. Turn out onto a lightly floured work surface and knead for 5 minutes or until smooth and elastic.

3 Return the dough to the bowl, add the seeds and knead until incorporated *(pic 2)*. Turn out onto a lightly floured work surface and knead for 3 minutes to distribute the seeds *(pic 3)*.

4 Shape the dough into a ball and place in a lightly oiled large bowl, turning to coat in the oil. Cover the bowl with plastic wrap and set aside in a warm, draught-free place for 30–45 minutes or until the dough has doubled in size.

5 Knock back the dough with just one punch to expel the air, then turn out onto a clean work surface. Shape into a round, about 20 cm (8 inches) in diameter, and place on a greased baking tray. Cover the dough with a damp tea towel (dish towel) and set aside in a warm, draught-free place for 30–45 minutes or until it has nearly doubled in size.

6 Meanwhile, preheat the oven to 220°C (425°F/Gas 7). Bake the bread for 10 minutes, then turn to ensure even cooking and bake for a further 12–15 minutes or until it sounds hollow when tapped on the base. Cool on the tray for 5 minutes, then transfer to a wire rack to cool to room temperature.

1

2

3

TIP This bread will keep, in an airtight bag, for 2–3 days or can be frozen, in a sealed freezer bag, for up to 8 weeks.

Rye bread

Rye flour is rather low in gluten (protein), so bread made from rye flour benefits from the addition of wheat flour, to develop structure and enable it to rise well. Rye-based doughs should not be allowed to get too warm when rising, as this makes the dough sticky and difficult to work with.

MAKES 15 cm (6 inch) loaf **PREPARATION TIME** 30 minutes (+ 12 hours standing and 1 hour 45–50 minutes proving)
COOKING TIME 45 minutes

205 g (7¼ oz/1⅔ cups) rye flour
150 g (5½ oz/1 cup) plain (all-purpose) wholemeal (whole-wheat) flour
2 g (¹⁄₁₂ oz/½ teaspoon) dried yeast
2 teaspoons salt
1½ teaspoons molasses
140 ml (4½ fl oz) lukewarm water

STARTER
110 g (3¾ oz/¾ cup) plain (all-purpose) wholemeal (whole-wheat) flour
30 g (1 oz/¼ cup) rye flour
2 g (¹⁄₁₂ oz/½ teaspoon) dried yeast
¾ teaspoon caster (superfine) sugar
250 ml (9 fl oz/1 cup) lukewarm water

1 For the starter, put all the ingredients in the bowl of a stand mixer and use the paddle attachment to mix at low speed for 2–3 minutes or until smooth *(pic 1)*. (Alternatively, if mixing by hand, put all the ingredients except the water in a bowl and mix well. Add the water in a steady stream while stirring constantly, then continue to stir vigorously for 3–4 minutes or until very smooth.) Cover the bowl with plastic wrap and set aside at room temperature for 12 hours. The mixture will be foamy.

2 Add the flours, yeast, salt, molasses and lukewarm water to the starter and use the paddle attachment to mix on low speed until a coarse dough forms. Switch to the dough hook attachment and knead for 5 minutes or until the

dough is smooth, but slightly sticky *(pic 2)*. If the dough is too dry, add a little water and if it is too wet, add a small amount of extra flour. (Alternatively, if mixing by hand, add all the ingredients to the starter and use a wooden spoon to mix until a coarse dough forms. Turn the dough out onto a lightly floured work surface and knead until a smooth, soft, slightly sticky dough forms.)

3 Shape the dough into a ball and place in a lightly oiled large bowl, turning to coat in the oil. Cover the bowl with plastic wrap and set aside at room temperature for 1 hour or until the dough has doubled in size.

4 Knock back the dough with just one punch to expel the air *(pic 3)*, then turn out onto a clean work surface. Shape the dough (it will be slightly sticky) into a 15 cm (6 inch) long log and place in a greased 9 x 15 cm (3½ x 6 inch) loaf (bar) tin. Cover with a tea towel (dish towel) and set aside at room temperature for 45–50 minutes or until nearly doubled in size.

5 Preheat the oven to 200°C (400°F/ Gas 6). Bake the bread for 45 minutes or until the loaf sounds hollow when tapped on the base. Cool for 5 minutes in the tin, then transfer to a wire rack to cool to room temperature.

TIP This bread will keep, in an airtight bag, for up to 3 days or can be frozen, in a sealed freezer bag, for up to 6 weeks.

Feta and olive pull-apart

Cutting bread dough into strips and placing them side by side in a tin creates a loaf that, once baked, can be pulled apart using your fingers. Pull-apart loaves usually have a savoury filling that makes them perfect for taking on a picnic or to serve as an accompaniment to an informal lunch or dinner.

MAKES 22.5 cm (8¾ inch) loaf   **PREPARATION TIME** 50 minutes (+ 2½ hours proving)   **COOKING TIME** 50 minutes

½ quantity basic white bread dough (see page 196)
80 g (2¾ oz/½ cup) pitted kalamata olives, coarsely chopped
150 g (5½ oz) feta cheese, crumbled
2½ tablespoons oregano leaves, coarsely chopped
1½ tablespoons olive oil

1 Follow the basic white bread recipe to the end of step 3. Knock back the dough with just one punch to expel the air and turn out onto a lightly floured work surface. Use a rolling pin to roll out the dough into a rectangle about 26 x 40 cm (10½ x 16 inches). With a long side facing you, scatter the olives, feta and oregano lengthways over half the dough, leaving a 1 cm (½ inch) border around the edges. Drizzle the oil over the filling. Grease an 8 x 22.5 cm (3¼ x 8¾ inch) loaf (bar) tin with olive oil.

2 Fold the dough over to enclose the filling (*pic 1*) and use your fingertips to press the edges of the dough all the way around to seal. Use a large sharp knife to cut the dough widthways into 10 even slices (*pic 2*). Working with one piece of dough at a time, roll up lengthways and place, cut side down, in the tin (*pic 3*), pushing in the ends to fit and taking care not to drop too much filling. Continue packing in the pieces of dough so they fit snugly in the tin, scattering with any dropped pieces of filling as you go.

3 Use your hands to press down on the surface of the dough to make it even, then cover with a tea towel (dish towel). Set aside in a warm, draught-free place for 1 hour or until the dough has risen to the top of the tin. Preheat the oven to 180°C (350°F/Gas 4).

4 Bake for 50 minutes or until the loaf is deep golden all over and the base sounds hollow when tapped. Cool in the tin for 5 minutes, then transfer to a wire rack.

VARIATION

Pesto, tomato and parmesan pull-apart: Omit the olives, feta and oregano. Spread 60 g (2¼ oz/¼ cup) pesto lengthways over half of the rolled dough, leaving a 1 cm (½ inch) border around the edges. Scatter 80 g (2¾ oz/ ¾ cup) finely grated parmesan cheese and 110 g (3¾ oz/½ cup) chopped semi-dried tomatoes over the pesto, then proceed as for the main recipe.

TIP This bread is best served on the day it is baked and is not suitable for freezing.

Cheats' sourdough

Making 'real' sourdough involves harnessing natural yeasts that are present in the air to act as a leavener, rather than using commercial yeast. Making true sourdough is a time-consuming and niche skill for the home baker, but this quick version using commercial yeast is a good approximation.

MAKES 35 cm (14 inch) loaf   **PREPARATION TIME** 30 minutes (+ 12 hours standing and 2 hours 45–50 minutes proving)
COOKING TIME 35 minutes

185 g (6½ oz/1¼ cups) plain
  (all-purpose) flour, plus extra, to dust
70 g (2½ oz/½ cup) plain (all-purpose)
  wholemeal (whole-wheat) flour
2 g (1/12 oz/½ teaspoon) dried yeast
1½ teaspoons salt
80 ml (2½ fl oz/⅓ cup) lukewarm water

STARTER

150 g (5½ oz/1 cup) plain (all-purpose)
  flour
50 g (1¾ oz/⅓ cup) plain (all-purpose)
  wholemeal (whole-wheat) flour
2 g (1/12 oz/½ teaspoon) dried yeast
1 teaspoon caster (superfine) sugar
250 ml (9 fl oz/1 cup) lukewarm water

1 For the starter, put all the ingredients in the bowl of a stand mixer and use the paddle attachment to mix at low speed for 2–3 minutes or until smooth *(pic 1)*. (Alternatively, if mixing by hand, put all the ingredients except the water in a bowl and mix well. Add the water in a steady stream while stirring constantly, then continue to stir vigorously for 3–4 minutes or until very smooth.) Cover the bowl with plastic wrap and set aside at room temperature for 12 hours. The mixture will be foamy.

2 Add the flours, yeast, salt and lukewarm water to the starter and use the paddle attachment to mix on low speed until a coarse dough forms. Switch to the dough hook attachment and knead the dough for 5 minutes or until smooth and slightly sticky. If the dough is too dry, add a little water and if it is too wet, add a little extra flour. (If mixing by hand, add all the ingredients

to the starter and use a wooden spoon to mix until a coarse dough forms. Turn the dough out onto a lightly floured work surface and knead until a smooth, soft, slightly sticky dough forms.)

3 Shape the dough into a ball and place in a lightly oiled large bowl, turning to coat in the oil. Cover the bowl with plastic wrap and set aside at room temperature (see tip) for 1 hour or until doubled in size. Knock back the dough with just one punch to expel the air, then cover the bowl with plastic wrap and set aside at room temperature for another hour or until doubled in size.

4 Knock back the dough. Turn out onto a lightly floured work surface and pat into a square, about 30 cm (12 inches). Roll it up, like a Swiss roll (jelly roll), then gently work with your hands to form a torpedo-like shape, about 35 cm (14 inches) long *(pic 2)*. Place on a baking tray lined with non-stick baking paper, cover with a tea towel (dish towel) and set aside at room temperature for 45–50 minutes or until nearly doubled in size.

5 Meanwhile, preheat the oven to 240°C (475°F/Gas 8) or the maximum temperature. Use a razor blade or sharp knife to make 3–4 diagonal slashes in the surface of the loaf *(pic 3)* and dust with flour. Bake for 10 minutes, then reduce the temperature to 180°C (350°F/Gas 4) and bake for a further 25 minutes or until the loaf sounds hollow when tapped on the base. Transfer to a wire rack to cool.

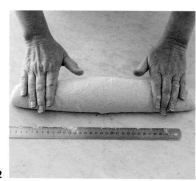

TIP It takes time to develop the flavour of this bread, so warmth is not required to accelerate proving. Store the loaf in an airtight bag for up to 3 days or freeze in a sealed freezer bag for up to 2 months.

Focaccia

Focaccia is associated with the cuisine of Liguria, a small region in northwest Italy also known as the Italian Riviera. It is eaten as a snack, as an accompaniment to meals or split and filled to make sandwiches. The simplest focaccia is topped simply with olive oil, to help it stay moist, and sea salt.

MAKES 22 x 36 cm (8½ x 14¼ inch) loaf   **PREPARATION TIME** 30 minutes (+ 1 hour proving)
COOKING TIME 25–30 minutes

Large pinch of caster (superfine) sugar
500 ml (17 fl oz/2 cups) lukewarm water
9 g (¼ oz/2½ teaspoons) dried yeast
50 ml (1½ fl oz) olive oil, plus extra,
   for drizzling
730 g (1 lb 9½ oz) plain (all-purpose)
   flour
3 teaspoons salt
Sea salt flakes and rosemary leaves,
   for sprinkling

1 Combine the sugar and 250 ml (9 fl oz/1 cup) of the lukewarm water in a large bowl, sprinkle over the yeast and set aside for 5–6 minutes or until foamy. Add the remaining lukewarm water and the olive oil, then use a wooden spoon to stir in about one-third of the flour and the salt, stirring until smooth. Gradually add the remaining flour, stirring until the mixture becomes too stiff to stir and then using your hands to mix. The dough should remain quite soft — you may not need all the flour.

2 Turn out onto a lightly floured work surface and knead for 7–8 minutes or until smooth and very elastic. Place in a lightly oiled large bowl, turning to coat in the oil. Cover the bowl with plastic wrap and set aside in a warm, draught-free place for 1 hour or until doubled in size.

3 Preheat the oven to 220°C (425°F/ Gas 7). Grease a 22 x 36 cm (8½ x 14¼ inch) baking dish with oil. Knock back the dough with just one punch to expel the air, then transfer to the greased dish. Use your hands to press the dough evenly into the dish *(pic 1)*. Use your fingertips to make deep dimples all over the surface *(pic 2)*. Drizzle with the extra olive oil *(pic 3)* and sprinkle with the salt and rosemary.

4 Bake for 25–30 minutes or until deep golden and cooked through. Turn out onto a wire rack to cool.

VARIATIONS

Green olive and oregano focaccia: Omit the sea salt flakes and rosemary. After making dimples in the dough with your fingers, press 215 g (7½ oz/1¼ cups) anchovy-stuffed green olives into the surface. Drizzle with the olive oil, then sprinkle with 2 teaspoons dried oregano.

Potato, sage and pecorino focaccia: Omit the rosemary. Add 125 g (4½ oz/ 1¼ cups) finely grated pecorino cheese to the dough with the flour. Before drizzling with olive oil and sprinkling with sea salt, scatter 300 g (10½ oz) very thinly sliced, scrubbed kipfler (fingerling) potatoes and a small handful of sage leaves over the dough.

1

2

3

TIP Focaccia is best eaten on the day it is made. It can be frozen, in a sealed freezer bag, for up to 4 weeks.

Naan

These teardrop-shaped breads are served as an accompaniment to savoury dishes and are traditionally used as a 'scoop', to replace a knife and fork. Authentic naan are slapped against the clay sides of an ultra-hot tandoor oven to cook, but a short blast under a grill (broiler) after baking is a good alternative.

MAKES 6 x 25 cm (10 inch) naan   **PREPARATION TIME** 45 minutes (+ 1 hour proving)   **COOKING TIME** 15 minutes

150 ml (5 fl oz) lukewarm milk
2 teaspoons caster (superfine) sugar
7 g (⅛ oz/2 teaspoons) dried yeast
450 g (1 lb/3 cups) plain
   (all-purpose) flour
1 teaspoon salt
1 teaspoon baking powder
2 tablespoons vegetable oil,
   plus extra, for greasing
150 g (5½ oz) plain yoghurt
1 egg, lightly whisked

1 Combine the milk and sugar in a small bowl, sprinkle over the yeast and set aside for 5–6 minutes or until foamy.

2 Sift the flour, salt and baking powder into a large bowl. Add the yeast mixture, oil, yoghurt and egg. Stir with a wooden spoon to form a coarse dough.

3 Turn out onto a lightly floured work surface and knead for 10 minutes or until smooth and elastic. Shape into a ball and place in an oiled bowl, turning to coat in the oil. Cover the bowl with plastic wrap and set aside in a warm, draught-free place for 1 hour or until doubled in size.

4 Preheat the oven to 240°C (475°F/ Gas 8). Preheat a large, heavy-based baking tray in the oven. If your oven has a separate grill (broiler), preheat that to high also.

5 Knock back the dough with just one punch to expel the air and divide it into 6 equal portions. Roll each portion into a ball, place on a lightly greased baking tray and cover with plastic wrap *(pic 1)*. Working with one ball at a time, use

a rolling pin to roll out on a lightly floured work surface into a rough oval, about 25 cm (10 inches) long and 13 cm (5 inches) wide *(pic 2)*.

6 Working quickly, remove the hot baking tray from the oven and slap 2 naan onto it. Immediately place in the oven and bake for 3 minutes or until puffed. Transfer to a large tea towel (dish towel) to keep warm *(pic 3)*. Repeat to cook the remaining naan.

7 If your grill is not separate to the oven, change the oven setting to grill and preheat on the highest heat, or use the preheated separate grill. Grill (broil) each naan, about 10 cm (4 inches) from the heat, for 40–45 seconds each side, until lightly scorched.

VARIATIONS

Coriander & garlic naan: Divide the dough into 12 balls. Working with 2 balls at a time, roll out to oval shapes about 25 cm (10 inches) long. Spread a crushed garlic clove over one rolled portion and sprinkle with 1 tablespoon finely chopped coriander (cilantro). Cover with the other rolled portion and press the edges to seal the filling inside. Cook as above.

Cheese naan: Divide the dough into 12 balls. Working with 2 balls at a time, roll out to oval shapes 25 cm (10 inches) long. Sprinkle one rolled portion with 1 tablespoon coarsely grated tasty cheddar cheese, cover with the other rolled portion and press the edges to seal the cheese inside. Cook as above.

1

2

3

TIP Naan are best eaten on the day they are made. They can be frozen, in a sealed freezer bag, for up to 8 weeks. Wrap in foil and reheat in a 150°C (300°F/Gas 2) oven for 5 minutes.

Grissini

Grissini are crisp bread sticks, originally from the area around Turin in northern Italy. They make a simple, tasty snack and are often served as a low-fuss appetiser with pre-dinner drinks. Grissini keep well and can be crisped in the oven if they become a little soft.

MAKES about 26   **PREPARATION TIME** 40 minutes (+ 1½ hours proving)   **COOKING TIME** 35 minutes

Large pinch of caster (superfine) sugar
150 ml (5 fl oz) lukewarm water
5 g (⅛ oz/1½ teaspoons) dried yeast
1 tablespoon extra virgin olive oil
225 g (8 oz/1½ cups) plain
    (all-purpose) flour
1 teaspoon salt

1 Combine the sugar and lukewarm water in a large bowl, sprinkle over the yeast and set aside for 5–6 minutes or until foamy. Stir in the olive oil. Add the flour and salt and use a wooden spoon to stir until a coarse dough forms.

2 Turn out onto a lightly floured work surface and knead for 5–6 minutes or until smooth and elastic. Place in an oiled bowl, turning to coat in the oil. Cover the bowl with plastic wrap and set aside in a warm, draught-free place for 1½ hours or until doubled in size.

3 Preheat the oven to 180°C (350°F/ Gas 4). Lightly grease 2 baking trays with oil. Knock back the dough with just one punch to expel the air. Turn out onto a lightly floured work surface and use a rolling pin to roll out to a rough rectangle, about 22 x 34 cm (8½ x 13½ inches) *(pic 1)*. Turn the dough so a long edge is facing you, then use a large, sharp knife to cut it widthways into 26 strips *(pic 2)*.

4 Use your hands to roll each strip into a thin log, about 26 cm (10½ inches) long *(pic 3)*. Some will be longer than others. Place on the greased trays and bake for 35 minutes or until golden and crisp. Transfer to wire racks to cool.

VARIATIONS

Parmesan grissini: Add 150 g (5½ oz/ 1½ cups) finely grated parmesan cheese with the flour. Cut the dough into 28 strips.

Garlic and oregano grissini: Add 1 tablespoon finely chopped garlic and 2 tablespoons dried oregano with the flour.

Fennel and pepper grissini: Add 1 tablespoon coarsely crushed fennel seeds and 2½ teaspoons freshly ground black pepper with the flour.

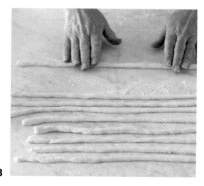

1

2

3

TIP Grissini will keep in an airtight container for up to 1 week. If they soften, place them in a preheated 180°C (350°F/Gas 4) oven for 5–6 minutes and they will become crisp again.

Pitta bread

This delicious flat bread is ubiquitous throughout the Arab world, where it is called khubz. Pitta bread has a distinctive 'pouch' inside, which develops as it bakes in a hot oven. Stack the freshly baked breads one on top of the other, then cover with a tea towel (dish towel) to keep them soft.

MAKES 8   **PREPARATION TIME** 25 minutes (+ 1½–2 hours proving)   **COOKING TIME** 15–20 minutes

Large pinch of sugar
310 ml (10¾ fl oz/1¼ cups) lukewarm water
7 g (⅛ oz/2 teaspoons) dried yeast
225 g (8 oz/1½ cups) plain (all-purpose) flour, plus extra, for dusting
200 g (7 oz/1⅓ cups) plain (all-purpose) wholemeal (whole-wheat) flour, plus extra, for dusting
1½ tablespoons olive oil
1 teaspoon salt

1 Combine the sugar and 125 ml (4 fl oz/½ cup) of the lukewarm water in a large bowl, sprinkle over the yeast and set aside for 5–6 minutes or until foamy. Combine the flours in a bowl. Add the remaining lukewarm water and half the flour to the yeast mixture and use a wooden spoon to stir vigorously for 3–4 minutes or until the mixture is well combined and very elastic.

2 Cover the bowl with plastic wrap and set aside for 10 minutes or until bubbly *(pic 1)*. Add the oil and salt and stir to combine, then gradually add the remaining flour, mixing well between each addition, until a soft, coarse dough forms. You may not need all the flour.

3 Turn out onto a lightly floured work surface and knead for 7–8 minutes or until smooth and elastic, adding a little extra flour if the dough remains sticky. Place in a lightly oiled large bowl, turning to coat in the oil. Cover the bowl with plastic wrap and set aside in a warm, draught-free place for 1½–2 hours or until doubled in size.

4 Preheat the oven to 240°C (475°F/ Gas 8) or to the maximum temperature. Knock back the dough with just one punch to expel the air, then turn out onto a lightly floured work surface and divide into 8 equal portions. Working with one portion at a time, roll into a ball and then use a rolling pin to roll out to a round about 22 cm (8½ inches) in diameter *(pic 2)*. Place the rounds on pieces of non-stick baking paper dusted with the extra plain flour. Dust each round of dough with a little extra wholemeal flour *(pic 3)*, then cover with tea towels (dish towels).

5 Preheat a baking tray in the oven. Dust the tray with extra plain flour and place 2–3 rounds of dough on it, depending on size. Bake for 5 minutes or until puffed. Transfer to a baking tray or plate, stacking them as you go, and cover with a tea towel. Continue baking the breads, one tray at a time, until they are all baked.

TIP Pitta bread is best eaten on the day it is made. It can be frozen, in a sealed freezer bag, for up to 8 weeks.

Pretzels

Pretzels originated in Europe and have come to be most closely associated with Germany. Commercial bakeries cook soft pretzels in a lye-water solution before baking, which helps make the crust brown and glossy and gives a unique flavour. However, plain water can be used and gives a delicious result.

MAKES 10 **PREPARATION TIME** 50 minutes (+ 45–55 minutes proving, 20 minutes standing and 15 minutes cooling)
COOKING TIME 30–36 minutes

375 ml (13 fl oz/1½ cups) lukewarm
   water
1 tablespoon sugar
9 g (¼ oz/2½ teaspoons) dried yeast
600 g (1 lb 5 oz/4 cups) plain
   (all-purpose) flour
1 tablespoon salt
1 egg, at room temperature,
   lightly whisked
2 teaspoons poppy seeds
1 tablespoon sea salt flakes

1 Combine the lukewarm water and sugar in a small bowl, sprinkle over the yeast and set aside for 5–6 minutes or until foamy.

2 Sift 560 g (1 lb 4¼ oz/3¾ cups) of the flour and the salt into a large bowl. Add the yeast mixture and use a wooden spoon to stir until a coarse dough forms. Turn out onto a lightly floured work surface and knead for 8 minutes, adding a little more flour, 1 tablespoon at a time, as needed. You may not need all the flour — the dough should be slightly sticky.

3 Put the dough in a lightly oiled bowl, turning to coat in the oil. Cover the bowl with plastic wrap and set aside in a warm, draught-free place for 45–55 minutes or until the dough has doubled in size. Knock back the dough with just one punch to expel the air and turn out onto a lightly floured work surface. Divide into 10 equal portions. Working with one portion at a time,

roll into a log about 55 cm (22 inches) long. If the dough sticks to your hands, dust your palms with flour.

4 Working with one log at a time, hold onto each end and make a loop *(pic 1)*. Twist the ends of the dough together once or twice *(pic 2)*, as you prefer, then bring them up to the top of the loop *(pic 3)* and press together to adhere. Place the shaped pretzels on a lightly greased baking tray, well spaced, and set aside for 20 minutes to rest.

5 Meanwhile, preheat the oven to 210°C (415°F/Gas 6–7). Lightly grease 2 baking trays with oil. Line 2 more baking trays with non-stick baking paper. Bring a large saucepan of water to the boil. Gently place 3–4 pretzels in the boiling water and cook for 1 minute, then gently turn, taking care not to damage their shape, and cook for a further minute, until puffed and set. Use a slotted spoon to carefully remove, drain well and transfer to a greased tray. Continue to boil the remaining pretzels. Once all the pretzels have been boiled, transfer them to the lined trays. Brush with the egg, sprinkle with poppy seeds and sea salt and bake for 15 minutes. Turn the trays to ensure even colouring and bake for a further 10–15 minutes or until the pretzels are golden and cooked through. Cool on the trays for 15 minutes, then serve warm.

1

2

3

TIP Pretzels are best eaten on the day they are made. They can be frozen, in sealed freezer bags, for up to 8 weeks.

Bagels

Bagels are twice-cooked, as they are boiled and then baked. Boiling gives them the dense, chewy texture for which they are so famous and 'sets' the crust, so they won't rise much in the oven. The bicarbonate of soda encourages browning during baking and contributes to their unique flavour.

MAKES 10   **PREPARATION TIME** 1 hour (+ overnight chilling and 1½–2 hours proving)   **COOKING TIME** 35 minutes

5 g (⅛ oz/1½ teaspoons) dried yeast
250 ml (9 fl oz/1 cup) room-temperature water
750 g (1 lb 10 oz/5 cups) plain (all-purpose) flour, approximately
250 ml (9 fl oz/1 cup) warm water
1½ tablespoons vegetable oil
90 g (3¼ oz/¼ cup) malt extract
2 teaspoons salt
1 tablespoon bicarbonate of soda (baking soda)
1 egg, whisked with 1 tablespoon water
Poppy and sesame seeds, for sprinkling

1 Put the yeast, room-temperature water and 375 g (13 oz/2½ cups) of the flour in a bowl and use a fork to stir until a coarse dough forms. Turn the dough out onto a very lightly floured work surface and knead for 4–5 minutes, until a smooth dough forms. Place the dough in a lightly floured bowl, turning to coat in the flour. Cover the bowl with plastic wrap and refrigerate overnight.

2 Use a large sharp knife to cut the dough into 7 or 8 pieces and place in the bowl of a stand mixer. Add the warm water, oil, malt extract, salt and 335 g (11¾ oz/2¼ cups) of the remaining flour. Use the dough hook attachment to knead on low speed for 10–15 minutes or until the dough is smooth and very elastic and comes away from the side of the bowl. The dough should be a little soft.

3 Cover the bowl with plastic wrap and set aside at room temperature for 1½–2 hours or until the dough has doubled in size.

4 Knock back the dough with just one punch to expel the air, then turn out onto a lightly floured work surface and divide into 10 equal portions. Preheat the oven to 180°C (350°F/Gas 4). Lightly grease 2 baking trays with oil.

5 Place 8–10 cm (3¼–4 inches) of water in a large, deep frying pan or shallow saucepan and bring to the boil. Add the bicarbonate of soda. Meanwhile, working with one portion of dough at a time, shape it into a ball on a lightly floured surface. Push your finger through the middle of the ball to form a hole, then pick it up and work it in your hands to enlarge the hole and form a ring around it, about 10–12 cm (4–4½ inches) in diameter *(pic 1)*.

6 Cook the bagels, in batches, in the boiling water for 2 minutes *(pic 2)*, then turn and boil for a further 90 seconds. Turn again, then use a slotted spoon to remove from the water and drain well. Transfer to the greased trays. Brush the bagels with the egg wash, then sprinkle with the poppy or sesame seeds *(pic 3)*. Bake for 20 minutes, swapping the trays halfway through cooking, or until golden and cooked through. Transfer to a wire rack to cool.

1

2

3

TIP Bagels are best eaten on the day they are made. They can be frozen, in sealed freezer bags, for up to 8 weeks.

Calzone

A calzone is technically a folded pizza that originated as snack food in the Italian city of Naples. Its name means 'pantaloons', as the folded shape supposedly resembles the leg of a man's trousers.

MAKES 4   **PREPARATION TIME** 25 minutes (+ 1 hour proving)   **COOKING TIME** 15 minutes

1 quantity pizza dough (see page 220)
Green salad, to serve

FILLING
200 g (7 oz) mozzarella cheese, thinly sliced
200 g (7 oz) sliced leg ham, any rind removed
2 roma (plum) tomatoes, thinly sliced
Small handful of basil leaves, torn

1 Preheat the oven to 240°C (475°F/ Gas 8) and lightly grease 2 baking trays. Make the pizza dough to the end of step 2, then knock it back with just one punch to expel the air. Divide the dough into 4 equal portions and roll each into a ball. Working with one ball at a time, use a rolling pin to roll out on a lightly floured work surface into a round, about 22 cm (8½ inches) in diameter *(pic 1)*.

2 Divide the cheese, ham, tomatoes and basil among the rounds, spreading them over half of each round and leaving a 1 cm (½ inch) border around the edge *(pic 2)*. Very lightly brush the border with water. Fold the uncovered dough over the filling to form a semi-circle, then use your fingertips to firmly press the edges to seal *(pic 3)*. Transfer to the greased baking trays.

3 Bake the calzone for 15 minutes, swapping the trays halfway through cooking, or until the crust is deep golden. Serve hot, with a green salad.

VARIATIONS

Mushroom calzone: Omit the filling. Heat 60 ml (2 fl oz/¼ cup) olive oil in a large frying pan over medium heat. Add 1 finely chopped onion, 3 crushed garlic cloves and 450 g (1 lb) finely chopped field mushrooms and cook, stirring often, for 8–10 minutes or until the vegetables are soft and any excess liquid has evaporated. Stir in 2½ teaspoons chopped thyme leaves and 125 g (4½ oz/ 1 cup) coarsely grated mozzarella cheese. Season with sea salt and freshly ground black pepper, to taste, and set aside to cool. Use to replace the filling.

Ricotta and spinach calzone: Omit the filling. Heat 1½ tablespoons olive oil in a large saucepan over medium heat. Add 1 finely chopped onion and 2 crushed garlic cloves and cook for 5 minutes or until softened. Add 40 g (1½ oz/¼ cup) currants and 3 chopped anchovies. Cook, stirring, for a further 1–2 minutes, then add 250 g (9 oz) baby spinach leaves. Cover and cook, stirring occasionally, for 3 minutes or until the spinach is wilted. Season with sea salt and freshly ground black pepper, to taste, and set aside to cool. Use to replace the filling, scattering each with 60 g (2¼ oz/¼ cup) firm fresh ricotta cheese, crumbled into large pieces, and 2 tablespoons finely grated parmesan or pecorino cheese before folding.

1

2

3

Tomato, salami and mozzarella pizza

Pizza dough is simple to make and produces a wonderful crisp, light base. Home-made tomato sauce for the base is worth the (minimal) effort and can be made while the dough is proving. A pizza stone will help you achieve a crisp crust — always put it in a cold oven and then preheat, or it can crack.

SERVES 4   **PREPARATION TIME** 40 minutes (+ 1 hour proving)   **COOKING TIME** 45 minutes–1 hour 15 minutes

DOUGH
Large pinch of caster (superfine) sugar
250 ml (9 fl oz/1 cup) lukewarm water
7 g (1/8 oz/2 teaspoons) dried yeast
2 tablespoons extra virgin olive oil
350 g (12 oz/2⅓ cups) plain
   (all-purpose) flour
1½ teaspoons salt

TOMATO SAUCE
1 tablespoon olive oil
1 small brown onion, finely chopped
1 tablespoon tomato paste
   (concentrated purée)
400 g (14 oz) tin chopped tomatoes
Small handful of small basil leaves

TOPPING
300 g (10½ oz) mozzarella cheese
200 g (7 oz) mild Italian-style salami
200 g (7 oz) cherry tomatoes, halved
50 g (1¾ oz) rocket (arugula) leaves

1 To make the dough, combine the sugar and 125 ml (4 fl oz/½ cup) of the water in a bowl, sprinkle over the yeast and set aside for 7–8 minutes or until foamy. Stir in the oil and remaining water, then add the flour and salt. Use your hands to mix until a coarse dough forms *(pic 1)*. Turn onto a lightly floured work surface and knead for 8 minutes, until smooth and elastic.

2 Transfer the dough to a lightly oiled large bowl, turning to coat in the oil. Cover the bowl with plastic wrap and set aside in a warm, draught-free place for 1 hour or until doubled in size.

3 Meanwhile, to make the tomato sauce, heat the oil in a small saucepan over medium heat. Add the onion and cook, stirring, for 5–6 minutes or until softened. Add the tomato paste and stir for 1 minute, then stir in the tomatoes. Reduce the heat to low and cook, stirring often, for 10 minutes or until thickened slightly. Cool, then stir in the basil.

4 If you have a pizza stone, put it in the oven. Preheat the oven to 240°C (475°F/ Gas 8). Knock back the dough with just one punch to expel the air, then turn out onto a lightly floured work surface. Divide into 4 equal portions and roll each into a ball *(pic 2)*. Working with one ball at a time, use a rolling pin to roll out into a round, 22 cm (8½ inches) in diameter. Transfer to lightly oiled baking trays or a floured work surface if using a pizza stone.

5 Divide the tomato sauce among the rounds *(pic 3)*, leaving a 1 cm (½ inch) border. Thinly slice the mozzarella and salami and scatter over the rounds with the tomatoes. Bake each tray of pizza for 12–15 minutes or until the dough is golden and the topping is bubbling, or carefully transfer the rounds to the pizza stone and cook as above. Serve the hot pizzas immediately, scattered with rocket, while the others are cooking.

VARIATION
Three-cheese and sage pizza: Replace the topping with 125 g (4½ oz) gorgonzola cheese, crumbled, 250 g (9 oz) mozzarella cheese, thinly sliced, 100 g (3½ oz) provolone piccante or parmesan cheese, finely grated, and a small handful of sage leaves.

TIP Pizza dough can be frozen, shaped into balls and placed in sealed freezer bags, for up to 1 month. The yeast may lose a little of its rising ability, but the difference will be minimal.

Gozleme

Gozleme are flat breads from Turkey, where they are a common snack food. In Turkey, a long thin rolling pin called an oklava is used to roll the dough and they are cooked on large griddles.

MAKES 4 **PREPARATION TIME** 40 minutes (+ 30 minutes proving) **COOKING TIME** 16–24 minutes

1 teaspoon caster (superfine) sugar
125 ml (4 fl oz/½ cup) lukewarm water
9 g (¼ oz/2½ teaspoons) dried yeast
450 g (1 lb/3 cups) plain (all-purpose) flour
½ teaspoon salt
160 ml (5¼ fl oz/⅔ cup) lukewarm milk
1 tablespoon olive oil
1 large brown onion, thinly sliced
2 garlic cloves, crushed
1 teaspoon paprika
¼ teaspoon cayenne pepper
100 g (3½ oz) baby spinach leaves, coarsely chopped
2 tablespoons finely chopped mint
100 g (3½ oz) firm, fresh ricotta cheese
200 g (7 oz) crumbled feta cheese
Lemon wedges, to serve

1 Combine the sugar and lukewarm water in a small bowl. Sprinkle over the yeast, then set aside for 7–8 minutes or until foamy.

2 Sift the flour and salt into a large bowl. Make a well in the centre, then add the yeast mixture and lukewarm milk. Use a flat-bladed knife in a cutting action to gradually mix together until a coarse dough forms. Turn out onto a lightly floured work surface and knead until smooth and elastic. Place in a lightly oiled bowl, turning to coat in the oil. Cover the bowl with plastic wrap and set aside in a warm, draught-free place for 30 minutes.

3 Meanwhile, heat the oil in a large frying pan over medium–high heat. Add the onion and cook, stirring, for 5 minutes. Add the garlic, paprika and cayenne pepper and cook for 1 minute or until aromatic. Add the spinach and cook, stirring occasionally, for 2 minutes or until just wilted. Transfer to a bowl, add the mint and stir to combine. Cool to room temperature.

4 Combine the ricotta and feta in a separate bowl. Divide the dough into 4 equal portions. Working with one portion at a time, use a rolling pin to roll out on a lightly floured work surface into a 20 x 35 cm (8 x 14 inch) rectangle, about 3 mm (⅛ inch) thick. Place one-quarter of the spinach mixture over half of the rectangle, leaving a 1 cm (½ inch) border. Top with one-quarter of the cheese mixture *(pic 1)*. Fold the dough over to enclose the filling *(pic 2)*, then press the edges together to seal.

5 Preheat a large non-stick frying pan or barbecue plate over medium heat. Lightly brush the pan or plate with a little oil. Cook the gozleme *(pic 3)*, one at a time, for 2–3 minutes each side or until cooked through. Transfer to a serving plate, cut into quarters and serve immediately with lemon wedges.

1

2

3

TIP Another classic gozleme filling is mashed potato, which is delicious with sheep's or goat's milk cheese sprinkled over. The addition of mint leaves, while not traditional, would also be nice.

Babka

MAKES 2   PREPARATION TIME 40 minutes (+ 1 hour 40 minutes proving, and cooling)   COOKING TIME 35 minutes

200 ml (7 fl oz) lukewarm milk
10 g (¼ oz/3 teaspoons) dried yeast
75 g (2¾ oz/⅓ cup) caster
    (superfine) sugar
4 egg yolks, at room temperature
2 eggs, at room temperature
2 teaspoons natural vanilla extract
600 g (1 lb 5 oz/4 cups) plain
    (all-purpose) flour, sifted
½ teaspoon salt
200 g (7 oz) unsalted butter, softened
1½ quantities glacé icing (see page 22)
Rose-pink food colouring (optional)

ALMOND FILLING
250 g (9 oz) marzipan, chopped
100 g (3½ oz/1 cup) almond meal
50 g (1¾ oz) unsalted butter, softened
1 egg, at room temperature

1 Combine the milk, yeast and a large pinch of the sugar in a small bowl. Set aside for 5–6 minutes or until foamy.

2 Put the yeast mixture, remaining sugar, the egg yolks, eggs and vanilla in the bowl of a stand mixer and beat on low speed until well combined. Gradually add 450 g (1 lb/3 cups) of the flour and the salt and beat until smooth. Add the butter a little at a time, alternating with the remaining flour, and beat until a soft dough forms. Turn out onto a lightly floured work surface and knead for 5 minutes or until smooth and elastic. Return to the bowl, cover with plastic wrap and set aside in a warm, draught-free place for 50 minutes or until doubled in size.

3 Grease and lightly flour 2 small 1 litre (35 fl oz/4 cup) kugelhopf tins.

4 Knock back the dough with one punch to expel the air, then turn out onto a lightly floured work surface and divide into 2 equal portions.

5 To make the almond filling, put all the ingredients in a bowl and use an electric mixer to beat for 2–3 minutes or until smooth.

6 Use a lightly floured rolling pin to roll out a portion of dough to a rectangle about 25 x 40 cm (10 x 16 inches) *(pic 1)*. Spread with half the filling, leaving a 2.5 cm (1 inch) border. Roll up firmly, starting at a long edge *(pic 2)*. Repeat with the remaining dough and filling.

7 Place the dough in the prepared tins, pinching the ends together to join *(pic 3)*. Press gently on the top with your hands to distribute the dough evenly. Cover each tin with a tea towel (dish towel). Set aside in a warm, draught-free place for 40–50 minutes or until the dough has risen to the top of each tin.

8 Preheat oven to 180°C (350°F/Gas 4). Bake the babkas for 35 minutes, covering with foil if they brown too quickly, or until an inserted skewer comes out clean. Leave in the tins for 10 minutes, then turn onto a wire rack to cool.

9 Tint the icing (frosting) with a few drops of food colouring. Drizzle over the cooled babkas and leave until set.

> **TIP** This recipe can be halved to make one babka, if preferred.
>   The babkas can also be baked in 10 x 20 cm (4 x 8 inch) loaf (bar) tins if kugelhopf tins are not available.
>   Un-iced babkas can be frozen, wrapped in plastic wrap and stored in a freezer bag, for up to 1 month.

Sticky pecan buns

The caramel and pecan topping on these sweet, more-ish buns means they require no spreads or accompaniments and makes them perfect to take on picnics and pack into lunchboxes.

MAKES 24   **PREPARATION TIME** 1 hour (+ 1½ hours proving)   **COOKING TIME** 15–18 minutes

700 g (1 lb 9 oz/4²⁄₃ cups) plain (all-purpose) flour

1 teaspoon salt

60 g (2¼ oz) chilled butter, cubed

110 g (3¾ oz/½ cup) caster (superfine) sugar

14 g (½ oz/1 tablespoon) dried yeast

375 ml (13 fl oz/1½ cups) lukewarm milk, plus 1 tablespoon extra, for brushing

1 egg, at room temperature, lightly whisked

75 g (2¾ oz) butter, extra, melted

165 g (5¾ oz/¾ cup, firmly packed) dark brown sugar

175 g (6 oz/½ cup) honey

115 g (4 oz/1 cup) coarsely chopped pecan halves

1 Sift the flour and salt together into a large bowl. Rub in the butter until the mixture resembles fine breadcrumbs. Stir in the caster sugar and yeast. Make a well in the centre and add the milk and egg. Stir to gradually incorporate the surrounding flour until a soft dough forms. Turn out onto a lightly floured work surface and knead for 5 minutes or until smooth and elastic. Shape into a ball and place in a lightly oiled bowl, turning to coat in the oil.

2 Cover with a tea towel (dish towel) and set aside in a warm, draught-free place for 1 hour 10 minutes or until the dough has doubled in size (pic 1).

3 Meanwhile, combine the melted butter, dark brown sugar and honey in a medium bowl. Pour into a 24 x 29 cm (9½ x 11½ inch) baking tin and sprinkle over the pecans (pic 2).

4 Preheat the oven to 200°C (400°F/Gas 6).

5 Turn the dough out onto a lightly floured work surface and knead until smooth. You may need a little more flour, up to 35 g (1¼ oz/¼ cup). The dough should be soft, but not sticky. Divide into 24 equal portions and knead each into a ball. Place the buns smooth-side down in the prepared tin (pic 3). Cover loosely with a tea towel and leave in a warm, draught-free place for 20 minutes or until the dough has doubled in size.

6 Brush the buns with the extra milk. Bake for 15–18 minutes or until they are golden brown and sound hollow when tapped on the top. Leave in the tin for 5 minutes before turning out of the tin (see tip). Serve the buns warm or at room temperature.

> **TIP** The sticky glaze will run over the buns when you turn the buns out of the tin.
> Sticky buns are best eaten on the day they are baked.

Challah

MAKES 2   **PREPARATION TIME** 40 minutes (+ 2 hours proving)   **COOKING TIME** 35–40 minutes

125 ml (4 fl oz/½ cup) lukewarm water
55 g (2 oz/¼ cup) caster
   (superfine) sugar
14 g (½ oz/1 tablespoon) dried yeast
90 g (3¼ oz/¼ cup) honey
100 g (3½ oz) butter, melted and cooled
4 egg yolks
3 eggs, at room temperature
675 g (1 lb 8 oz/4½ cups) plain
   (all-purpose) flour
2½ teaspoons salt
1 teaspoon poppy seeds

1 Combine the lukewarm water and a pinch of the sugar in the bowl of a stand mixer. Sprinkle over the yeast, then set aside for 5–6 minutes or until foamy. Add the remaining sugar, honey, butter, egg yolks and 2 of the whole eggs and use the paddle attachment to beat until combined.

2 Add half the flour and the salt and mix on low speed until smooth. Change to the dough hook, then gradually add the remaining flour, kneading on low speed for 8 minutes or until the dough is smooth and elastic.

3 Cover the bowl with plastic wrap and set aside in a warm, draught-free place for 1 hour or until it has doubled in size. Line a large baking tray with non-stick baking paper.

4 Knock back the dough with just one punch to expel the air, then turn out onto a lightly floured work surface and knead for 1 minute or until smooth and elastic. Halve the dough, then divide one of the halves into thirds. Using your hands, roll each third into a log, about 36 cm (14¼ inches) long *(pic 1)*. Arrange the 3 logs closely together in a line, then press together firmly at one end to join. Overlap the logs to form a tight plait (braid) *(pic 2)*, then press the ends together to join. Transfer to the baking tray. Repeat with the remaining dough.

5 Whisk the remaining egg, then brush over the loaves. Sprinkle with the poppy seeds *(pic 3)*. Cover the loaves loosely with a tea towel (dish towel) and set aside in a warm, draught-free place for 1 hour or until well risen (the loaves will not double in size).

6 Preheat the oven to 180°C (350°F/ Gas 4). Bake the challah loaves for 35–40 minutes, covering with foil after 30 minutes to prevent excessive browning, or until golden and cooked through. Transfer to a wire rack to cool. Serve the challah as an accompaniment to savoury meals.

> **TIP** You can refrigerate the dough at the end of step 2 and let it rise slowly overnight. The chilled dough is easier to shape, although the second rising will take longer (up to 2 hours).
>
> The challah will keep, wrapped in plastic wrap, for up to 2 days. Alternatively, wrap and seal in a freezer bag or airtight container and freeze for up to 6 weeks. Thaw at room temperature.

Brioche

MAKES 16   **PREPARATION TIME** 40 minutes (+ 2½–3 hours proving)   **COOKING TIME** 15–18 minutes

675 g (1 lb 8 oz/4½ cups) plain
   (all-purpose) flour
14 g (½ oz/1 tablespoon) dried yeast
75 g (2¾ oz/⅓ cup) caster
   (superfine) sugar
2 teaspoons salt
125 ml (4 fl oz/½ cup) lukewarm water
6 eggs, at room temperature
230 g (8 oz) unsalted butter, softened,
   plus extra, for greasing
1 egg yolk, whisked with 2 teaspoons
   water, for brushing

1 Put 150 g (5½ oz/1 cup) of the flour, the yeast, sugar, salt and water in the bowl of a stand mixer and beat on medium speed for 2–3 minutes, until very smooth. Add the eggs one at a time, beating well after each addition. Reduce the speed to low and gradually add 300 g (10½ oz/2 cups) of the remaining flour, beating until smooth.

2 Add the butter a little at a time, beating after each addition to incorporate. When all the butter has been added and the mixture is smooth, add the remaining flour and beat to combine well. The mixture should be soft and very elastic.

3 Scrape down the side of the bowl, cover with plastic wrap and set aside in a warm, draught-free place for 1½ hours or until doubled in size. Gently deflate the dough using a wooden spoon *(pic 1)*. Cover and set aside at room temperature for another 1–1½ hours or until nearly doubled in size once more. (Alternatively, cover the bowl with plastic wrap and refrigerate for 12 hours.)

4 Preheat the oven to 200°C (400°F/ Gas 6). Lightly grease sixteen 7 cm (2¾ inch) (top measurement) brioche moulds. Divide the dough into 16 equal portions. Working with one portion at a time, remove a piece almost the size of a tablespoon from each portion of dough, then use your hands to roll the larger piece into a smooth ball. Place in a greased tin, then use a bread knife to cut a small cross in the middle, all the way through to the base *(pic 2)*. Roll the smaller piece of dough into a ball, squeeze the end of it to taper it slightly and then push the tapered end into the cut in the dough *(pic 3)*.

5 Brush lightly with the egg yolk mixture. Bake for 15–18 minutes or until deep golden and cooked through. Leave in the tins for 5 minutes, then turn out onto a wire rack to cool.

VARIATION

Rosemary and parmesan brioche (makes two 10 x 22 cm/4 x 8½ inch loaves): Reduce the sugar to 55 g (2 oz/¼ cup). Add 2 tablespoons finely chopped rosemary leaves to the dough with the eggs. After the second rise, divide the dough in half and then roll each piece out on a lightly floured surface to a rectangle, about 25 x 30 cm (10 x 12 inches). Brush each rectangle with beaten egg, then scatter 125 g (4½ oz/ 1¼ cups) finely grated parmesan cheese over each piece, leaving a 2 cm (¾ inch) border. Starting at a short side, roll each rectangle up and then tuck under the ends. Place each in a greased 8 x 19 cm (4 x 7½ inch) loaf (bar) tin, seam side down. Brush with beaten egg, sprinkle with rosemary leaves and bake in an oven preheated to 180°C (350°F/ Gas 4) for 45 minutes or until deep golden and cooked through. Cover with foil if browning too quickly. Leave in the tins for 10 minutes, then carefully turn out onto a wire rack to cool.

1

2

3

TIP Brioche are best served on the day they are baked, though they will keep, stored in an airtight container, for up to 3 days. They are best served toasted after the first day. They can also be frozen, in an airtight container or sealed freezer bag, for up to 6 weeks.

Kugelhopf

Legend has it that Marie Antoinette's fondness for enriched yeast breads made cakes such as the kugelhopf very popular in France. It is certainly a favourite in the Alsace region, where it is baked at night and served the following morning as it's believed this cake tastes best when slightly stale.

SERVES 12–14 **PREPARATION TIME** 30 minutes (+ 2½ hours proving) **COOKING TIME** 45 minutes

13 blanched almonds
85 g (3 oz/½ cup) raisins
60 ml (2 fl oz/¼ cup) kirsch
500 g (1 lb 2 oz/3⅓ cups) plain
   (all-purpose) flour
1 teaspoon salt
150 g (5½ oz) chilled butter, cubed
110 g (3¾ oz/½ cup) caster
   (superfine) sugar
10 g (¼ oz/3 teaspoons) dried yeast
185 ml (6 fl oz/¾ cup) lukewarm milk
2 eggs, at room temperature,
   lightly whisked
2 teaspoons finely grated lemon zest
Icing (confectioners') sugar, to dust

1 Brush a 2.5 litre (87 fl oz/10 cup), 14 cm (5½ inch) (top measurement) kugelhopf tin with melted butter to grease. Place the almonds in the grooves of the tin.

2 Combine the raisins and kirsch in a small bowl and set aside to soak.

3 Sift the flour and salt into a large bowl. Rub in the butter until the mixture resembles breadcrumbs. Stir in the sugar and yeast. Make a well in the centre and add the milk and egg. Stir to gradually incorporate the surrounding flour until a soft dough forms. Turn out onto a lightly floured surface and knead for 5–10 minutes or until the dough is smooth and elastic. Shape the dough into a ball and place in a lightly oiled bowl, turning to coat in the oil.

4 Cover the bowl with a tea towel (dish towel) and leave in a warm, draught-free place for 1½ hours or until the dough has doubled in size (*pic 1*).

5 Turn the dough onto a lightly floured work surface. Add the raisin mixture and zest, and knead until well combined (*pic 2*). You may need to add more flour, up to 75 g (2¾ oz/½ cup) to ensure the dough is soft, but not sticky. Roll the dough into a log shape, long enough to fit the tin. Carefully place in the greased tin (*pic 3*) and press down to even up the surface. Cover with a tea towel and set aside in a warm, draught-free place for 1 hour or until doubled in size. Preheat the oven to 180°C (350°F/Gas 4).

6 Bake the kugelhopf for 45 minutes or until golden and an inserted skewer comes out clean. Remove from the oven and turn out onto a wire rack to cool. Serve dusted with the icing sugar.

1

2

3

Orange, cardamom and plum jam brioche

Scandinavia provided the inspiration for the wonderful flavour combination in these buns. The Vikings used to trade goods for spices when they travelled along the rivers of Russia and cardamom soon became a popular flavouring for their baked goods. These buns make a delicious breakfast or brunch.

MAKES 16   **PREPARATION TIME** 45 minutes (+ 3–3½ hours proving)   **COOKING TIME** 20 minutes

675 g (1 lb 8 oz/4½ cups) plain
   (all-purpose) flour
14 g (½ oz/1 tablespoon) dried yeast
75 g (2¾ oz/⅓ cup) caster
   (superfine) sugar
2 teaspoons salt
125 ml (4 fl oz/½ cup) lukewarm water
Finely grated zest of 2 oranges
6 eggs, at room temperature
230 g (8 oz) unsalted butter,
   chopped and softened
2½ teaspoons ground cardamom
125 g (4½ oz/½ cup) plum or
   cherry jam
1 egg yolk, whisked with
   2 teaspoons water
50 g (1¾ oz/½ cup) flaked almonds

1 Combine 150 g (5½ oz/1 cup) of the flour, the yeast, sugar, salt and lukewarm water in the bowl of a stand mixer and beat on medium speed for 2–3 minutes, until very smooth. Beat in the orange zest. Add the eggs one at a time, beating well after each addition. Reduce the speed to low and gradually add 300 g (10½ oz/2 cups) of the remaining flour, beating until the mixture is smooth.

2 Add the butter a little at a time, beating well after each addition to incorporate the butter. When all the butter is added and the mixture is smooth, add the remaining flour and the cardamom and beat until smooth and well combined. The mixture should be soft and very elastic.

3 Scrape down the side of the bowl, then cover with plastic wrap and set aside in a warm, draught-free place for 1½ hours or until the dough has doubled in size. Use a wooden spoon to gently deflate the dough, then cover again and set aside at room temperature for 1–1½ hours or until the dough has nearly doubled in size once more (alternatively, cover with plastic wrap and refrigerate for 12 hours).

4 Take two 12-hole 185 ml (6 fl oz/ ¾ cup) muffin tins and line 16 of the holes with paper cases. Knock back the dough with just one punch to expel the air, then turn out onto a clean work surface and use a large sharp knife to divide the dough into 16 equal portions. Roll each portion into a ball.

5 Working with one ball of dough at a time, use a finger to make a deep indentation, then pinch the edges of the dough around the indentation up a little to form a cavity *(pic 1)*. Place a teaspoonful of plum or cherry jam in the cavity *(pic 2)*, then bring the dough up over the filling to enclose it and shape into a ball *(pic 3)*. Place the balls in the lined muffin holes, seam sides down. Set aside at room temperature for 30 minutes to rise.

6 Preheat the oven to 180°C (350°F/ Gas 4). Brush each brioche with the egg yolk mixture, then sprinkle with the flaked almonds. Bake for 20 minutes or until golden.

1

2

3

TIP This recipe can be halved successfully to make 8 brioche.
   The brioche are best eaten on the day they are made. They can be frozen, wrapped in plastic wrap and stored in a sealed freezer bag, for up to 6 weeks.

Chocolate and cinnamon babka

MAKES 2 **PREPARATION TIME** 40 minutes (+ 1 hour 30–40 minutes proving) **COOKING TIME** 35 minutes

200 ml (7 fl oz) lukewarm milk
75 g (2¾ oz/⅓ cup) caster
   (superfine) sugar
10 g (¼ oz/3 teaspoons) dried yeast
4 egg yolks, at room temperature
2 eggs, at room temperature
2 teaspoons natural vanilla extract
600 g (1 lb 5 oz/4 cups) plain
   (all-purpose) flour
½ teaspoon salt
200 g (7 oz) unsalted butter,
   chopped and softened

FILLING
110 g (3¾ oz/½ cup, firmly packed)
   light brown sugar
30 g (1 oz/¼ cup) unsweetened
   cocoa powder, sifted
1 teaspoon ground cinnamon
75 g (2¾ oz) butter, softened
100 g (3½ oz) dark chocolate,
   finely chopped

ICING
280 g (10 oz/2¼ cups) icing
   (confectioners') sugar, sifted
30 g (1 oz) unsalted butter

1 Combine the lukewarm milk and a large pinch of the sugar in a small bowl. Sprinkle over the yeast, then set aside for 5–6 minutes or until foamy.

2 Put the yeast mixture, remaining sugar, the egg yolks, eggs and vanilla in a large bowl. Use an electric mixer to beat on low speed until well combined. Gradually add 450 g (1 lb/3 cups) of the flour and the salt and beat until smooth. Add the butter a little at a time, alternating with the remaining flour, and beat until a soft dough forms. Turn out onto a lightly floured work surface and knead for 5 minutes or until smooth and elastic. Return to the bowl, cover with plastic wrap and set aside in a

warm, draught-free place for 50 minutes or until doubled in size.

3 Grease and lightly flour two 16 cm (6¼ inch) diameter (top measurement) kugelhopf tins.

4 Knock back the dough, then turn out onto a lightly floured work surface and divide in half.

5 To make the filling, combine all the ingredients in a bowl.

6 Working with one portion of dough at a time, use a rolling pin to roll out on a lightly floured work surface to a rectangle, 25 x 40 cm (10 x 16 inches). Scatter over half the filling, leaving a 2.5 cm (1 inch) border *(pic 1)*. With a long side facing you, roll up firmly, like a Swiss roll (jelly roll), to form a log *(pic 2)*.

7 Place the logs in the prepared tins, pinching the ends together *(pic 3)*. Press gently with your hands to even the surfaces. Cover with a tea towel (dish towel). Set aside in a warm, draught-free place for 40–50 minutes or until the dough has risen to the tops of the tins.

8 Preheat oven to 180°C (350°F/Gas 4). Bake the babkas for 35 minutes, covering with foil if they brown too fast, or until an inserted skewer comes out with no dough on it. Set aside for 10 minutes, then turn onto a wire rack to cool.

9 To make the icing (frosting), put the icing sugar, butter and 1½ tablespoons water in a small heatproof bowl over a saucepan of simmering water (make sure the base of the bowl doesn't touch the water). Stir until the icing is glossy and smooth. Drizzle over the babkas and allow to set before serving.

1

2

3

TIP This recipe can be halved successfully. The babkas can also be baked in two 10 x 22 cm (4 x 8½ inch) loaf (bar) tins if kugelhopf tins are not available.
   Un-iced babkas can be frozen, wrapped in plastic wrap and stored in a sealed freezer bag, for up to 1 month.

Lemon and apricot savarin

Savarin is a rich yeasted cake, soaked in a rum or kirsch syrup and often served with lashings of whipped cream, thought to have originated in Poland with inspiration from the babka and kugelhopf. This version is flavoured using lemon and the southern Italian liqueur, limoncello.

MAKES 22 cm (8½ inch) diameter cake **PREPARATION TIME** 30 minutes (+ 1 hour soaking and 1 hour 40 minutes proving)
COOKING TIME 25 minutes

7 g (⅛ oz/2 teaspoons) dried yeast
2½ tablespoons caster (superfine) sugar
60 ml (2 fl oz/¼ cup) warm milk
2 eggs, whisked
Finely grated zest of 1 lemon
150 g (5½ oz/1 cup) plain (all-purpose) flour, sifted
½ teaspoon salt
60 g (2¼ oz) unsalted butter, softened
100 g (3½ oz) whole dried apricots, soaked in boiling water for 1 hour
Whipped cream, to serve

SYRUP
350 g (12 oz) caster (superfine) sugar
80 ml (2½ fl oz/⅓ cup) strained freshly squeezed lemon juice
2 tablespoons limoncello, brandy or gin

1 Combine the yeast, sugar and milk in the bowl of a stand mixer and set aside for 4–5 minutes or until the yeast has softened. Add the egg, then use the paddle attachment to mix until well combined *(pic 1)*. Add the lemon zest, flour and salt while beating on low speed, then continue to beat for 5–6 minutes or until smooth and elastic. Cover with plastic wrap and set aside in a warm, draught-free place for 1 hour or until bubbling and risen (the mixture will not quite double in size).

2 Gradually add the butter while beating constantly using the paddle attachment, until the mixture is smooth and the butter is incorporated. Grease and flour a 22 cm (8½ inch), 1 litre (35 fl oz/4 cup) savarin tin. Use a slotted spoon to remove the apricots from the liquid and place, slightly overlapping, around the tin. Brush with the soaking liquid. Spoon in the batter *(pic 2)*, cover the tin with a slightly damp tea towel (dish towel) and set aside in a warm, draught-free place for 40 minutes or until risen to the top of the tin.

3 Preheat the oven to 180°C (350°F/ Gas 4). Bake for 25 minutes or until a skewer inserted into the centre of the cake comes out clean.

4 Meanwhile, to make the syrup, combine the sugar and 310 ml (10¾ fl oz/1¼ cups) water in a saucepan over medium–low heat. Slowly bring to a simmer and cook for 5 minutes or until the sugar has dissolved. Remove from the heat and stir in the lemon juice and limoncello, brandy or gin.

5 Use a skewer to prick the surface of the hot cake and spoon over some of the warm syrup *(pic 3)*. When the syrup has been absorbed, spoon over some more, and continue adding syrup this way until the cake has absorbed it all. Carefully turn the savarin out onto a plate and cool. Serve with the cream.

VARIATION
Currant and rum savarin: Omit the apricots and lemon zest and add 75 g (2¾ oz/½ cup) currants to the batter. Reduce the water in the syrup to 275 ml (9½ fl oz) and omit the lemon juice and limoncello, brandy or gin. Allow the syrup to cool, then stir in 125 ml (4 fl oz/½ cup) rum.

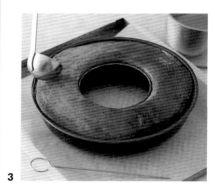

TIP The savarin will keep, in an airtight container, for up to 3 days. A savarin tin is a shallow ring tin with a rounded base, available from speciality kitchenware shops.

Stollen

Stollen is a dense bread flavoured with dried fruit, citrus zest, mixed peel and almonds that is traditionally eaten at Christmas. Many versions exist in Germany, where it originated, with the most famous being Dresden Stollen. The marzipan is optional, but it does make the loaf rather special.

MAKES 35 cm (14 inch) loaf **PREPARATION TIME** 1 hour (+ overnight soaking and 3 hours 15 minutes proving)
COOKING TIME 50 minutes

120 g (4¼ oz/⅔ cup) raisins
105 g (3½ oz/⅔ cup) currants
55 g (2 oz/⅓ cup) mixed peel
   (mixed candied citrus peel)
80 g (2¾ oz/½ cup) chopped
   blanched almonds
40 ml (1¼ fl oz) rum or brandy
2 tablespoons lukewarm water
55 g (2 oz/¼ cup) caster
   (superfine) sugar
7 g (⅛ oz/2 teaspoons) dried yeast
125 ml (4 fl oz/½ cup) lukewarm milk
335 g (11¾ oz/2¼ cups) plain
   (all-purpose) flour
1 teaspoon finely grated lemon zest
1 teaspoon finely grated orange zest
2 egg yolks, lightly whisked
1 teaspoon natural vanilla extract
60 g (2¼ oz) butter, melted and cooled
½ teaspoon salt
200 g (7 oz) marzipan (see tip)
1 egg, whisked with 1 tablespoon water
1½ tablespoons melted butter, extra
40 g (1½ oz/⅓ cup) icing
   (confectioners') sugar, approximately

1 Combine the dried fruits, peel, nuts and rum or brandy in a bowl, cover and set aside at room temperature overnight.

2 Combine the lukewarm water and a pinch of the caster sugar, sprinkle over the yeast and set aside for 5–6 minutes or until foamy. Add the milk and 150 g (5½ oz/1 cup) of the flour and stir until smooth. Cover with plastic wrap and set aside in a warm, draught-free place for 30 minutes or until it begins to bubble.

3 Transfer to the bowl of a stand mixer, add the zests, egg yolks, vanilla, remaining caster sugar and the butter and use the paddle attachment to beat until well combined. Change to the dough hook, add the remaining flour and the salt and knead on low speed for 10 minutes or until smooth and elastic. Cover with plastic wrap and set aside in a warm, draught-free place for 2 hours or until the dough has doubled in size.

4 Knock back the dough, then cut it into 6 portions. Add the fruit mixture and use the dough hook to knead on low speed for 6–7 minutes or until well combined. Turn out onto a lightly floured work surface.

5 Use your hands and a rolling pin to roll and press the dough to form an oval, about 32 cm (12¾ inches) long and 24 cm (9½ inches) at the widest part, with slightly pointed ends *(pic 1)*. Roll the marzipan into a log, about 30 cm (12 inches) long. Brush the edges of the dough with the egg wash. Place the marzipan along the centre *(pic 2)*, then fold each side over the marzipan (they will overlap slightly). Pinch firmly along the seam to join *(pic 3)*. Pinch the ends. Place on a lined baking tray, cover with a tea towel (dish towel) and set aside in a warm, draught-free place for 45 minutes or until risen.

6 Preheat the oven to 180°C (350°F/Gas 4). Bake the stollen for 50 minutes, covering with foil if it browns too quickly, or until a skewer inserted into the thickest part comes out clean. Brush lightly with extra butter, dredge heavily in sifted icing sugar, then allow to cool.

1

2

3

TIP Marzipan is available from supermarkets. Almond paste is not the same thing and will not give the desired result.
   Stollen will keep in an airtight container for up to 2 weeks.

Jam doughnuts

A version of the berliner (also called bismarck and krapfen), a type of doughnut popular in Germany and Central Europe, these jam-filled treats are not hard to make, though it is hard to stop eating them! It's important to keep your deep-frying oil at the correct temperature to avoid any greasiness.

MAKES 12   **PREPARATION TIME** 30 minutes (+ 1 hour 40–50 minutes proving)   **COOKING TIME** 32 minutes

185 ml (6 fl oz/³⁄₄ cup) lukewarm milk
55 g (2 oz/¹⁄₄ cup) caster (superfine) sugar, plus extra, for rolling
10 g (¹⁄₄ oz/3 teaspoons) dried yeast
3 egg yolks
375 g (13 oz/2¹⁄₂ cups) plain (all-purpose) flour
1 teaspoon salt
100 g (3¹⁄₂ oz) chilled unsalted butter, chopped
85 g (3 oz/¹⁄₄ cup) raspberry jam
1.25 litres (44 fl oz/5 cups) vegetable oil

1 Combine the milk and a large pinch of the sugar in a medium bowl. Sprinkle over the yeast, then set aside for 5–6 minutes or until foamy. Stir in the remaining sugar and the egg yolks and mix until well combined.

2 Combine the flour and salt in a large bowl. Use your fingertips to rub in the butter until the mixture resembles fine breadcrumbs. Add the milk mixture and use a flat-bladed knife to stir until a coarse dough begins to form. Turn out onto a lightly floured work surface and knead for 5–6 minutes or until a smooth, soft, elastic dough forms. Place the dough in a lightly oiled bowl, turning to coat in the oil. Cover the bowl with plastic wrap and set aside in a warm, draught-free place for 1 hour or until doubled in size.

3 Knock back the dough with just one punch to expel the air, then turn out onto a lightly floured work surface. Divide into 12 equal portions. Roll each portion into a ball *(pic 1)*, then flatten slightly. Place on a lightly greased tray or board, allowing room for spreading, and cover with a tea towel (dish towel). Set aside for 40–50 minutes or until risen (they will not quite double in size).

4 Heat the oil in a medium saucepan until 160°C (315°F) or until a cube of bread dropped into the oil turns golden brown in 30–35 seconds. Cook the doughnuts, in batches, for 8 minutes or until deep golden and cooked through, turning once during cooking. Use a slotted spoon *(pic 2)* to transfer onto paper towels to drain and cool.

5 Put the jam in a small disposable piping (icing) bag fitted with a small plain nozzle. Push the nozzle into the side of the doughnuts and squeeze a little jam into each *(pic 3)*. Roll the doughnuts in the extra sugar to coat.

2

3

1

TIP Doughnuts are best eaten on the day they are made and are not suitable to freeze.

Chocolate and prune loaf

This more-ish bread is also delicious toasted and spread with firm, fresh ricotta cheese. If you'd like to give it a jaffa flavour, substitute big, sticky raisins for the prunes and add the finely grated zest of 1 orange when adding the flour, cocoa and salt to the dough.

MAKES 2 x 22 cm (8½ inch) loaves **PREPARATION TIME** 40 minutes (+ 2½ hours proving) **COOKING TIME** 45 minutes

80 ml (2½ fl oz/⅓ cup) warm water
55 g (2 oz/¼ cup) caster (superfine)
  sugar
7 g (⅛ oz/2 teaspoons) dried yeast
125 ml (4 fl oz/½ cup) milk
25 g (1 oz) unsalted butter, chopped
  and softened
1 egg, lightly whisked
1 teaspoon natural vanilla extract
2½ tablespoons Dutch unsweetened
  cocoa powder (see tip)
1 teaspoon salt
300 g (10½ oz/2 cups) plain
  (all-purpose) flour
75 g (2¾ oz) dark chocolate, chopped
200 g (7 oz/1 cup) pitted prunes, halved
Icing (confectioners') sugar, to dust

1 Combine the warm water and a pinch of the caster sugar in a large bowl, then sprinkle over the yeast and set aside for 7–8 minutes or until foamy.

2 Meanwhile, put the milk, remaining caster sugar and the butter in a small saucepan and stir over medium–low heat for 2–3 minutes to dissolve the sugar. Set aside to cool until lukewarm, then add to the yeast mixture with the egg and vanilla and stir to combine.

3 Sift the cocoa, salt and flour together, then add to the yeast mixture. Use a wooden spoon to stir until the mixture starts to come together and forms a soft, coarse dough. Turn out onto a lightly floured work surface and knead for 6–7 minutes or until smooth and elastic, adding a little extra flour if the

dough feels too sticky. Take care not to add too much extra flour as it will make the loaf heavy.

4 Put the dough in a lightly oiled bowl, turning to coat in the oil. Cover the bowl with plastic wrap and set aside in a warm, draught-free place for 1½ hours or until doubled in size.

5 Knock back the dough with just one punch to expel the air, then transfer to a lightly floured work surface and divide into 2 equal portions. Working with one portion at a time, use a rolling pin to roll out to a rough rectangle, about 18 x 28 cm (7 x 11¼ inches) *(pic 1)*. Turn the dough so a short side is facing you, then scatter over half each of the chocolate *(pic 2)* and prunes, leaving a 2 cm (¾ inch) border. Roll the dough up, like a Swiss roll (jelly roll), then gently roll the log a little more to elongate it to about 22 cm (8½ inches) *(pic 3)* and make it roughly even in thickness. Transfer to a lightly greased baking tray, cover with a tea towel (dish towel) and set aside for 1 hour or until risen (the logs will not double in size).

6 Preheat the oven to 180°C (350°F/ Gas 4). Use a large sharp knife or razor blade to cut 4–5 diagonal slashes in the top of each log, taking care not to deflate the dough. Bake for 40 minutes or until the loaves sound hollow when tapped on the base. Transfer to a wire rack to cool. Dust the loaves with icing sugar to serve.

1

2

3

TIP Dutch cocoa powder is treated with alkaline, which mellows the flavour, lowers its acidity and makes it more soluble.
  These loaves are best eaten on the day they are made. They can be frozen, in a sealed freezer bag, for up to 6 weeks.

Kulich

Kulich is a Russian yeast-raised cake made over the Easter period. It is traditionally baked in a very tall, straight-sided tin, however this recipe uses dariole moulds to make individual cakes. The rich dough, which resembles a thick batter, is very slow rising — don't be fooled into thinking it's not working.

MAKES 6 small kulich   **PREPARATION TIME** 40 minutes (+ 7½ hours proving, and cooling/setting)   **COOKING TIME** 20 minutes

60 ml (2 fl oz/¼ cup) warm milk

75 g (2¾ oz/⅓ cup) caster (superfine) sugar

9 g (¼ oz/2½ teaspoons) dried yeast

300 g (10½ oz/2 cups) plain (all-purpose) flour

65 g (2¼ oz) unsalted butter, melted and cooled

4 egg yolks

2 tablespoons honey

1 tablespoon rum or brandy

½ teaspoon natural vanilla extract

½ teaspoon ground cardamom

½ teaspoon salt

3 egg whites

75 g (2¾ oz/½ cup) currants

60 g (2¼ oz/⅓ cup) sultanas (golden raisins)

40 g (1½ oz/¼ cup) mixed peel (mixed candied citrus peel)

Sugar flowers, to decorate

ICING

90 g (3¼ oz/¾ cup) icing (confectioners') sugar, sifted

2 teaspoons lemon juice

Few drops of almond extract

1 Combine the warm milk and a teaspoon of the sugar in the bowl of a stand mixer. Sprinkle over the yeast. Mix in 35 g (1¼ oz/¼ cup) of the flour. Cover the bowl with plastic wrap and set aside for 30 minutes or until risen.

2 Use the paddle attachment to beat in the remaining sugar, the butter, egg yolks, honey, rum or brandy and vanilla until combined. Beat in the remaining flour, the cardamom and salt, then continue to beat for 2 minutes or until a soft, smooth batter forms *(pic 1)*.

3 Use an electric mixer with a whisk attachment to whisk the egg whites in a clean, dry bowl until firm peaks form, then add to the dough. Use the dough hook to knead for 3–4 minutes *(pic 2)* or until combined. Add the fruits and mixed peel and knead until well combined. Cover with plastic wrap and set aside in a warm, draught-free place for 6 hours or until well risen.

4 Grease the sides of six 250 ml (9 fl oz/1 cup) dariole moulds and line the bases with non-stick baking paper. Divide the mixture among the prepared moulds — the moulds should be half full. Cover loosely with plastic wrap and set aside in a warm, draught-free place for 1 hour or until the dough has risen to the tops of the moulds *(pic 3)*.

5 Preheat the oven to 180°C (350°F/ Gas 4). Place the moulds on a baking tray and bake for 20 minutes or until a skewer inserted into the centre of a kulich comes out clean. Cool in the tins for 2 minutes, then carefully turn out onto a wire rack to cool completely.

6 To make the icing (frosting), combine all the ingredients in a bowl, adding 1–2 teaspoons of water or enough to form a thick glaze. Stand the cakes upright and drizzle over the icing, allowing it to run down the sides a little. Decorate with sugar flowers and set aside for 30 minutes to allow the icing to set before serving.

1

2

3

TIP Kulich are best eaten on the day they are made. They can be frozen, un-iced, in a sealed freezer bag, for up to 6 weeks.

Fruit bread

With a delicious combination of apricot, pear, peach and cranberries, as well as walnuts, spices and orange zest, this bread is positively loaded with flavour. It's a very flexible recipe, so feel free to experiment with other combinations — raisins, figs and hazelnuts, for example, will also work well.

MAKES 24 cm (9½ inch) diameter loaf **PREPARATION TIME** 45 minutes (+ 3–4 hours proving)
COOKING TIME 45–50 minutes

90 g (3¼ oz/¼ cup) honey
185 ml (6 fl oz/¾ cup) lukewarm water
9 g (¼ oz/2½ teaspoons) dried yeast
200 g (7 oz/1⅓ cups) plain
    (all-purpose) flour
200 g (7 oz/1⅓ cups) plain
    (all-purpose) wholemeal
    (whole-wheat) flour
1 teaspoon salt
2 teaspoons ground cinnamon
¼ teaspoon ground cloves
1 egg, lightly whisked
Finely grated zest of 1 orange
100 g (3½ oz/¾ cup) coarsely
    chopped dried apricots
100 g (3½ oz/¾ cup) coarsely
    chopped dried pears
100 g (3½ oz/¾ cup) coarsely
    chopped dried peaches
105 g (3½ oz/⅔ cup) sweetened
    dried cranberries
125 g (4½ oz/1 cup) coarsely
    chopped walnut pieces
1 egg yolk, whisked with
    2½ teaspoons water
40 g (1½ oz/¼ cup) poppy seeds

1 Combine the honey and lukewarm water in the bowl of a stand mixer, sprinkle over the yeast and set aside for 5–6 minutes or until foamy.

2 Add the flours, salt, cinnamon, cloves, egg and orange zest. Use the dough hook attachment to knead for 8 minutes or until an elastic, slightly sticky dough forms. Cover the bowl with plastic wrap and set aside in a warm, draught-free place for 1½–2 hours or until doubled in size.

3 Knock back the dough with just one punch to expel the air. Use a flat-bladed knife to cut the dough, still in the bowl, into 5–6 pieces. Add the fruits and walnuts (pic 1). Use the dough hook on low speed to knead the dough for 5–6 minutes or until the fruits and nuts are well incorporated.

4 Turn the dough out onto a lightly floured work surface and shape it into a slightly flattened ball, about 18 cm (7 inches) in diameter (pic 2).

5 Lightly grease a baking tray. Brush the dough all over with the egg wash, then sprinkle with the poppy seeds. Place on the tray, cover with a tea towel (dish towel) and set aside in a warm, draught-free place for 1½–2 hours or until risen (pic 3). (The loaf will be not quite doubled in size.)

6 Preheat the oven to 180°C (350°F/ Gas 4). Bake the fruit bread for 45–50 minutes or until the base sounds hollow when tapped. Transfer to a wire rack to cool.

1

2

3

TIP This bread will keep, wrapped tightly in plastic wrap or stored in an airtight container, for up to 3 days. It can be frozen, in a sealed freezer bag, for up to 6 weeks.

Hot cross buns

In 16th-century England, bakers were restricted by law to making spiced buns only on certain occasions. One of these was Good Friday, when the symbolic 'cross buns' were sold warm, as the rhyme 'one a penny, two a penny, hot cross buns' attests. This recipe can easily be doubled.

MAKES 8   **PREPARATION TIME** 50 minutes (+ 3 hours 15 minutes proving)   **COOKING TIME** 22 minutes

80 g (2¾ oz) caster (superfine) sugar
60 ml (2 fl oz/¼ cup) warm water
7 g (⅛ oz/2 teaspoons) dried yeast
125 ml (4 fl oz/½ cup) lukewarm milk
35 g (1¼ oz) butter, melted
410 g (14½ oz/2¾ cups) plain
   (all-purpose) flour
2 teaspoons ground cinnamon
½ teaspoon ground nutmeg
¼ teaspoon ground cloves
1 teaspoon salt
105 g (3½ oz/⅔ cup) currants
120 g (4¼ oz/⅔ cup) raisins
40 g (1½ oz/¼ cup) mixed peel
   (mixed candied citrus peel)
1 egg, whisked
1 teaspoon natural vanilla extract

DECORATION

2 tablespoons plain (all-purpose) flour
115 g (4 oz/⅓ cup) apricot jam

1 Combine a pinch of the sugar and the warm water in a large bowl. Sprinkle over the yeast, then set aside for 7–8 minutes or until foamy. Add half the milk, half the melted butter and 110 g (3¾ oz/¾ cup) of the flour and stir until smooth and combined. Cover the bowl with plastic wrap and set aside in a warm, draught-free place for 45 minutes or until doubled in size.

2 Combine the remaining sugar, the spices, salt, dried fruits and mixed peel. Stir into the yeast mixture with the egg, vanilla and the remaining milk and butter. Add the remaining flour and mix until a coarse dough forms. Turn out onto a lightly floured work surface and knead for 5–6 minutes or until the dough is soft, smooth and elastic.

3 Put the dough in a lightly oiled bowl, turning to coat in the oil. Cover the bowl with plastic wrap and set aside in a warm, draught-free place for 1 hour or until doubled in size.

4 Knock back the dough with just one punch to expel the air. Turn out onto a clean work surface and use a large sharp knife to cut into 8 equal portions. Lightly grease a baking tray. Roll each portion of dough into a ball *(pic 1)* and place on the greased tray. Cover with a tea towel (dish towel) and set aside in a warm, draught-free place for 1½ hours or until nearly doubled in size.

5 Preheat the oven to 180°C (350°F/ Gas 4). To make the decoration, combine the flour with 2½ tablespoons water or enough to make a firm paste, beating with a wooden spoon until smooth. Place in a small piping (icing) bag fitted with a small plain nozzle and pipe a cross on top of each bun *(pic 2)*. Bake the buns for 20 minutes or until an inserted skewer comes out clean. Transfer to a wire rack to cool.

6 Put the jam and 2 tablespoons water in a small saucepan over low heat and stir constantly for 1–2 minutes or until warm and combined. Pass through a sieve, then use a pastry brush to brush over the buns *(pic 3)*.

1

2

3

TIP Hot cross buns are best eaten on the day they are made. They can be frozen, without the glaze, in a sealed freezer bag, for up to 6 weeks.

Pies & Tarts

Tomato and fennel quiches with basil pesto

These mini quiches make excellent party or finger food. Any remaining basil pesto can be tossed through pasta with roasted cherry tomatoes or served with barbecued chicken or lamb.

MAKES 24   **PREPARATION TIME** 25 minutes (+ 15 minutes chilling)   **COOKING TIME** 23 minutes

1 quantity parmesan shortcrust pastry (see page 25)
1 tablespoon olive oil
1 medium fennel bulb, trimmed, thinly sliced
75 g (2¾ oz/¾ cup, loosely packed) coarsely grated cheddar cheese
2 eggs
160 ml (5¼ fl oz/⅔ cup) pouring (whipping) cream
80 ml (2½ fl oz/⅓ cup) milk
12 cherry tomatoes, halved

BASIL PESTO
55 g (2 oz/2 cups, firmly packed) basil leaves
2 garlic cloves, coarsely chopped
40 g (1½ oz/¼ cup) toasted pine nuts
35 g (1¼ oz/⅓ cup) finely grated parmesan cheese
125 ml (4 fl oz/½ cup) olive oil

1 Grease two 12-hole (40 ml/1¼ fl oz/ 2 tablespoon) flat-based patty pan tins with oil or butter. Divide the pastry into 2 portions and roll out a portion on a lightly floured work surface to 3 mm (⅛ inch) thick. Use a round 6.5 cm (2½ inch) cutter to cut discs from the pastry. Press the pastry discs into the greased holes and prick all over with a fork. Repeat with the remaining pastry portion to line the remaining greased patty pans. Cover with plastic wrap and refrigerate for 15 minutes.

2 Preheat the oven to 200°C (400°F/ Gas 6).

3 Heat the oil in a large frying pan over medium–high heat. Add the fennel and cook, stirring, for 4–5 minutes or until light golden and soft *(pic 1)*. Divide the fennel and cheese evenly among the pastry shells.

4 Whisk the eggs, cream and milk in a small bowl until combined. Season well with salt and freshly ground black pepper. Transfer to a jug and divide evenly among the pastry shells. Top each with a cherry tomato half *(pic 2)*.

5 Bake the quiches for 18 minutes or until the filling is just set. Set aside for 5 minutes before removing from the trays.

6 Meanwhile, to make the basil pesto, blend or process the basil, garlic, pine nuts and parmesan in a food processor until almost smooth. With the motor running, gradually add the oil in a thin, steady stream, until thick and well combined *(pic 3)*. Season with salt and freshly ground black pepper.

7 Serve the quiches warm or at room temperature, topped with a little pesto.

1

2

3

TIP Keep in an airtight container in the refrigerator for up to 2 days. To reheat, return to the trays and put in a preheated 180°C (350°F/ Gas 4) oven for 5–8 minutes.

Silverbeet pie

This pie is similar to spanakopita, the famous spinach and feta pie so common throughout Greece. You don't need to make the pastry yourself so it is quick and easy to put together, perfect for a picnic.

SERVES 8   **PREPARATION TIME** 20 minutes   **COOKING TIME** 1½ hours

1 tablespoon olive oil

2 spring onions (scallions), thinly sliced

1 bunch (about 545 g/1 lb 3½ oz) silverbeet (Swiss chard), trimmed and thinly sliced

2 tablespoons finely chopped dill

1 tablespoon finely chopped mint

2 teaspoons finely grated lemon zest

310 g (11 oz/1⅓ cups) firm, fresh ricotta cheese

4 eggs, lightly whisked

200 g (7 oz/1½ cups) crumbled feta cheese

10 sheets filo pastry

100 g (3½ oz) butter, melted

Lemon wedges, to serve

1 Heat the oil in a large frying pan over medium heat. Add the spring onions and cook, stirring occasionally, for 5 minutes. Add the silverbeet, cover and cook for 3 minutes or until wilted. Transfer to a colander to drain and cool completely. Use your hands to squeeze the mixture in the colander to remove as much liquid as possible.

2 Combine the dill, mint, zest, ricotta and egg in a bowl. Add the spinach mixture and feta, and season with salt and freshly ground black pepper. Stir until well combined.

3 Preheat the oven to 180°C (350°F/ Gas 4). Lay one sheet of filo on a clean work surface, keeping the remaining sheets covered with a damp tea towel (dish towel) to prevent them drying out. Brush with some of the melted butter, then lay another sheet of filo on top. Repeat with the remaining sheets to make two stacks, each with 5 sheets of filo. Cut each stack widthways to make six 13 cm (5 inch) wide rectangles *(pic 1)*.

4 Grease the base and side of a round 22 cm (8½ inch) diameter spring-form cake tin. Place the filo rectangles over the base and side of the tin to line it fully, allowing the filo to overhang the side of the tin *(pic 2)*.

5 Spoon the spinach mixture into the filo-lined tin. Fold the overhanging filo over to enclose the filling *(pic 3)*. Brush with the remaining melted butter. Bake for 1 hour 20 minutes or until cooked through. Cool in the tin for at least 10 minutes before removing. Serve the pie warm or at room temperature with lemon wedges.

1

2

3

TIP This pie is best eaten on the day it is baked.

Individual meat pies

MAKES 4   **PREPARATION TIME** 45 minutes (+ 30 minutes chilling)   **COOKING TIME** 3 hours 5–10 minutes

2 tablespoons plain (all-purpose) flour

600 g (1 lb 5 oz) chuck steak, cut into
1 cm (½ inch) pieces

60 ml (2 fl oz/¼ cup) olive oil

4 brown onions, thinly sliced

1 medium carrot, finely chopped

1 celery stalk, finely chopped

2 garlic cloves, crushed

1 teaspoon caster (superfine) sugar

125 ml (4 fl oz/½ cup) red wine

500 ml (17 fl oz/2 cups) beef stock

200 g (7 oz) Swiss brown mushrooms,
trimmed and quartered

1 quantity shortcrust pastry
(see pages 24–25)

1 egg, lightly whisked

1 Place the flour in a large bowl and season with sea salt and freshly ground black pepper. Add the beef, toss to coat in the flour and shake off any excess.

2 Heat 1 tablespoon of the oil in a large heavy-based flameproof casserole over medium–high heat. Add half the beef and cook, turning often, for 5 minutes or until browned all over. Transfer to a plate and repeat with the remaining beef, adding a little extra oil if necessary.

3 Heat half the remaining oil in the casserole. Add the onions, carrot and celery and cook over medium heat, stirring occasionally, for 10–12 minutes or until soft. Add the garlic and sugar and cook, stirring, for 30 seconds.

4 Add the wine and bring to the boil. Reduce the heat to low and simmer, uncovered, for 2 minutes or until slightly reduced. Return the beef to the casserole with the stock. Bring to the boil, then reduce the heat and simmer, covered, for 1 hour. Uncover and cook for a further 1 hour or until the meat is very tender and the liquid has thickened.

5 Meanwhile, heat the remaining oil in a frying pan over medium–high heat. Add the mushrooms and cook, stirring, for about 5 minutes or until browned all over. Add to the beef mixture and stir to combine. Transfer to a bowl and cool to room temperature.

6 Preheat the oven to 180°C (350°F/ Gas 4). Divide the pastry into 2 portions, one twice as big as the other *(pic 1)*. Use a lightly floured rolling pin to roll out the smaller portion of pastry on a lightly floured work surface until 3 mm (⅛ inch) thick. Use the top of an 11 cm (4¼ inch) (top diameter), 7.5 cm (3 inch) (base diameter) pie tin to cut 4 rounds from the pastry *(pic 2)*.

7 Divide the larger portion of pastry into 4 equal portions and roll each out on a lightly floured work surface, taking care not to overwork the dough or it will become too soft, into a 15 cm (6 inch) diameter round. Carefully ease each round into a pie tin, using your fingertips to press them into the base and side. Roll the rolling pin over the tops of the tins to trim the excess pastry.

8 Divide the beef mixture among the pastry-lined tins *(pic 3)*. Brush the top edges of the pastry with a little egg. Place the smaller pastry rounds on top to cover the beef mixture and use a lightly floured fork to press the edges together. Use a small sharp knife to make 2 slits in the top of each pastry lid. Brush the tops lightly with egg and bake for 40 minutes or until golden. Set aside for 10 minutes to cool slightly, then remove from the tins. Serve hot.

TIP These pies are best eaten on the day they are made. If you have more pies than you need, freeze them in sealed freezer bags for up to 2 months. Thaw overnight in the refrigerator and reheat in an oven preheated to 180°C (350°F/ Gas 4) for 20–25 minutes.

Quiche lorraine

Quiche is an open tart with an egg-based filling that originated in Lorraine, France. Bacon, eggs and cheese feature in the traditional quiche lorraine filling, though it's easy to vary the flavours once you have mastered the classic recipe. Try our variations, then create your own flavour combinations.

SERVES 4–6   **PREPARATION TIME** 30 minutes (+ 45 minutes chilling)   **COOKING TIME** 1 hour

1 quantity shortcrust pastry
  (see pages 24-25)
2 teaspoons olive oil
1 brown onion, finely chopped
4 bacon rashers (slices), rind removed,
  finely chopped
50 g (1¾ oz/½ cup, loosely packed)
  coarsely grated gruyère cheese
¼ cup snipped chives
3 eggs
250 ml (9 fl oz/1 cup) pouring
  (whipping) cream
125 ml (4 fl oz/½ cup) milk

1 Roll the pastry out between 2 sheets of non-stick baking paper to a disc 4 mm (¼ inch) thick. Roll the pastry around the rolling pin and carefully ease it into a 3.5 cm (1½ inch) deep, 24 cm (9½ inch) fluted, loose-based tart (flan) tin, pressing it into the edges with your fingertips (see page 28). Trim any excess pastry by rolling the rolling pin over the top of the tin. Cover with plastic wrap and place in the refrigerator for 15 minutes to rest.

2 Preheat the oven to 200°C (400°F/ Gas 6). Place the tart tin on a baking tray. Line the pastry shell with non-stick baking paper, then fill with baking beads, dried beans or rice. Bake for 10 minutes, then remove the beads and paper. Bake for a further 10 minutes or until the pastry is light golden-brown and just cooked through.

3 Meanwhile, heat the oil in a frying pan over medium heat. Add the onion and bacon and cook, stirring, for 3–5 minutes or until the bacon is crisp.

Transfer onto paper towels to drain and set aside to cool *(pic 1)*.

4 Reduce the oven temperature to 180°C (350°F/Gas 4). Sprinkle the bacon mixture, cheese and chives over the cooked pastry shell *(pic 2)*. Whisk the eggs in a medium jug, then whisk in the cream and milk. Pour into the pastry shell *(pic 3)*. Bake the quiche for 35–40 minutes or until the filling has just set. Remove from the oven and leave in the tin for 5 minutes before removing. Serve the quiche warm or at room temperature, cut into wedges.

VARIATIONS

Pancetta and zucchini quiche: Use 1 quantity herb shortcrust pastry (see page 25). Replace the bacon with 150 g (5½ oz) pancetta slices, cut into thin strips. Cook 2 small zucchini, thinly sliced, with the pancetta and onion, and cook for 6–8 minutes. Replace the gruyère with cheddar cheese and the chives with chopped basil.

Spinach and feta quiche: Use 1 quantity parmesan shortcrust pastry (see page 25). Omit the bacon. Add 150 g (5½ oz) baby spinach leaves and 1 tablespoon lemon juice to the cooked onion and cook for a further 1–2 minutes or until the spinach wilts. Replace the gruyère with 100 g (3½ oz) crumbled feta cheese and 50 g (1¾ oz/ ½ cup) finely grated parmesan cheese.

TIP Keep in an airtight container in the refrigerator for up to 2 days.

Pissaladière

SERVES 4–6   **PREPARATION TIME** 30 minutes (+ 30 minutes cooling)   **COOKING TIME** 40–45 minutes

60 ml (2 fl oz/¼ cup) olive oil

1 kg (2 lb 4 oz) brown onions, halved and thinly sliced

½ teaspoon salt

4 sheets (25 x 25 cm/10 x 10 inches) frozen ready-rolled puff pastry, thawed

1 egg, lightly whisked

20–30 anchovies, halved lengthways

95 g (3¼ oz/½ cup) kalamata olives, pitted and halved

10 thyme sprigs

1 Heat a large heavy-based frying pan over medium–low heat. Add the oil, onions and salt and cook, stirring often, for 20–25 minutes or until the onions are soft and caramelised (*pic 1*). Transfer to a bowl and set aside for 30 minutes or until cooled to room temperature.

2 Preheat the oven to 220°C (425°F/ Gas 7). Line 2 baking trays with non-stick baking paper.

3 Place a pastry sheet on each lined tray. Brush lightly with the whisked egg (*pic 2*) and then place another sheet of pastry on top of each.

4 Use a very sharp knife to mark a 1 cm (½ inch) border around each pastry square, cutting only through the top sheet of pastry (*pic 3*).

5 Divide the cooled onion mixture between the pastry squares and spread it out in an even layer to the border of each. Arrange the anchovies on top in a lattice pattern. Dot with the olive halves. Strip the leaves from the thyme sprigs and scatter over the top. Lightly brush the pastry border with a little of the remaining whisked egg.

6 Bake the pissaladière for 20 minutes or until the pastry is puffed and golden. Serve warm or at room temperature.

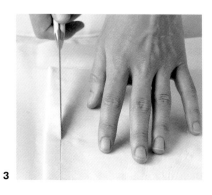

1

2

3

TIP You can use a 375 g (13 oz) block of ready-made puff pastry if you prefer. Use a lightly floured rolling pin to roll it out on a lightly floured work surface to 25 x 40 cm (10 x 16 inches) and about 4 mm (¼ inch) thick. Cut it in half and then place on the lined trays. Refrigerate for 15 minutes or until firm. Do not brush with egg. When marking the border, cut only halfway into the pastry.

Caramelised tomato tart

Peeling and seeding tomatoes may seem a chore, but such refinements give a professional finish to your cooking. This elegant tart, with its summery flavours, would make a lovely dinner party entrée.

SERVES 6–8   **PREPARATION TIME** 55 minutes (+ 50 minutes chilling and 15 minutes cooling)   **COOKING TIME** 1 hour

1 quantity shortcrust pastry
   (see pages 24–25)
50 g (2½ oz/½ cup) finely grated
   parmesan cheese
9 (about 1 kg/2 lb 4 oz) firm, ripe
   roma (plum) tomatoes
30 g (1 oz) butter
1 tablespoon light brown sugar
1 tablespoon balsamic vinegar
1 egg yolk, lightly whisked
Sprigs of small marjoram leaves,
   to garnish

1 Make the pastry as directed, adding the parmesan after the butter has been rubbed in.

2 Cut a small cross in the base of each tomato. Bring a large saucepan of water to the boil. Add the tomatoes and cook for about 30 seconds or until the skins begin to peel away from the flesh. Drain and refresh under cold water. Peel the skins, then cut the tomatoes in half lengthways. Use a small spoon to carefully scrape the seeds and juice into a bowl, leaving the centre membranes as they will help the tomatoes hold their shape *(pic 1)*. Strain the seeds and juice through a fine sieve into a small jug. Discard the solids. Reserve the juice.

3 Melt the butter in a large frying pan over medium heat. Add the sugar and vinegar and cook, stirring, for 1 minute. Add the tomato halves and cook for 1–2 minutes, carefully turning once, or until softened slightly. Remove from the pan and set aside to cool completely. Add the reserved tomato juice to the pan and bring to the boil. Reduce the

heat to low and simmer, uncovered, for 2 minutes or until reduced by half *(pic 2)*. Transfer to a small jug.

4 Meanwhile, use a lightly floured rolling pin to roll out the pastry on a lightly floured work surface to a rectangle, about 16 x 42 cm (6¼ x 16½ inches). Roll the pastry around the rolling pin and carefully ease into a 2 cm (¾ inch) deep, 12 x 35 cm (4½ x 14 inch) fluted loose-based tart (flan) tin, pressing it into the base and sides with your fingertips (see page 28). Roll the rolling pin over the tin to trim the excess pastry, then refrigerate for 20 minutes to chill.

5 Preheat the oven to 200°C (400°F/ Gas 6). Line the pastry shell with non-stick baking paper and fill with baking beads, dried beans or uncooked rice. Bake for 20 minutes, reduce the temperature to 180°C (350°F/Gas 4) and remove the paper and weights. Brush the pastry base with the egg yolk.

6 Return the tart shell to the oven and bake for a further 10 minutes or until the base is golden and dry. Arrange the tomatoes, cut side down, in the pastry shell *(pic 3)*. The tighter you pack them in, the better the result will be, as they will collapse a little during cooking.

7 Bake the tart for 20 minutes or until the pastry is cooked through. Leave in the tin to cool for 15 minutes. Warm the reduced tomato juice. Serve the tart drizzled with the tomato juice and sprinkled with the marjoram sprigs.

TIP This tart is best eaten on the day it is baked.

Mini prawn and avocado tartlets

What's really special about these beautiful little tarts is that once you've cooked the pastry shells, the work is virtually done. The filling requires no cooking and can be put in place just before serving.

MAKES 48   **PREPARATION TIME** 35 minutes (+ 1 hour chilling, and cooling)   **COOKING TIME** 15 minutes

1 quantity shortcrust pastry
  (see pages 24–25)
24 (about 400 g/14 oz) cooked medium
  prawns (shrimp), peeled and deveined
2–3 tablespoons lemon or lime juice
1 small (200 g/7 oz) avocado
200 g (7 oz) punnet small grape
  tomatoes, quartered
2 long red chillies, seeded and
  finely diced
48 coriander (cilantro) leaves

1 Preheat the oven to 180°C (350°F/ Gas 4).

2 Cut the pastry into 2 equal portions. Use a rolling pin to roll out each portion between 2 sheets of non-stick baking paper until 2–3 mm (¹⁄₁₆–¹⁄₈ inch) thick. Refrigerate for 20 minutes to chill.

3 Remove one pastry portion from the refrigerator. Peel off the top sheet of paper. Use a round 5 cm (2 inch) pastry cutter to cut out 24 circles. Press each circle gently into a 1 cm (½ inch) deep, 4 cm (1½ inch) diameter (base measurement) fluted tartlet tin *(pic 1)*. Roll the rolling pin gently over the tins to trim the excess pastry, then place the tins on a baking tray and refrigerate. Repeat with the remaining portion of pastry to line another 24 tartlet tins. Refrigerate for 10 minutes or until all the pastry is well chilled.

4 Line each pastry shell with a small square of non-stick baking paper and fill with baking beads. Bake for 8 minutes. Remove the paper and beads and bake for a further 5–7 minutes or until the pastry is golden and crisp. Cool for 2 minutes in the tins, then transfer to a wire rack to cool completely.

5 Slice the prawns in half lengthways and place in a medium bowl *(pic 2)*. Drizzle with half the lemon juice and season with salt and freshly ground black pepper. Finely dice the avocado and place in a separate bowl with the tomatoes, chillies and remaining lemon juice. Season well with salt and pepper.

6 Spoon a teaspoonful of the avocado and tomato mixture into each pastry case *(pic 3)*. Top each with a prawn half and a coriander leaf. Serve immediately.

TIP The pastry shells can be made up to 2 days in advance. Keep in an airtight container.

Roast onion tart

Perfect for a lunch party or light dinner, this tart needs no more than a simple green salad as an accompaniment. Roasting the onions makes them wonderfully sweet and smooth.

MAKES 26 cm (10½ inch) tart   **PREPARATION TIME** 55 minutes (+ 1 hour chilling)   **COOKING TIME** 1 hour 35–40 minutes

1 quantity pâte brisée (see page 26)
700 g (1 lb 9 oz) brown onions (about 6)
90 ml (3 fl oz) olive oil
1¼ tablespoons balsamic vinegar
1 tablespoon caster (superfine) sugar
2 eggs
1 egg yolk
225 ml (7¾ fl oz) pouring (whipping) cream
225 ml (7¾ fl oz) milk
100 g (3½ oz/1 cup) finely grated parmesan cheese
2½ teaspoons thyme leaves, plus thyme sprigs, to garnish

1 Use a rolling pin to roll out the pastry on a lightly floured work surface to a circle, about 36 cm (14¼ inches) in diameter. Gently ease the pastry into a 2.5 cm (1 inch) deep, round 26 cm (10½ inch) fluted loose-based tart (flan) tin (see page 28). Roll the rolling pin over the tin to trim the excess pastry, then refrigerate for 30 minutes.

2 Preheat the oven to 180°C (350°F/ Gas 4). Line the pastry shell with non-stick baking paper and fill with baking beads, dried beans or uncooked rice. Bake for 25 minutes, then remove from the oven. Remove the paper and weights and set the pastry shell aside.

3 Peel the onions, leaving the root ends intact. Cut in half, then cut each half into thirds lengthways and place in a single layer on a baking tray. Drizzle the olive oil, then the vinegar, over the onions and sprinkle with the sugar. Roast for 35 minutes, turning occasionally, or until deep golden and soft (*pic 1*).

4 Meanwhile, whisk together the eggs and egg yolk in a medium bowl. Whisk in the cream and milk. Season with sea salt and freshly ground black pepper.

5 Scatter the parmesan over the pastry shell, then arrange the onions on top in concentric circles (*pic 2*). Place the tin on a baking tray, then carefully pour the cream mixture over the onions (*pic 3*). Scatter over the thyme leaves, then bake for 35–40 minutes or until the filling is just set. Remove from the oven and allow to cool slightly. Serve the tart warm or at room temperature, garnished with the thyme sprigs.

1

2

3

TIP You can vary the cheese and herbs if you like. Try cheddar and snipped chives, blue cheese and chopped sage, or gruyère and finely chopped rosemary.

Lemon tart

This is a gorgeous, silky smooth, lemony tart ideal for those who prefer a not-so-sweet dessert. Try replacing the lemon zest and juice with lime zest and juice for a slightly different flavour.

SERVES 8   **PREPARATION TIME** 30 minutes (+ 1 hour chilling)   **COOKING TIME** 50 minutes

1 quantity sweet shortcrust pastry (see pages 24–25)

5 eggs, at room temperature

220 g (7¾ oz/1 cup) caster (superfine) sugar

Finely grated zest of 2 lemons

125 ml (4 fl oz/½ cup) strained freshly squeezed lemon juice

150 ml (5 fl oz) pouring (whipping) cream

Cream or vanilla ice cream, to serve

1 Use a lightly floured rolling pin to roll out the pastry on a lightly floured work surface to 4 mm (¼ inch) thick. (Alternatively, roll out the pastry between 2 sheets of non-stick baking paper.) Roll the pastry around the rolling pin and carefully ease it into a 2.5 cm (1 inch) deep, 24 cm (9½ inch) fluted, loose-based tart (flan) tin, pressing it into the edges with your fingertips (see page 28). Trim any excess pastry by rolling the rolling pin over the top of the tin. Cover with plastic wrap and place in the refrigerator for 30 minutes.

2 Preheat the oven to 200°C (400°F/ Gas 6).

3 Line the pastry shell with non-stick baking paper and fill with baking beads, rice or beans. Bake for 10 minutes. Remove the beads or rice and paper and bake for a further 10 minutes or until light golden.

4 Just before the pastry shell is ready, prepare the filling. Use a balloon whisk to whisk together the eggs, sugar and lemon zest until well combined (*pic 1*). Add the lemon juice and cream and gently whisk to combine. Strain the filling into a jug (*pic 2*).

5 Remove the pastry shell from the oven and reduce the oven temperature to 180°C (350°F/Gas 4). Pour the filling into the hot pastry shell (*pic 3*). Return to the oven and bake for 30 minutes or until just set in the centre. Cool the tart in the tin, placed on a wire rack. Serve with cream or vanilla ice cream.

1

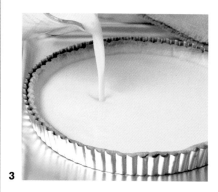

2

3

TIP To really enjoy the fragrant lemon in this tart it is best made and served on the same day. It can, however, be stored in an airtight container in the refrigerator for up to 3 days. Bring to room temperature before serving.

Free-form apple and rhubarb tart

Crisp buttery pastry encasing a slightly tart fruit filling is a superb combination and you'll come back to this recipe often. The fact that there are no special tin requirements, as the pastry is simply folded over the filling, is less intimidating for pastry novices, too. It's best served straight from the oven.

SERVES 6–8   **PREPARATION TIME** 30 minutes (+ 1 hour chilling)   **COOKING TIME** 50–55 minutes

2 medium (about 300 g/10½ oz) apples
(such as granny smith or
golden delicious)
20 g (¾ oz) butter
2 tablespoons light brown sugar
1 tablespoon orange juice
4 rhubarb stalks, trimmed, cut into
5 cm (2 inch) lengths
1 quantity brown sugar shortcrust
pastry (see page 25)
1 tablespoon raw sugar
Vanilla custard or ice cream, to serve

1 Preheat the oven to 200°C (400°F/ Gas 6).

2 Peel and core the apples, then cut into thin wedges. Melt the butter in a medium frying pan over medium heat. Add the apples and cook, turning occasionally, for 2–3 minutes or until light golden. Add the brown sugar and orange juice and cook, stirring, for 1 minute or until the sugar dissolves. Add the rhubarb and cook, stirring, for 2–3 minutes or until the rhubarb starts to soften *(pic 1)*. Set aside to cool to room temperature.

3 Use a lightly floured rolling pin to roll the pastry out on a piece of non-stick baking paper to a 30 cm (12 inch) round, about 4 mm (¼ inch) thick. Transfer the pastry, still on the paper, to a large baking tray. Spread the fruit mixture over the pastry, leaving a 4 cm (1½ inch) border around the edge *(pic 2)*. Fold the border up and over the filling *(pic 3)*. Sprinkle the upturned pastry edge with the raw sugar. Place the tart in the fridge for 20 minutes for the pastry to firm up slightly.

4 Bake the tart for 40–45 minutes or until the pastry is golden and crisp. Serve cut into wedges and accompanied by the custard or ice cream.

1

2

3

Linzertorte

Arguably the oldest cake in the world (the word *torte* is German for 'cake'), the Linzertorte is from the town of Linz in Austria. It always uses ground almonds in the pastry, has a lattice pattern on top, and is filled with jam (traditionally, redcurrant jam).

SERVES 10   **PREPARATION TIME** 40 minutes (+ 30 minutes chilling)   **COOKING TIME** 48 minutes

160 g (5¾ oz/1 cup) almonds
300 g (10½ oz/2 cups) plain
  (all-purpose) flour
1 teaspoon baking powder
2½ teaspoons ground cinnamon
½ teaspoon ground cloves
250 g (9 oz) unsalted butter, softened
220 g (7¾ oz/1 cup) caster
  (superfine) sugar
1 teaspoon natural vanilla extract
Finely grated zest of 1 orange
2 egg yolks
500 g (1 lb 2 oz) raspberry jam
1 egg yolk, extra, lightly whisked
2½ tablespoons flaked almonds

1 Preheat the oven to 180°C (350°F/ Gas 4). Spread the almonds on a baking tray and toast for 8 minutes or until aromatic. Set aside to cool. Transfer to a food processor and process until finely ground *(pic 1)*.

2 Sift the flour, baking powder and spices into a bowl. Use an electric mixer to beat the butter, sugar, vanilla and orange zest in a separate medium bowl until pale and creamy. Add the egg yolks one at a time, beating well after each addition. Add the flour mixture and ground toasted almonds and use a flat-bladed knife and then your hands to mix until a soft dough forms.

3 Turn the dough out onto a lightly floured work surface and shape into a disc. Wrap in plastic wrap and refrigerate for 30 minutes.

4 Preheat the oven to 180°C (350°F/ Gas 4). Divide the dough into 3 portions, then combine 2 of them.

Use a lightly floured rolling pin to roll out the larger portion on a lightly floured work surface to a 30 cm (12 inch) round, taking care not to work the dough too much as it will become very soft. Roll the pastry around the rolling pin and carefully ease it into a 2 cm (¾ inch) deep, 24 cm (9½ inch) fluted, loose-based tart (flan) tin, pressing it into the edges with your fingertips (see page 28). Trim any excess by rolling the rolling pin over the top of the tin.

5 Spread the jam into the pastry shell to cover the base evenly. Roll the remaining dough out between 2 sheets of non-stick baking paper to a rectangle about 20 x 26 cm (8 x 10½ inches) and about 5 mm (¼ inch) thick. Use a fluted pastry wheel or a large sharp knife to cut the remaining portion of dough into 1.5 cm (⅝ inch) wide strips *(pic 2)*. Arrange the strips over the jam to form a lattice pattern *(pic 3)*, taking care as the dough will be quite fragile and may break easily. Re-roll any scraps as necessary to make enough strips to form the lattice.

6 Use a small sharp knife to trim the edges of the strips. Lightly brush the strips with the extra egg yolk and sprinkle the tart with flaked almonds.

7 Bake for 40 minutes or until deep golden and the pastry is cooked through. Leave in the tin to cool. Serve at room temperature.

1

2

3

TIP Keep the linzertorte in an airtight container for up to 3 days.

Individual berry tarts

MAKES 10 **PREPARATION TIME** 25 minutes (+ 1–1½ hours chilling and cooling) **COOKING TIME** 20 minutes

1 quantity pâte sucrée (see page 27)
165 g (5¾ oz/½ cup) good-quality
   berry jam
250 g (9 oz) mascarpone cheese
125 ml (4 fl oz/½ cup) pouring
   (whipping) cream
2 tablespoons icing (confectioners')
   sugar, sifted, plus extra, to dust
½ vanilla bean, split lengthways and
   seeds scraped
350 g (12 oz) mixed fresh berries,
   such as raspberries, blackberries
   and blueberries

1 Make the pastry as directed, rolling it into a 10 cm (4 inch) long log before wrapping in plastic wrap and refrigerating for 30–60 minutes or until firm (see tip).

2 Cut the pastry log into 10 even discs *(pic 1)*. Place a disc between 2 sheets of non-stick baking paper and then use a rolling pin to roll out to about 12 cm (4½ inches) in diameter. Place the pastry round in a 6 cm (2½ inch) diameter (base measurement) tart (flan) tin with removable base and use your fingertips to press it gently into the base and side *(pic 2)*. Trim any overhanging pastry by rolling the rolling pin over the top of the tin. Place on a baking tray. Repeat with the remaining pastry discs to make 10 pastry shells in total. Refrigerate for 30 minutes.

3 Meanwhile, preheat the oven to 200°C (400°F/Gas 6).

4 Line the pastry shells with non-stick baking paper and fill with baking beads *(pic 3)*, dried beans or uncooked rice. Bake for 10 minutes, then remove the weights and paper. Bake for a further 8–10 minutes or until golden and cooked through. Remove from the oven and cool completely in the tins.

5 Divide the jam among the pastry shells and spread to coat the bases. Place the mascarpone, cream, icing sugar and vanilla seeds in a medium bowl. Use a balloon whisk to gently whisk until very soft peaks form, being careful not to overwork the mascarpone. Divide the mixture among the tart cases and top with the berries. Dust with extra icing sugar to serve.

VARIATION

Individual cherry tarts: Use good-quality cherry jam instead of the berry jam and use 650 g (1 lb 7 oz) cherries, pitted, instead of the mixed berries.

1

2

3

> **TIP** Rolling the pastry into a log shape makes it easier to divide it into 10 equal portions. You can simply slice off discs that are then rolled into rounds just the right size for the tins.

Rich chocolate tart

This luscious, not-too-sweet tart is best made using a semi-sweet chocolate with 70% cocoa solids for the ganache filling and Dutch cocoa powder for the pastry. Don't let plastic wrap or any other covering touch the surface of the ganache filling when chilling the tart or it will lose its beautiful sheen.

SERVES 10 **PREPARATION TIME** 30 minutes (+ 4 hours chilling and 30 minutes cooling) **COOKING TIME** 25 minutes

1 quantity chocolate pâte sucrée
  (see page 27)
Dutch unsweetened cocoa powder,
  to dust (optional)
Double (thick/heavy) cream or
  vanilla or coffee ice cream, to serve

CHOCOLATE GANACHE FILLING
300 g (10½ oz) dark chocolate
  (70% cocoa solids), chopped
310 ml (10¾ fl oz/1¼ cups) pouring
  (whipping) cream
60 ml (2 fl oz/¼ cup) brandy, dark rum
  or Frangelico

1 Use a lightly floured rolling pin to roll out the pastry on a cool, lightly floured work surface to a large rectangle, about 22 x 45 cm (8½ x 17¾ inches) and 3 mm (⅛ inch) thick.

2 Line an 11.5 x 34.5 cm (4½ x 13¾ inch) tart (flan) tin (base measurement) with a removable base *(pic 1)* with the pastry, gently easing it into the tin with your fingertips and making sure it fits snugly against the sides and on the base (see page 28). Trim any overhanging pastry by rolling the rolling pin over the top of the tin. Place on a baking tray and refrigerate for 30 minutes or until it is well chilled.

3 Preheat the oven to 200°C (400°F/Gas 6).

4 Line the pastry shell with non-stick baking paper and fill with baking beads, dried beans or uncooked rice. Bake for 10 minutes. Remove the paper and weights, reduce the oven temperature to 180°C (350°F/Gas 4) and bake for a further 15 minutes or until cooked through and dry to the touch. Remove from the oven, place on a wire rack and cool to room temperature.

5 Meanwhile, to make the chocolate ganache filling, put the chocolate in a medium heatproof bowl. Place the cream in a small saucepan and bring just to a simmer. Pour the hot cream over the chocolate *(pic 2)* and stand for 2 minutes. Stir until the chocolate melts and the mixture is completely smooth. Stir in the brandy, rum or Frangelico, then set aside for 30 minutes, stirring occasionally, until the ganache has cooled to room temperature.

6 Pour the ganache filling into the cooled tart shell *(pic 3)*, then gently tap the tin on the bench to even the surface (don't smooth with the back of a spoon or a spatula as it will leave streaks over the surface of the tart). Refrigerate for 3 hours or until the filling is set.

7 Dust the tart with the cocoa, if using. Use a warmed, dry knife to cut the tart into thick slices and serve accompanied by cream or ice cream.

1

2

3

Lemon meringue pie

SERVES 8–10   **PREPARATION TIME** 30 minutes (+ 4 hours chilling and 30 minutes cooling)   **COOKING TIME** 1 hour

1 quantity sweet shortcrust pastry
(see pages 24–25)

LEMON FILLING
10 egg yolks, at room temperature
220 g (7¾ oz/1 cup) caster
(superfine) sugar
Finely grated zest of 3 lemons
40 g (1½ oz/⅓ cup) cornflour
(cornstarch)
160 ml (5¼ fl oz/⅔ cup) strained,
freshly squeezed lemon juice
200 g (7 oz) unsalted butter, chilled and
cut into 1 cm (½ inch) dice

ITALIAN MERINGUE
165 g (5¾ oz/¾ cup) caster
(superfine) sugar
3 egg whites, at room temperature
Pinch of cream of tartar

1 Preheat the oven to 180°C (350°F/
Gas 4). Use a lightly floured rolling pin
to roll out the pastry on a lightly floured
work surface to a 4 mm (⅛ inch) thick
round. Ease it into a 22 cm (8½ inch)
diameter, 4.5 cm (1¾ inch) deep pie tin,
making sure it fits snugly, then trim the
excess. Refrigerate for 20 minutes.

2 Line the pastry shell with non-stick
baking paper and fill with baking beads,
dried beans or uncooked rice. Bake for
20 minutes, then remove the paper and
weights and bake for 20–25 minutes or
until golden and cooked through. Cool
to room temperature on a wire rack.

3 Invert the pastry onto your hand,
then place on a baking tray. To make
the lemon filling, place the egg yolks,
sugar and lemon zest in a saucepan and
use a balloon whisk to whisk until well
combined. Combine the cornflour with
125 ml (4 fl oz/½ cup) water. Add to
the pan with the lemon juice and whisk

to combine. Add the butter. Place over
medium heat and whisk constantly for
2 minutes or until the butter has melted.
Continue whisking for 3–4 minutes or
until thick and almost boiling (do not
allow it to boil) *(pic 1)*. Immediately
pour it into the pastry shell and use a
palette knife dipped in boiling water to
spread to the edges (see tip). Cool, then
refrigerate for 3 hours or until set.

4 To make the Italian meringue,
combine the sugar with 80 ml (2½ fl oz/
⅓ cup) water in a small saucepan and
stir over medium heat until the sugar
dissolves. Brush down the side of the
pan with a pastry brush dipped in
water to remove any sugar crystals.
Increase the heat to high and bring to
the boil. Cook, brushing down the pan
occasionally *(pic 2)*, until the mixture
reaches thread stage (110°C/230°F) on
a sugar thermometer. At this point, put
the egg whites and cream of tartar in a
medium bowl and use an electric mixer
with a whisk attachment to whisk on
medium–high speed until soft peaks
form. Continue cooking the sugar
syrup until it reaches hard ball stage
(118°C/244°F), then, with the motor
running on high, gradually pour it
onto the egg whites in a steady stream.
Whisk constantly for 6–7 minutes, until
the meringue is very thick and glossy,
and has cooled to room temperature.

5 Preheat the grill (broiler) to medium.
Spoon the meringue over the filling and
use a palette knife to spread, swirling as
you go *(pic 3)*. Put on the middle shelf
of the oven and grill for 30 seconds.
Check the colour and grill for 30 seconds
more if needed, turning the pie if it's
colouring unevenly. Stand for 5 minutes.
Use a sharp knife dipped in very hot
water and dried to cut the pie into slices.

1

2

3

TIP The filling for this pie may
seem very thick when you pour
it into the pastry shell, but this
is exactly how it needs to be so
that it will cut well and hold its
shape once set.

Tarte tatin

The Tatin sisters, who ran a hotel in France in the early 1900s, created this upside-down tart. It is traditionally made with apples, though pears are a common substitute.

SERVES 6–8   **PREPARATION TIME** 25 minutes (+ cooling)   **COOKING TIME** 1 hour 5 minutes

3 large (600 g/1 lb 5 oz) granny
   smith apples
75 g (2¾ oz) unsalted butter, chopped
150 g (5½ oz/⅔ cup) caster
   (superfine) sugar
1 sheet (24 x 24 cm/9½ x 9½ inches)
   frozen butter puff pastry,
   thawed slightly (see tip)
Crème fraîche, thick (double/heavy)
   cream, pouring custard (see pages
   348–49) or ice cream, to serve

1 Peel, core and halve the apples. Cut each apple half into 3 wedges. Combine the butter and sugar in a 21 cm (8¼ inch) (base measurement) ovenproof cast-iron pan and place over medium heat. Cook, stirring occasionally, for 5 minutes or until the butter has melted and the mixture is bubbling. Remove from the heat and arrange the apple wedges over the base of the pan (*pic 1*). You may have some apple left over.

2 Return the pan to medium heat and cook for 15 minutes or until the apples are tender and golden underneath (*pic 2*). Remove the pan from the heat and allow the apple mixture to cool completely. Preheat the oven to 180°C (350°F/Gas 4).

3 Cut the pastry into a 24 cm (9½ inch) round. Place the pastry over the cooled apples, then carefully tuck it around the apples, pushing it gently down the inside of the pan and onto the apples (*pic 3*). Bake for 40–45 minutes or until the pastry is deep golden and cooked through, and the apple juices are bubbling. Remove from the oven and set aside for 10 minutes to cool slightly.

4 Invert the tarte tatin onto a serving plate. Serve immediately, cut into wedges, with crème fraîche, cream, pouring custard or ice cream.

VARIATION

Pear and honey tarte tatin: Use 4 firm, ripe beurre bosc or william pears instead of the apples. Peel, core and cut the pears into quarters. Replace half the sugar with 115 g (4 oz/⅓ cup) honey.

1

2

3

TIP You can use 1 quantity sweet shortcrust pastry (see pages 24–25), rolled out to 5 mm (¼ inch) thick and cut into a 24 cm (9½ inch) round instead of puff pastry.

Pistachio and fig tart

Frangipane is a traditional French tart filling, invented by a 16th century cook of the same name, or so the story goes. It is made using finely ground almonds, although hazelnuts or pistachios, as used here, are delicious alternatives. Plums, apricots, peaches or poached pears would also be lovely in this tart.

SERVES 8–10 **PREPARATION TIME** 35 minutes (+ 1 hour chilling and 30 minutes standing) **COOKING TIME** 55–60 minutes

1 quantity pâte sucrée (see page 27)
6 firm ripe figs (85 g/3 oz each)
Icing (confectioners') sugar, to dust
Thick (double/heavy) cream, vanilla
   ice cream or pouring custard
   (see pages 348–49), to serve

**PISTACHIO AND
ROSEWATER FRANGIPANE**

250 g (9 oz) unsalted pistachios
2 tablespoons plain (all-purpose) flour
125 g (4½ oz) unsalted butter,
   at room temperature
110 g (3¾ oz/½ cup) caster
   (superfine) sugar
3 eggs
1½ teaspoons rosewater, or to taste
50 g (1¾ oz/½ cup) flaked almonds

1 Remove the pastry from the refrigerator and set aside at room temperature for 20–30 minutes or until slightly pliable. Use a lightly floured rolling pin to roll out the pastry on a cool, lightly floured work surface to a round about 3 mm (⅛ inch) thick. Gently ease the pastry into a round 28 cm (11¼ inch) fluted loose-based tart (flan) tin, making sure it fits snugly against the side and on the base (see page 28). Trim any overhanging pastry by rolling the rolling pin over the top of the tin. Place on a baking tray and refrigerate for 30 minutes.

2 Meanwhile, preheat the oven to 200°C (400°F/Gas 6).

3 Line the pastry shell with non-stick baking paper and fill with baking beads, dried beans or uncooked rice. Bake for 10 minutes, then remove the paper and weights. Reduce the oven temperature to 180°C (350°F/Gas 4) and bake the pastry shell for a further 10 minutes. Transfer to a wire rack and cool to room temperature.

4 Cut each fig into 8 wedges and arrange over the cooled pastry (pic 1).

5 To make the pistachio and rosewater frangipane, put the pistachios and flour in a food processor bowl and process until the nuts are very finely ground. Use an electric mixer to beat the butter and sugar in a medium mixing bowl until pale and creamy. Add the eggs one at a time, beating well after each addition. Add the pistachio mixture and rosewater and stir until well combined. Carefully spread the frangipane over the figs to cover (pic 2). Scatter the almonds evenly over the frangipane.

6 Bake for 35–40 minutes or until the frangipane is cooked through and the tart is golden. Transfer to a wire rack and cool to room temperature.

7 Dust the tart with icing sugar (pic 3). Cut into wedges and serve with cream, vanilla ice cream or pouring custard.

1

2

3

TIP This tart is best eaten on the day it is baked.

Double-crust apple pie

This traditional apple pie has a melt-in-the-mouth pastry shell and sweet apple filling, thickened with almond meal and given a slight tang by the addition of lemon juice. It's comfort cooking at its best.

SERVES 8   **PREPARATION TIME** 40 minutes (+ 30 minutes chilling, and cooling)   **COOKING TIME** 50 minutes

2 quantities sweet shortcrust pastry (see pages 24–25)
1 egg, lightly whisked
1 tablespoon sugar, to sprinkle
Vanilla ice cream or pouring (whipping) cream, to serve

FILLING
1.2 kg (2 lb 10 oz) granny smith apples
2 tablespoons lemon juice
25 g (1 oz/¼ cup) almond meal
110 g (3¾ oz/½ cup) sugar
1 teaspoon ground cinnamon
¼ teaspoon ground nutmeg
Finely grated zest of 1 lemon

1 Make the 2 quantities of pastry separately and place in the refrigerator to rest, as directed.

2 To make the filling, peel the apples, cut into quarters and cut away the core. Slice each quarter into wedges about 2 cm (¾ inch) thick. Put the apples in a large, deep frying pan with the lemon juice, cover with a tight-fitting lid and cook over medium–low heat, stirring occasionally, for 5–7 minutes or until just soft. Transfer the apples to a colander and set aside to drain and cool to room temperature.

3 Meanwhile, use a rolling pin to roll out each pastry disc between 2 sheets of non-stick baking paper to 3 mm (⅛ inch) thick. Place one portion on a large baking tray, still between the baking paper, and refrigerate until required. Use the remaining pastry to line a 4.5 cm (1¾ inch) deep, round

22 cm (8½ inch) pie tin, easing it gently into the base (see page 28) and allowing it to overhang the top edge (do not trim). Place on a baking tray and refrigerate until required.

4 Preheat the oven to 200°C (400°F/ Gas 6). When the apples have cooled, remove the pastry shell and the rolled pastry from the refrigerator. Sprinkle the almond meal over the base of the pastry shell. Put the apples in a large bowl, add the combined sugar and spices and the lemon zest and gently fold through to combine.

5 Spoon the apple mixture into the pastry shell, then brush the edges of the pastry with the egg *(pic 1)*. Peel the paper away from the rolled pastry and invert the pastry on top of the pie, over the apples. Remove the paper on top and gently press the edges of the pastry to seal *(pic 2)*, then trim with a sharp knife around the outside edge of the tin. Press and fold the pastry back inside the rim of the tin. Brush the top with egg and sprinkle with the sugar. Cut a small cross in the top of the pie to allow steam to escape *(pic 3)*.

6 Bake for 25 minutes, then turn the pie around in the oven to ensure even cooking and bake for a further 20 minutes or until the pastry is cooked through and deep golden. Serve warm with vanilla ice cream or cream.

1

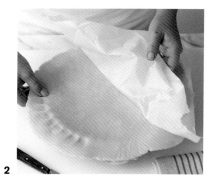
2

3

Peach pie

SERVES 8–10   **PREPARATION TIME** 40 minutes (+ 1 hour chilling)   **COOKING TIME** 1 hour

850 g (1 lb 14 oz) yellow peaches
110 g (3¾ oz/½ cup) caster
　(superfine) sugar
45 g (1¾ oz/⅓ cup) slivered almonds
Whipped cream, to serve

SHORTCAKE PASTRY
175 g (6 oz) unsalted butter, softened
110 g (3¾ oz/½ cup) caster
　(superfine) sugar
1½ teaspoons natural vanilla extract
1 egg, lightly whisked
260 g (9¼ oz/1¾ cups) self-raising
　flour
80 g (2¾ oz/¾ cup) almond meal

1 To make the shortcake pastry, use an electric mixer to beat the butter and sugar in a medium bowl until pale and creamy. Add the vanilla and egg and beat until well combined. Combine the flour and almond meal in a bowl, add to the butter mixture and stir with a wooden spoon, and then your hands, until well combined. Shape into a disc, wrap in plastic wrap and refrigerate for 1 hour or until firm.

2 Meanwhile, cut the peach flesh from the stones. Chop the flesh into 1 cm (½ inch) pieces, then put in a medium saucepan with the sugar and 60 ml (2 fl oz/¼ cup) water. Cover and cook over medium heat, stirring occasionally, for 15 minutes or until the peaches are very tender *(pic 1)*.

3 Transfer the peach mixture to a sieve set over a bowl to drain, reserving the juices. Put the peaches in a heatproof bowl and set aside. Pour the cooking liquid into a small saucepan. Boil for 5 minutes or until thick and syrupy. Add to the peaches, then refrigerate for 20 minutes or until cooled to room temperature.

4 Preheat the oven to 180°C (350°F/ Gas 4). Lightly brush a 9.5 cm x 33.5 cm (3¾ x 13¼ inch) (base measurement) fluted loose-based tart (flan) tin with melted butter to grease.

5 Divide the pastry into 3 portions. Wrap one portion in plastic wrap and return to the refrigerator. Combine the remaining portions. Pinch off small amounts of pastry and press into the greased tin to evenly line the sides and base *(pic 2)* (it should be about 5 mm/ ¼ inch thick). Roll a rolling pin over the top of the tin to trim any excess pastry.

6 Spoon the cooled peach mixture evenly into the pastry shell. Coarsely grate the reserved chilled pastry over the peach filling to cover evenly *(pic 3)*. Sprinkle with the almonds.

7 Bake for 35 minutes or until the pastry is golden and cooked through. Transfer to a wire rack and cool to room temperature. Slice and serve with the whipped cream.

TIP This pastry is simple to make and perfect to use when the pie filling is slightly wet, as in this recipe. Try using it in your favourite pie and tart recipes.

You can add 2½ teaspoons finely chopped rosemary to the flour and almond meal when making the pastry if you wish.

This pie is also delicious accompanied by pouring custard (see pages 348–49).

Pecan pie

The pecan nut is native to the Americas and was an important food source in pre-colonial times. Its name is a native American word originally referring to any nut that required a stone to crack it open.

SERVES 8 **PREPARATION TIME** 20 minutes (+ 30 minutes chilling) **COOKING TIME** 1 hour

1 quantity sweet shortcrust pastry
  (see pages 24–25)
40 g (1½ oz) butter, melted
110 g (3¾ oz/½ cup, firmly packed)
  dark brown sugar
175 g (6 oz/½ cup) golden syrup
1 teaspoon natural vanilla extract
2 eggs, lightly whisked
200 g (7 oz/2 cups) pecan halves
2 tablespoons apricot jam
Thick (double/heavy) or whipped
  cream, to serve

1 Preheat the oven to 200°C (400°F/ Gas 6). Use a lightly floured rolling pin to roll out the pastry on a lightly floured work surface to a 30 cm (12 inch) diameter circle, taking care not to overwork the dough or it will become too soft. Roll the pastry around the rolling pin and ease it into a 3 cm (1¼ inch) deep, round 24 cm (9½ inch) fluted loose-based tart (flan) tin, pressing it into the base and side with your fingertips (see page 28). Roll the rolling pin over the tin to trim the excess pastry.

2 Line the pastry shell with non-stick baking paper and fill with baking beads, dried beans or uncooked rice. Bake for 20 minutes, then remove the paper and weights. Reduce the temperature to 160°C (315°F/Gas 2–3).

3 Meanwhile, put the butter, sugar, golden syrup, vanilla and egg in a bowl and whisk until well combined *(pic 1)*. Scatter the pecans evenly over the tart shell *(pic 2)*. Pour over the golden syrup mixture *(pic 3)*. Bake for 40 minutes or until the filling is browned and firm to touch. Place on a wire rack and cool the pie in the tin.

4 Put the jam in a small saucepan and heat until warm. Push through a sieve to remove any solids. Brush the sieved jam over the top of the pie to glaze. Serve at room temperature with the cream.

1

2

3

TIP Pecan pie will keep for 2–3 days in an airtight container. Like most cooked pastries, it should not be refrigerated if possible, as refrigeration spoils the texture of cooked pastry.

Portuguese custard tarts

These tarts are called *pastéis de nata*, or cream pastries, in their homeland of Portugal. They are notoriously difficult to make as the pastry requires a high temperature and the custard a low one, however this recipe for the home cook is achievable and gives an authentic result.

MAKES 12   **PREPARATION TIME** 1 hour 15 minutes (+ 1 hour 20 minutes chilling)   **COOKING TIME** 20–25 minutes

165 g (5¾ oz/¾ cup) caster (superfine) sugar, plus 1 tablespoon, extra
250 ml (9 fl oz/1 cup) milk
50 g (1¾ oz/⅓ cup) plain (all-purpose) flour
1 vanilla bean, split lengthways and seeds scraped
1 x 10 cm (4 inch) long strip lemon zest
4 egg yolks
185 ml (6 fl oz/¾ cup) pouring (whipping) cream
1 teaspoon ground cinnamon
½ quantity puff pastry (see pages 32–33)

1 Preheat the oven to 240°C (475°F/ Gas 8). Position an oven shelf at the top of the oven. (Tarts need to be cooked at the top of the oven where it's hottest.) Lightly grease a 12-hole 80 ml (2½ fl oz/ ⅓ cup) muffin tin.

2 Combine the sugar and 125 ml (4 fl oz/½ cup) water in a small saucepan over low heat. Cook, stirring, until the sugar dissolves. Bring to a simmer over medium heat and simmer for 5–7 minutes or until the mixture reaches soft-ball stage (112°C/235°F) on a sugar thermometer. Remove from the heat and set aside.

3 Meanwhile, put 60 ml (2 fl oz/ ¼ cup) of the milk and the flour in a small bowl and stir until smooth. Place the remaining milk, vanilla seeds and pod, and lemon zest in a small saucepan. Bring to the boil, then remove from the heat. Add the flour mixture,

stirring constantly until smooth. Add the egg yolks, stirring constantly until well combined. Stir in the cream until combined. Add the sugar syrup in a slow, steady stream, stirring constantly until combined. Transfer to a heatproof jug and set aside to cool slightly while you roll out the pastry.

4 Combine the extra sugar and cinnamon in a small bowl. Use a lightly floured rolling pin to roll out the pastry on a clean work surface to a 30 x 35 cm (12 x 14 inch) rectangle. With a long side facing you, sprinkle the pastry with the cinnamon mixture. Starting at the side closest to you, roll up the pastry tightly to form a 35 cm (14 inch) long log *(pic 1)*. Cut the log into 12 slices, about 3 cm (1¼ inches) wide *(pic 2)*.

5 Working with one slice at a time, place, cut side down, on a lightly floured work surface. Gently press with the heel of your hand to flatten slightly, then use a lightly floured rolling pin to roll out the pastry to form a 9 cm (3½ inch) round *(pic 3)*. Use a round 9 cm (3½ inch) pastry cutter to trim the edges as necessary. Gently press each round into a greased muffin hole, using your fingertips to carefully press them into the base and side of each hole. Divide the custard mixture among the pastry shells. Bake for 6–10 minutes or until the custard is firm to touch and beginning to brown in patches. Cool in the tin for 5 minutes, then transfer to a wire rack to cool completely.

1

2

3

TIP These tarts are best eaten on the day they are baked.

Rosemary and honey rice-custard tart

This tart is inspired by the flavours and ingredients of Italy, where rice is often used this way in desserts. A spoonful of lightly sweetened apple purée would make the perfect accompaniment, though the tart is wonderful served simply as is.

MAKES 26 cm (10½ inch) tart **PREPARATION TIME** 20 minutes (+ 1 hour–1 hour 15 minutes chilling) **COOKING TIME** 1 hour

1 quantity pâte sucrée (see page 27)
1 tablespoon finely chopped rosemary, plus extra sprigs, to garnish
110 g (3¾ oz/½ cup) short-grain white rice
250 ml (9 fl oz/1 cup) milk
300 ml (10½ fl oz) pouring (whipping) cream
175 g (6 oz/½ cup) honey
1 teaspoon natural vanilla extract
1 egg
2 egg yolks

1 Make the pastry as directed, adding the rosemary to the flour. Use a rolling pin to roll out the chilled pastry on a lightly floured work surface to a 36 cm (14¼ inch) diameter circle and ease into a 2.5 cm (1 inch) deep, round 26 cm (10½ inch) fluted loose-based tart (flan) tin, using your fingertips to press it into the base and side of the tin (see page 28). Roll the rolling pin over the top of the tin to trim the excess pastry. Refrigerate for 30 minutes.

2 Preheat the oven to 180°C (350°F/ Gas 4). Line the pastry shell with non-stick baking paper and fill with baking beads, dried beans or uncooked rice. Bake for 15 minutes, then remove the paper and weights and bake for a further 6–7 minutes or until light golden and dry on the base *(pic 1)*. Transfer to a wire rack to cool slightly.

3 Meanwhile, combine the rice, milk and 125 ml (4 fl oz/½ cup) of the cream in a small saucepan and bring to a simmer over medium heat. Reduce the heat to low and cook, covered, for 18–20 minutes, stirring occasionally, or until the rice is nearly tender and the mixture is very thick. Remove from the heat, stir in the honey and vanilla and set aside to cool slightly *(pic 2)*.

4 Add the remaining cream, the egg and egg yolks and stir to combine well. Pour the mixture into the pastry shell *(pic 3)* and bake for 35 minutes or until the filling is just set. Transfer to a wire rack and cool in the tin. Serve the tart at room temperature, sprinkled with rosemary sprigs.

1

2

3

TIP This tart is best eaten on the day it is baked.

Pastries

Pork, apple and fennel sausage rolls

Sausage rolls are perennially popular, especially for casual finger food at a party. Making your own, using good-quality ingredients, is so simple and gives such fabulous results that you'll never look back.

MAKES 12   **PREPARATION TIME** 1 hour (+ 1 hour 20 minutes chilling/cooling)   **COOKING TIME** 35–40 minutes

1 tablespoon fennel seeds

1 tablespoon olive oil

1 small fennel bulb, trimmed and
    finely chopped

2 garlic cloves, finely chopped

60 g (2¼ oz/½ cup) chopped pancetta

Pinch of allspice

300 g (10½ oz) good-quality pork
    sausages, removed from their casings

300 g (10½ oz) minced (ground) pork

60 g (2¼ oz/1 cup, lightly packed)
    fresh breadcrumbs, made from
    day-old bread

1 small green apple (about 100 g/
    3½ oz), peeled and coarsely grated

¼ cup roughly chopped flat-leaf
    (Italian) parsley

1 egg yolk

1 quantity rough puff pastry
    (see pages 36–37)

1 egg, lightly whisked with
    2 teaspoons water

1 tablespoon sesame seeds

1 Heat a small non-stick frying pan over medium heat. Add 3 teaspoons of the fennel seeds and cook, shaking the pan, for 30 seconds or until aromatic. Use a mortar and pestle or spice grinder to grind the seeds to a powder.

2 Heat the olive oil in a medium frying pan over medium–low heat. Add the chopped fennel and cook, stirring, for 5 minutes. Add the garlic and pancetta and cook for a further 5 minutes or until the fennel is golden and tender. Add the ground fennel and the allspice and cook for 30 seconds or until aromatic. Set aside to cool.

3 Combine the sausage meat, minced pork, cooled fennel mixture, breadcrumbs, apple, parsley and egg yolk in a large bowl. Season well with salt and freshly ground black pepper.

4 Preheat the oven to 200°C (400°F/ Gas 6). Line 2 large baking trays with non-stick baking paper.

5 Cut the pastry in half widthways, then roll each piece out on a lightly floured work surface to a 25 cm (10 inch) square. Cut each pastry sheet in half. Divide the mince mixture into 4 equal portions. Shape each portion into a log and place on the centre of each piece of pastry (*pic 1*). Brush the edges of the pastry well with the egg wash. Fold the pastry over to enclose the filling, overlapping the edges and pressing to seal (*pic 2*). Transfer to a tray and refrigerate for 20 minutes to rest.

6 Line 2 more baking trays with non-stick baking paper. Place the sausage rolls on a chopping board, seam side down. Cut each roll into 3 equal pieces (*pic 3*). Transfer to the lined trays, allowing room for spreading.

7 Combine the remaining fennel seeds and the sesame seeds in a small bowl. Brush the sausage rolls with the egg wash and sprinkle with the seed mixture. Bake for 15 minutes, then reduce the temperature to 180°C (350°F/Gas 4), swap the trays around and cook for 10–15 minutes more or until puffed and golden.

1

2

3

TIP The uncooked sausage rolls can be frozen, in sealed freezer bags, for up to 2 months. There is no need to defrost them before cooking, but allow an extra 5 minutes to cook them through.

Potato and pea samosas

The samosa has been a popular snack food throughout parts of Asia for centuries, although most people associate them with India. Vegetable-based fillings are more common than those with meat. Traditional accompaniments include chutney and yoghurt, chopped onions and coriander.

MAKES 16   **PREPARATION TIME** 1 hour 10 minutes (+ 1 hour resting/cooling)   **COOKING TIME** 1 hour 15 minutes

500 g (1 lb 2 oz) all-purpose potatoes
120 ml (4 fl oz) vegetable oil, plus extra, for deep-frying
1 onion, finely chopped
110 g (3¾ oz/¾ cup) frozen peas, thawed and drained well
2 teaspoons finely grated ginger
2 garlic cloves, finely chopped
1 small green chilli, finely chopped
4 tablespoons finely chopped coriander (cilantro)
1 teaspoon salt
1 teaspoon ground cumin
¾ teaspoon ground coriander
¾ teaspoon garam masala
1½ tablespoons lemon juice
260 g (9¼ oz/1 cup) plain yoghurt
2 tablespoons finely chopped mint
225–260 g (8–9¼ oz/1½–1¾ cups) plain (all-purpose) flour
60 ml (2 fl oz/¼ cup) chilled water

1 Put the potatoes in a saucepan, cover with cold water and bring to the boil. Reduce the heat and simmer for 25–35 minutes or until tender. Drain the potatoes and allow to cool, then peel and cut into 1 cm (½ inch) pieces.

2 Heat 2 tablespoons of the oil in a large frying pan over medium–high heat. Cook the onion, stirring, for 6 minutes. Add the peas, ginger, garlic, chilli, half the chopped coriander and 2 tablespoons water. Reduce the heat to medium–low, cover and cook, stirring occasionally, for 3 minutes.

3 Reduce the heat to low, add the potatoes, half each of the salt and cumin, the ground coriander, garam masala and the lemon juice. Cook for 3–4 minutes, stirring occasionally. Transfer to a bowl.

4 Combine the yoghurt, remaining chopped coriander, remaining cumin and the mint. Refrigerate until required.

5 Sift 225 g (8 oz/1½ cups) of the flour and the remaining salt into a bowl. Add the remaining 80 ml (2½ fl oz/⅓ cup) oil and mix to combine. Gradually mix in the chilled water with a flat-bladed knife, using a cutting action, until a dough forms. Turn out and knead on a clean work surface for 5 minutes, adding the remaining flour, 1 tablespoon at a time, if it seems too wet. Shape into a ball and place in an oiled bowl, turning to coat in the oil. Cover with plastic wrap and set aside for 30 minutes.

6 Knead the pastry briefly, then divide into 8 equal portions. Roll each into a ball, place on a lightly greased baking tray and cover with plastic wrap. Working with one ball at a time, roll out to a 16 cm (6¼ inch) diameter circle, then cut in half. Pick up a semi-circle and dampen the straight side with a little water *(pic 1)*. Shape it into a cone, pinching the edges to seal. Spoon in 2 tablespoons of filling *(pic 2)*, then dampen the edges and pinch to seal, pleating slightly. Place on a lined tray. Repeat with remaining dough and filling.

7 Fill a small, deep saucepan one-third full with the extra oil and heat to 180°C (350°F). Fry the samosas, 3–4 at a time, for 6 minutes, turning once, or until golden and crisp. Drain on paper towels. Serve with the herbed yoghurt.

1

2

3

TIP If you like some chilli heat in your samosas, add ⅛ teaspoon chilli powder with the ground coriander and garam masala.
When in season, use fresh podded peas rather than frozen.

Chicken, bacon and mushroom vol-au-vents

MAKES 4   **PREPARATION TIME** 1 hour 20 minutes (+ 1 hour 35 minutes chilling)   **COOKING TIME** 50–60 minutes

1 quantity puff pastry (see pages 32–33)
   (see tip)
1 egg, lightly whisked with
   2 teaspoons water
225 g (8 oz) skinless chicken
   breast fillet
375 ml (13 fl oz/1½ cups) chicken stock
1 bay leaf
1 thyme sprig
1 tablespoon olive oil
75 g (2¾ oz) lean bacon, chopped
100 g (3½ oz) button mushrooms, sliced
2 small garlic cloves, crushed
1 French shallot, finely chopped
60 ml (2 fl oz/¼ cup) white wine
2 tablespoons cornflour (cornstarch),
   mixed with 60 ml (2 fl oz/¼ cup) water
60 ml (2 fl oz/¼ cup) pouring
   (whipping) cream
Thinly sliced spring onion (scallion),
   to garnish

1 Preheat the oven to 220°C (425°F/ Gas 7). Line 2 baking trays with non-stick baking paper.

2 Use a rolling pin to roll out the pastry to a 36 cm (14¼ inch) square, then use a round 9 cm (3½ inch) pastry cutter to cut out 12 rounds. Place 4 rounds on a lined tray and use a round 6 cm (2½ inch) cutter to mark a small round in the centre of each, without cutting through *(pic 1)*. These are the bases.

3 Place the remaining pastry rounds on the other lined tray and use the smaller cutter to cut out the centre of each to make rings of an even thickness *(pic 2)*.

4 Brush the outer ring of each pastry base with egg wash, taking care not to brush the sides or the pastry won't rise properly. Carefully place a pastry ring

on top of a pastry base *(pic 3)*. Brush the top of the ring with egg wash and place another ring on top. Repeat with the remaining bases, egg wash and rings. Refrigerate for 15 minutes or until well chilled. Brush the top ring of each pastry with egg wash, avoiding the sides.

5 Bake for 20 minutes or until puffed and golden. Remove any uncooked pastry from the centre and bake for 5–10 minutes or until the bases are golden and crisp. Cool on a wire rack.

6 Place the chicken and stock in a small saucepan. If the chicken isn't covered, add a little extra stock or water. Add the bay leaf and thyme and bring to a gentle simmer over medium heat. Reduce the heat to medium–low, cover and cook for 4–5 minutes. Remove from the heat and set aside for 10 minutes or until the chicken is just cooked through. Transfer the chicken to a plate and reserve the cooking liquid. Use 2 forks to shred the chicken and place in a medium bowl.

7 Heat the oil in a medium non-stick frying pan over medium–high heat. Add the bacon and cook, stirring, for 5 minutes. Add the mushrooms and garlic and cook, stirring, for a further 3 minutes. Add the shallot, season well and then mix into the chicken. Return the pan to the heat, add the wine and cook until reduced by half, then add the reserved cooking liquid. Bring to the boil, then reduce the heat and simmer for 2 minutes. Add the cornflour mixture and cream and stir until thickened. Remove the herbs. Add the chicken mixture and heat through. Season to taste. Spoon into the pastry cases and serve warm, sprinkled with spring onion.

1

2

3

TIP You can use 3 square 24 cm (9½ inch) sheets ready-made puff pastry or 4 large (8 cm/3¼ inch) ready-made vol-au-vent cases.
   Unfilled vol-au-vents can be kept in an airtight container for up to 2 days. Before filling, heat in a preheated 180°C (350°F/Gas 4) for 5–7 minutes or until crisp.

Cornish pasties

This style of pasty was regular lunchtime fare for labourers working in the area around Cornwall in England during the 18th century. Today the Cornish pasty enjoys protected status under the European Commission, so only pasties made in Cornwall or to a traditional recipe can carry this name.

MAKES 8　　**PREPARATION TIME** 1 hour (+ 30 minutes resting)　　**COOKING TIME** 45–50 minutes

PASTRY

600 g (1 lb 5 oz/4 cups) plain (all-purpose) flour
1 teaspoon salt
150 g (5½ oz) chilled butter, chopped
150 g (5½ oz) chilled lard (see tip), chopped
80 ml (2½ fl oz/⅓ cup) chilled water

FILLING

100 g (3½ oz) swede (rutabaga), peeled
100 g (3½ oz) potato, peeled
½ brown onion
350 g (12 oz) trimmed rump steak, cut into 8 mm (⅜ inch) pieces
1 tablespoon plain (all-purpose) flour
Milk, for brushing
1 egg yolk, whisked with 1½ tablespoons water

1 To make the pastry, combine the flour and salt in a large bowl. With your palms facing upwards, use your fingertips to rub in the butter and lard, lifting the flour mixture up as you rub to aerate it, until the mixture resembles fine breadcrumbs. Add almost all the chilled water and mix with a flat-bladed knife, using a cutting action, to form a dough, adding the remaining water if necessary. Knead briefly until the dough just comes together. Shape into a disc, wrap in plastic wrap and refrigerate for 30 minutes to rest.

2 Preheat the oven to 180°C (350°F/ Gas 4) and line a large baking tray with non-stick baking paper. Cut the swede, potato and onion into 8 mm (⅜ inch) pieces. Combine with the meat in a large bowl. Scatter over the flour, season well with sea salt and freshly ground black pepper, then toss well.

3 Roll the pastry out on a lightly floured work surface until it is 5 mm (¼ inch) thick. Using a 16 cm (6¼ inch) plate or bowl as a guide, cut out 8 rounds from the pastry *(pic 1)*, gathering up the scraps and re-rolling as necessary. Brush the edges of the rounds lightly with milk, then divide the meat mixture among them, placing it along the centre and leaving a 1 cm (½ inch) border at each end *(pic 2)*.

4 Bring the sides of the pastry up to meet at the top, then press together. Crimp the edges together to seal well, using your fingers to push the edges into a decorative 'wave' *(pic 3)*. Place the pasties on the lined tray and brush all over with the egg wash. Bake for 45–50 minutes or until the pastry is deep golden. Cool slightly on the trays, then serve hot or at room temperature.

1

2

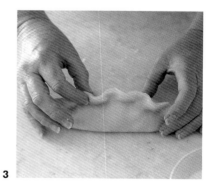
3

TIP Lard gives the pastry a beautiful, rich flaky quality but if it is hard to get, or you prefer, simply replace it with the equivalent weight in butter.

Raisin and custard spirals

These utterly delicious pastries use the same leavened pastry as croissants but are far easier to make as there is less precise measuring and cutting involved. They make an irresistible morning treat.

MAKES 10   **PREPARATION TIME** 1½ hours (+ 4–4½ hours proving and 1½ hours chilling)   **COOKING TIME** 33 minutes

1 quantity leavened puff pastry
   (see pages 38–39)
½ quantity crème pâtissière (see
   page 349), reducing the plain
   (all-purpose) flour to 1 tablespoon
1 egg yolk, whisked with
   2 teaspoons water
130 g (4½ oz/¾ cup) raisins
115 g (4 oz/⅓ cup) apricot jam

1 Roll out the dough on a lightly floured work surface to a neat rectangle, about 28 x 60 cm (11¼ x 24 inches). Try to keep the edges as straight as possible.

2 With a short side facing you, use a large sharp knife to trim the edges so they are straight. Spread the cooled crème pâtissière over the dough (*pic 1*), leaving a 1 cm (½ inch) border at the far end. Brush the border very lightly with the egg yolk mixture. Scatter the raisins evenly over the crème pâtissière.

3 Line 2 baking trays with non-stick baking paper. Starting at the short side facing you, roll the dough up into a short, thick log (*pic 2*). Use a sharp serrated knife to cut the log in half

widthways, then cut each portion into 5 slices, each about 2.5 cm (1 inch) wide (*pic 3*). Place on the lined trays, cut-side down and allowing room for spreading. Set aside in a warm, draught-free place for 1½ hours or until puffed and risen.

4 Preheat the oven to 200°C (400°F/ Gas 6). Lightly brush the pastries all over with the egg yolk mixture. Bake for 30 minutes, swapping the trays halfway through to ensure even cooking, or until golden and crisp. Transfer to a wire rack to cool.

5 Combine the jam and 1 tablespoon water in a small saucepan and bring to a simmer, stirring until smooth. Remove from the heat and push through a sieve to remove any solids, then brush over the cooled pastries to glaze.

1

2

3

TIP These pastries are best eaten on the day they are baked.

Chocolate éclairs

One of the great classics of the French pastry repertoire, home-made éclairs never fail to impress.
If you are short on time, simply fill them with sweetened whipped cream flavoured with vanilla.

MAKES 16 **PREPARATION TIME** 1½ hours (+ 40 minutes cooling/setting) **COOKING TIME** 44 minutes–1 hour

1 quantity choux pastry
(see pages 40–41)
1 quantity crème pâtissière
(see page 349), adding 1 tablespoon
unsweetened cocoa powder when
sifting the flour and cornflour
125 g (4½ oz) dark chocolate,
melted

CHOCOLATE GLACÉ ICING
210 g (7½ oz/1¾ cups) icing
(confectioners') sugar
15 g (½ oz) unsweetened
cocoa powder
60–80 ml (2–2½ fl oz/¼–⅓ cup)
boiling water
½ teaspoon natural vanilla extract

1 Preheat the oven to 200°C (400°F/
Gas 6). Line 2 baking trays with
non-stick baking paper. Spoon the
pastry into a large piping (icing) bag
fitted with a 1.5 cm (⅝ inch) plain
nozzle (see page 42).

2 Pipe 10 cm (4 inch) lengths onto a
lined tray, allowing room for spreading
(pic 1). Sprinkle the baking tray lightly
with water to create steam in the oven
and encourage the puffs to rise. Bake
for 12–15 minutes. Reduce the heat to
180°C (350°F/Gas 4) and bake for a
further 10–15 minutes, or until golden
and puffed. Transfer to a wire rack and
use a small sharp knife to split each

pastry in half to allow the steam to
escape *(pic 2)*. Increase the temperature
to 200°C (400°F/Gas 6) and pipe the
remaining choux pastry into 10 cm
(4 inch) lengths on the other lined tray.
Cook the remaining pastries as before,
then transfer to the wire rack and split
in half. Allow to cool completely, then
carefully remove any uncooked dough
from inside each split pastry.

3 Make the crème pâtissière and
while it is still warm, stir in the melted
chocolate. Spoon the chocolate crème
pâtissière into a large piping bag with
a 1.5 cm (⅝ inch) plain nozzle. Pipe
the crème onto the bottom half of the
pastries *(pic 3)*, then cover with the
tops of the pastries.

4 To make the chocolate glacé icing
(frosting), sift the icing sugar and cocoa
into a large bowl. Use a whisk to slowly
stir in 60 ml (2 fl oz/¼ cup) of the
boiling water to form a smooth icing
with a light coating consistency. Stir
in the vanilla. Add a little more water,
a few drops at a time, if necessary, to
reach the desired consistency. Spread
about 1 tablespoon of icing over the top
of each éclair. Set aside for 20 minutes
or until the icing is set.

1

2

3

TIP Éclairs are best eaten as
soon as possible after filling and
icing. Keep refrigerated, but return
to room temperature to serve.
Unfilled éclairs can be kept
in an airtight container for up to
2 days or frozen in an airtight
container for up to 2 weeks.

Honey and nut filo rolls

These mouthwatering morsels have all the exotic flavours of the Middle East, including cinnamon, honey and pistachio nuts. In that part of the world, it is usual for pastries, many of which are made using filo pastry, to be doused in a rich, sweet syrup.

MAKES 48   **PREPARATION TIME** 50 minutes (+ cooling)   **COOKING TIME** 15–20 minutes

140 g (5 oz/1 cup) pistachios
140 g (5 oz/1 cup) walnut pieces
1 teaspoon ground cinnamon
55 g (2 oz/¼ cup) caster
    (superfine) sugar
150 g (5½ oz) unsalted butter, chopped
1½ tablespoons vegetable oil
16 sheets filo pastry (each measuring
    27.5 x 43 cm/11 x 17 inches)
30 g (1 oz/¼ cup) pistachios,
    extra, finely chopped

SYRUP
350 g (12 oz/1 cup) honey
330 g (11½ oz/1½ cups) caster
    (superfine) sugar
10 whole cloves

1 Preheat the oven to 180°C (350°F/ Gas 4). Line 2 baking trays with non-stick baking paper. Place the pistachios, walnuts, cinnamon and sugar in the bowl of a food processor and pulse until coarsely ground.

2 Heat the butter in a small saucepan over low heat until just melted. Add the oil and set aside. Lay the filo pastry flat on a work surface and cover with a clean tea towel (dish towel), then a slightly damp tea towel to prevent it drying out. Take 1 sheet of pastry and place it flat on the work surface. Brush with a little of the butter mixture, then top

with another sheet of filo *(pic 1)*. Repeat with 2 more sheets of filo, brushing each sheet with the butter mixture. Sprinkle over 70 g (2½ oz/½ cup) of the nut mix.

3 Cut the pastry stack in half lengthways, then cut each strip into 6 evenly sized rectangles. Working with one rectangle at a time and starting with a shorter edge, roll up tightly into a cigar shape *(pic 2)*. Place on baking trays lined with non-stick baking paper. Brush with a little more butter mixture. Repeat with the remaining filo pastry, nut mix and butter mixture. Bake for 15–20 minutes or until golden.

4 Meanwhile, to make the syrup, combine all the ingredients in a saucepan over medium heat and stir until the sugar dissolves. Boil for 5 minutes, then remove from the heat.

5 Cool the filo rolls on the trays for 5 minutes, then transfer to a large tray. Drizzle two-thirds of the syrup over the warm filo rolls *(pic 3)*, then allow them to cool to room temperature.

6 To serve, arrange the filo rolls on a serving platter, drizzle with the remaining syrup and sprinkle with the extra pistachios.

TIP This recipe can be halved successfully, if desired.
   The filo rolls will keep, covered with plastic wrap or in an airtight container, at room temperature for up to 3 days; do not refrigerate.

Baklava

This popular Middle Eastern treat consists of paper-thin filo pastry, buttered and layered with a nut and spice filling, then covered with a sweet syrup. Filo pastry is available fresh or frozen from supermarkets. Fresh filo is easier to work with, less fragile and won't tear as much as the frozen variety.

MAKES about 18 pieces   **PREPARATION TIME** 30 minutes (+ cooling)   **COOKING TIME** 30 minutes

400 g (14 oz/3½ cups) walnut halves, finely chopped
155 g (5½ oz/1 cup) almonds, finely chopped
½ teaspoon ground cinnamon
½ teaspoon mixed (pumpkin pie) spice
1 tablespoon caster (superfine) sugar
16 sheets filo pastry
200 g (7 oz) butter, melted
1 tablespoon olive oil

SYRUP
440 g (15½ oz/2 cups) sugar
330 ml (11¼ fl oz/1⅓ cups) water
3 whole cloves
3 teaspoons lemon juice

1 Preheat the oven to 180°C (350°F/ Gas 4). Brush the base and sides of a shallow 18 x 28 cm (7 x 11¼ inch) tin with melted butter to grease.

2 Put the walnuts, almonds, spices and sugar in a medium bowl and mix well. Lay the filo pastry flat on a work surface and cover with a clean tea towel (dish towel), then a slightly damp tea towel to prevent it drying out. Combine the butter and oil. Take 1 sheet of pastry and place it flat on the work surface. Brush liberally with the butter mixture, then fold it in half crossways. Trim the edges to fit the greased tin and then

place in the tin. Repeat with 3 more pastry sheets to cover the base, brushing liberally with the butter mixture and trimming edges as needed *(pic 1)*.

3 Sprinkle one-third of the nut mixture over the pastry in the tin *(pic 2)*. Repeat this process to make 2 more layers each of pastry and nut mixture, then finish with another pastry layer. Press the top down with your hands so that the pastry and nuts stick to each other.

4 Brush the top of the pastry with the remaining butter and oil mixture. Use a large sharp knife to cut the baklava lengthways into 4 even strips, then diagonally into diamonds. Bake the baklava for 30 minutes or until the pastry is golden and crisp.

5 Meanwhile, to make the syrup, combine all the ingredients in a small saucepan and stir over low heat until the sugar dissolves. Bring to the boil, then reduce the heat and simmer, without stirring, for 10 minutes. Set aside to cool. Discard the cloves.

6 Pour the cooled syrup over the hot baklava *(pic 3)*, transfer to a wire rack and allow to cool in the tin. Cut into diamonds to serve.

1

2

3

TIP Keep in an airtight container, layered with non-stick baking paper, for up to 5 days.

Ricotta and raisin strudel

Originating in Austria, strudel is traditionally made with a very thin, stretched dough that is spread with a filling, then rolled up and baked. This recipe can easily be doubled to make two strudels — double the ingredients, then halve the dough before rolling out and divide the filling among the two rectangles.

SERVES 8–10   **PREPARATION TIME** 45 minutes (+ 30 minutes resting)   **COOKING TIME** 40 minutes

175 g (6 oz) plain (all-purpose) flour, plus 2 teaspoons, extra
½ lightly whisked egg (see tip)
2 tablespoons vegetable oil
Large pinch of salt
2 teaspoons strained, freshly squeezed lemon juice
60 ml (2 fl oz/¼ cup) room-temperature water, approximately
250 g (9 oz) firm, fresh ricotta cheese
30 g (1 oz) butter, softened, plus 80 g (2¾ oz) butter, melted, extra
75 g (2¾ oz/⅓ cup) caster (superfine) sugar
½ vanilla bean, split lengthways and seeds scraped
2 eggs, extra, at room temperature, separated
65 g (2¼ oz/¼ cup) sour cream
2 tablespoons raisins
Finely grated zest of 1 lemon
Icing (confectioners') sugar, to dust

1 Put the flour, egg, oil, salt and lemon juice in the bowl of a stand mixer fitted with a dough hook attachment. Add the water and mix on low speed until combined. Increase the speed to medium–low and mix for 5 minutes or until smooth and elastic. (Alternatively, knead the dough by hand on a lightly floured work surface.) Add a little extra water if it is too dry; it should be firm. Turn out onto a clean surface and shape into a ball. Cover with a large warmed bowl and set aside for 30 minutes.

2 Meanwhile, use a spatula to beat the ricotta until almost smooth; set aside. Put the butter, caster sugar, vanilla and egg yolks in a bowl and use an electric mixer to beat until pale. Add the sour cream and extra flour and beat until just combined. Stir in the raisins and zest.

3 Use a clean, dry electric mixer to whisk the egg whites in a clean, dry bowl until firm peaks form. Stir the ricotta into the butter mixture until smooth, then add the egg whites and mix until well combined. Set aside.

4 Preheat the oven to 220°C (425°F/ Gas 7). Line a large baking tray with non-stick baking paper.

5 Knead the dough for 5 minutes, then shape into a ball and brush lightly with the extra melted butter. Place a large tea towel (dish towel) or cloth on a work surface and dust lightly with half the extra flour. Place the dough on the cloth and dust lightly with the remaining flour. Use a rolling pin to roll out to a rectangle, about 30 x 45 cm (12 x 17¾ inches) *(pic 1)*. Put your hands under the dough and gently stretch it out *(pic 2)*, working from the centre, to about 45 x 60 cm (17¾ x 24 inches). Brush with butter, then spoon the filling across the dough, starting 10 cm (4 inches) in from a short side and stopping about 5 cm (2 inches) in from each end.

6 Use the cloth to help you fold the dough over to enclose the filling *(pic 3)*. Using the cloth as a guide, roll up the pastry and transfer to the baking tray, seam side down. Fold the ends under. Brush with melted butter and bake for 40 minutes, brushing with butter every 10 minutes, until golden and crisp. Cool on the tray for 10 minutes, then dust with the icing sugar and serve.

1

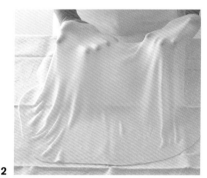

2

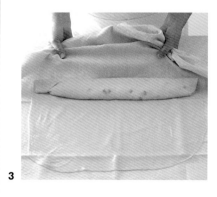

3

TIP To measure half an egg, crack an egg into a small measuring jug and lightly whisk, then use half the amount it measures on the jug.
Strudel is best eaten on the day it is baked.

Eccles cakes

These little pastries take their name from the English town of Eccles, where they originated. They are similar to the Chorley cake, also named after an English town, though they are made using flaky pastry rather than shortcrust. Both these pastries are traditionally served with Lancashire cheese.

MAKES 12   **PREPARATION TIME** 1 hour (+ 1½ hours chilling)   **COOKING TIME** 25–30 minutes

1 quantity flaky pastry
   (see pages 34–35)
1 egg white, whisked
Caster (superfine) sugar, to sprinkle

FILLING
20 g (¾ oz) unsalted butter
60 g (2¼ oz/⅓ cup, lightly packed)
   dark brown sugar
115 g (4 oz/¾ cup) currants
40 g (1½ oz/¼ cup) mixed peel
   (mixed candied citrus peel)
1 teaspoon finely grated lemon zest
2 teaspoons lemon juice
¾ teaspoon mixed (pumpkin pie) spice

1 To make the filling, put the butter and sugar in a small saucepan over low heat and cook, stirring, for 2–3 minutes or until the butter melts and the mixture is smooth. Transfer to a bowl, add the remaining ingredients and stir to mix well. Set aside to cool.

2 Line 2 baking trays with non-stick baking paper. Roll out the pastry on a lightly floured work surface to a

rectangle, about 32 x 42 cm (12¾ x 16½ inches) and 4 mm (¼ inch) thick. Use a round 10 cm (4 inch) pastry cutter to cut out 12 rounds. Place on the lined trays and refrigerate for 20 minutes.

3 Preheat the oven to 200°C (400°F/ Gas 6).

4 Divide the filling among the rounds on the trays, placing it in a heap in the centre of each and leaving a border of about 1 cm (½ inch) *(pic 1)*. Working with one at a time, bring the edges up and over to fully enclose the filling and form a ball, pressing the edges to seal *(pic 2)*. Use your hand to press down on the pastry balls to flatten them *(pic 3)*. Turn them over — the filling should start showing through the pastry.

5 Brush the pastries with the egg white and sprinkle with the sugar. Use a small sharp knife to cut three small slits in the top of each pastry. Bake the pastries for 20–25 minutes or until deep golden. Transfer to a wire rack to cool.

1

2

3

TIP Eccles cakes will keep, stored in an airtight container, for up to 5 days.

Croissants

Croissants are not particularly difficult to make, but they do require patience and practice. To achieve a neat crescent shape, it's important to keep the sides of the dough straight and measure accurately.

MAKES 10 **PREPARATION TIME** 1 hour 20 minutes (+ 3½–4½ hours proving and 1½ hours chilling)
COOKING TIME 17–22 minutes

1 quantity leavened puff pastry
  (see pages 38–39)
2 egg yolks, whisked with
  1½ tablespoons water

1 Use a rolling pin to roll out the pastry on a lightly floured work surface to a neat 35 x 53 cm (14 x 21 inch) rectangle, keeping the edges as straight as possible and rotating the pastry often so you are always rolling away from yourself.

2 Use a large sharp knife to trim the edges so they are straight, forming a 32 x 48 cm (12¾ x 19 inch) rectangle, discarding the offcuts. Cut the pastry in half lengthways, making the cut as straight as possible. Don't separate the two strips. Measure and mark 16 cm (6¼ inch) intervals along either side of the cut down the centre of the pastry (pic 1). On the two outside edges, measure and mark the first 8 cm (3¼ inches), then mark 16 cm (6¼ inch) intervals the rest of the way along. Make straight, diagonal cuts into the pastry to join the marks on each strip and form triangles (pic 2).

3 Separate each pastry triangle, then elongate each one slightly by giving it a brief roll lengthways with a rolling pin. Working with one triangle at a time, place the short side nearest you and gently stretch the two ends to lengthen slightly. Make a 5 mm (¼ inch) cut into the base of each triangle, at the centre.

4 Roll the croissant up by rolling the base towards the tip (pic 3). Turn the roll so the tip of the triangle is facing you, then bend to form a crescent shape.

5 Place on lined baking trays, cover with tea towels (dish towels) and set aside in a warm, draught-free place for 1–1½ hours or until puffed and risen. The croissants will not double in size.

6 Preheat the oven to 220°C (425°F/Gas 7). Brush the croissants all over with the egg wash. Bake for 2 minutes, then reduce the heat to 180°C (350°F/Gas 4). Bake for a further 15–20 minutes or until golden and puffed. Transfer to a wire rack. Serve warm or allow to cool.

VARIATIONS

Chocolate croissants: Roll the pastry out to a 34 x 50 cm (13½ x 20 inch) rectangle, then trim the edges to give a neat 32 x 48 cm (12¾ x 19 inch) rectangle. Cut the pastry in half lengthways, then neatly cut each strip into 6 rectangles, 8 cm (3¼ inches) wide. Coarsely chop 150 g (5½ oz) dark chocolate. Working with one rectangle at a time, place on a work surface with a short side facing you. Place a row of chopped chocolate along the end, then roll the bottom edge over to enclose. Make another row of chocolate and roll again to enclose, then roll up completely. Continue from step 5.

Ham and cheese croissants: Before rolling, place a thin 50 g (1¾ oz) slice of ham and a thin 50 g (1¾ oz) slice of gruyère cheese along the centre of the triangle, tearing them to roughly fit. Continue from step 4 (you will need to push them firmly to form crescents). Place an extra slice of gruyère on each croissant before baking, if desired.

1

2

3

> **TIP** Croissants are best eaten on the day they are baked but they can be frozen, in an airtight container or in sealed freezer bags, for up to 6 weeks. Reheat in the oven before serving.

Apple turnovers

Crisp puff pastry enclosing a sweet fruit filling with a hint of spice is a wonderful combination. You can experiment with other fruit fillings, such as cooked pears, plums, cherries or apricots. Just make sure you simmer or drain away any excess liquid or the pastry may burst and/or become soggy.

MAKES 6 **PREPARATION TIME** 1 hour (+ 1 hour 50 minutes chilling, and cooling) **COOKING TIME** 35 minutes

1 quantity puff pastry (see pages 32–33)
1 egg yolk, whisked with
 1½ tablespoons water
55 g (2 oz/¼ cup) coffee crystals
 or raw (demerara) sugar

FILLING

3 large granny smith apples, peeled
 and cut into small pieces
130 g (4½ oz/¾ cup) raisins
75 g (2¾ oz/⅓ cup) caster
 (superfine) sugar
1 teaspoon ground cinnamon

1 To make the filling, put all the ingredients in a saucepan and add 60 ml (2 fl oz/¼ cup) water. Cover the pan tightly and cook over medium heat for 8–10 minutes or until the apple is soft. Remove the lid and cook for a further 3–4 minutes or until the excess liquid has evaporated. Remove from the heat and set aside to cool.

2 Use a rolling pin to roll out the pastry on a lightly floured work surface to a rectangle, about 24 x 36 cm (9½ x 14¼ inches). Use a lightly floured round 12 cm (4½ inch) pastry cutter or saucer

of the same size to cut out 6 rounds. Working with one round at a time, roll out to an oval, about 20 cm (8 inches) long and 12 cm (4½ inches) wide *(pic 1),* taking care not to stretch the dough or the pastry will shrink. Transfer to a tray and refrigerate for 30 minutes.

3 Preheat the oven to 200°C (400°F/ Gas 6). Working with one oval at a time, brush the edges lightly with the egg wash. Divide the filling among the ovals, placing it over half of each oval and leaving a 1 cm (½ inch) border *(pic 2).* Fold the uncovered pastry over the filling, pressing the edges together gently to seal. Do not crimp or fold, as this will prevent the pastry puffing up properly around the edges. Brush each pastry with egg wash and sprinkle with the coffee crystals. Make two small slashes on top of each pastry using the tip of a small sharp knife *(pic 3),* then transfer to a lightly greased tray. Bake for 20 minutes or until puffed and golden. Transfer to a wire rack to cool to room temperature.

1

2

3

TIP Turnovers are best eaten on the day they are baked.

Christmas mince pies

Although English mince pies originally contained minced (ground) meat, these days the filling is fruit based. Fruit mince can be made several months before Christmas and stored in an airtight container in the refrigerator. These sublime tarts are not hard to make and the work can be spread over a few days.

MAKES 12   **PREPARATION TIME** 1½ hours (+ 1 hour chilling and 8 hours soaking)   **COOKING TIME** 2 hours 25 minutes

**2 quantities sweet shortcrust pastry
(see pages 24–25)**

**2 egg yolks, whisked with
1½ tablespoons water**

Icing (confectioners') sugar, to dust

FRUIT MINCE

**1 large granny smith apple, peeled,
cored and finely chopped**

**65 g (2¼ oz/½ cup) suet mix
(see tip)**

120 g (4¼ oz/⅔ cup) raisins

**85 g (3 oz/½ cup) sultanas
(golden raisins)**

75 g (2¾ oz/½ cup) currants

**55 g (2 oz/⅓ cup) mixed peel
(mixed candied citrus peel)**

**100 g (3½ oz/½ cup, lightly packed)
dark brown sugar**

Finely grated zest of 1 lemon

Finely grated zest of 1 small orange

2½ tablespoons lemon juice

2½ tablespoons orange juice

**40 g (1½ oz/¼ cup) chopped
blanched almonds**

1 teaspoon ground cinnamon

¼ teaspoon ground nutmeg

Large pinch of ground cloves

80 ml (2½ fl oz/⅓ cup) brandy

1 To make the fruit mince (mincemeat), combine all the ingredients in a large heatproof bowl and toss to combine well *(pic 1)*. Cover with plastic wrap and set aside for 8 hours or overnight to soak.

2 Preheat the oven to 120°C (235°F/ Gas ½). Remove the plastic wrap and cover the bowl with foil. Place in the oven and cook for 2 hours, stirring occasionally. Remove from the oven and set aside to cool *(pic 2)*.

3 Working with one quantity of pastry at a time, roll out on a lightly floured work surface until 5 mm (¼ inch) thick. Using a round 10 cm (4 inch) and a round 7.5 cm (3 inch) pastry cutter, cut out 12 rounds of pastry each. Gather the offcuts together and re-roll as required.

4 Use the large pastry rounds to line a 12-hole 80 ml (2½ fl oz/⅓ cup) muffin tin, pressing into the base and side with your fingertips. Divide the fruit mince among the pastry shells. Working with one small pastry round at a time, brush around the edge lightly with the egg wash and place, egg side down, on a filled pastry shell, pressing the edges to join *(pic 3)*. Refrigerate for 30 minutes.

5 Meanwhile, preheat the oven to 180°C (350°F/Gas 4). Brush the tarts lightly with the egg wash and bake for 25 minutes or until the pastry is deep golden. Cool in the tin for 10 minutes, then carefully transfer to a wire rack to cool completely. Serve at room temperature, dusted with icing sugar.

VARIATION

Vegetarian mince pies: Replace the suet with 75 g (2¾ oz) grated chilled unsalted butter.

1

2

3

> **TIP** Suet is derived from the fat around beef kidneys. Suet mix is available from the baking section of the supermarket.
> These tarts will keep, in an airtight container, for up to 10 days.

Walnut, cinnamon and brown sugar palmiers

MAKES 12   **PREPARATION TIME** 20 minutes   **COOKING TIME** 20–25 minutes

150 g (5½ oz/⅔ cup, firmly packed) light brown sugar
85 g (3 oz/⅔ cup) chopped walnuts
1½ teaspoons ground cinnamon
1 egg
1 egg yolk
3 sheets (25 x 25 cm/10 x 10 inch) frozen butter puff pastry, thawed

1 Preheat the oven to 200°C (400°F/ Gas 6). Line 2 baking trays with non-stick baking paper. Combine the sugar, walnuts and cinnamon in a bowl.

2 Whisk together the egg and yolk in a small bowl until well combined. Place a piece of non-stick baking paper on your work surface. Put a pastry sheet on top and brush with a little of the whisked egg. Scatter evenly with a third of the sugar mixture. Brush another pastry sheet with a little egg and then place, brushed side down, over the first pastry sheet to cover the sugar mixture. Brush the top of the pastry with a little more egg, then scatter over half the remaining sugar mixture *(pic 1)*. Repeat with the remaining pastry sheet, egg and sugar mixture to make 1 more layer. Use your fingers to press down on the pastry so the layers stick together a little.

3 Starting with the pastry edge nearest you, roll the pastry up tightly (like a Swiss roll/jelly roll) until it reaches halfway across. Roll the opposite side

of the pastry up tightly so they meet in the middle *(pic 2)*. Use a sharp knife to cut the log into 12 even slices. Working with one slice at a time, place between two sheets of non-stick baking paper and roll with a rolling pin to flatten to about 6 mm (¼ inch) and enlarge *(pic 3)*. Transfer to the lined trays.

4 Bake the palmiers for 20–25 minutes, swapping the trays around halfway through cooking, until they are deep golden and crisp.

VARIATION

Rosemary, sugar and clove twists: Replace the sugar, walnuts and cinnamon with 30 g (1 oz/½ cup) coffee crystals (or other very coarse sugar), 1½ tablespoons chopped rosemary leaves and ¼ teaspoon ground cloves. Reduce the pastry to 2 sheets and layer as before, scattering half the rosemary mixture between the sheets and half on top. Press down firmly with your fingers so the pastry sticks together. Instead of rolling the pastry, use a large sharp knife to cut it into 12 even strips. Carefully twist each strip several times, then place on the lined trays. Bake for 20 minutes, swapping trays as before, or until the pastry is deep golden and crisp.

1

2

3

TIP Palmiers are best eaten on the day of making but will keep in an airtight container for up to 2 days.

Lemon beignets

A beignet, which means 'fritter' in French, is a fried and sugared pastry that is not dissimilar to a doughnut, only without the hole in the centre. The recipe is very versatile, so try replacing the lemon zest with orange zest or adding raisins, currants or chopped candied peel if you like.

MAKES 24   **PREPARATION TIME** 30 minutes   **COOKING TIME** 16–20 minutes

1 quantity choux pastry (see pages 40–41), increasing the sugar to 2 tablespoons
2 tablespoons finely grated lemon zest
1.25 litres (44 fl oz/5 cups) vegetable oil, for deep frying
Caster (superfine) sugar, to dredge

1 Make the choux pastry according to the recipe, beating in the lemon zest with the final addition of egg.

2 Heat the oil in a medium saucepan until it reaches 180°C (350°F) or until a cube of bread dropped into the oil turns golden brown in 15 seconds. Take a heaped teaspoon of the batter and use another teaspoon to push it into the oil *(pic 1)*. Cook 5–8 beignets at a time so you don't crowd the pan (this will depend on the size of your pan). Cook for 4 minutes, turning halfway through cooking, or until deep golden and cooked through. Use a slotted spoon to remove the beignets from the oil *(pic 2)*, drain well and transfer to a plate lined with paper towels. Repeat to cook the remaining batter.

3 Dredge the hot beignets in sugar to coat well *(pic 3)* and serve warm.

1

2

3

TIP Beignets are best eaten on the day they are baked.

Paris brest

This delicious choux pastry cake was created in 1891 by a French pastry chef to commemorate the Paris–Brest–Paris bicycle race. It was made in a ring shape to represent a wheel.

MAKES 1 cake   **PREPARATION TIME** 1 hour 20 minutes (+ chilling)   **COOKING TIME** 45 minutes

**1 quantity choux pastry
(see pages 40–41)**
80 g (2¾ oz/¾ cup) flaked almonds
**1½ quantities crème pâtissière
(see page 349)**
**185 ml (6 fl oz/¾ cups) pouring
(whipping) cream, whipped to
firm peaks**
**165 g (5¾ oz/¾ cup) caster
(superfine) sugar**
Icing (confectioners') sugar, to dust

1 Preheat the oven to 200°C (400°F/ Gas 6). Line a large baking tray with non-stick baking paper, mark a 22 cm (8½ inch) diameter circle and then turn the paper upside down.

2 Spoon the choux pastry into a large piping (icing) bag fitted with a 1 cm (½ inch) plain nozzle (see page 42). Pipe the dough onto the baking paper, following the circle, to make a ring with a thickness of about 2.5 cm (1 inch) *(pic 1)*. Pipe another circle of dough around the inside, leaving a 3 mm (⅛ inch) gap to allow for spreading *(pic 2)*. Pipe a third circle over the gap between the 2 rings, then use your fingers to very lightly smooth the surface slightly *(pic 3)*.

3 Scatter 25 g (1 oz/¼ cup) of the flaked almonds over the pastry, then bake for 25 minutes or until the pastry is golden and puffed. Transfer to a wire rack to cool completely.

4 Meanwhile, refrigerate the crème pâtissière until completely chilled. Fold through the whipped cream and refrigerate again until firm.

5 Line another baking tray with non-stick baking paper. Combine the sugar and 60 ml (2 fl oz/¼ cup) water in a saucepan over low heat. Cook, stirring, for 5 minutes or until the sugar dissolves. Increase the heat to high and bring to the boil. Boil, without stirring, for 5–7 minutes, regularly brushing down the side of the pan with a pastry brush dipped in water to avoid crystallisation. When the mixture is deep golden, remove from the heat and add the remaining almonds. Pour immediately onto the lined tray and set aside to cool and harden. Break up into small pieces, then process in a food processor to a fine powder. Stir into the chilled crème pâtissière.

6 Use a sharp serrated knife to slice the Paris Brest in half horizontally. Remove any uncooked dough. Place the bottom half on a serving plate or platter. Spoon the crème pâtissière into a large piping (icing) bag fitted with a 1 cm (½ inch) plain nozzle. Pipe the filling onto the base. Top with the remaining pastry ring and dust with the icing sugar.

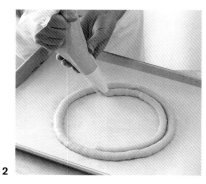

TIP Paris Brest is best eaten on the day it is made, as the praline quickly melts and loses its texture. If you would like a garnish, sliced fresh strawberries are a wonderful accompaniment.

Strawberry, rhubarb and vanilla mille feuille

This is a simplified version of mille feuille. Weighting the pastry sheets as they cook, by placing a baking tray on top, results in wonderfully crisp and more-ish pastry layers.

SERVES 6   **PREPARATION TIME** 30 minutes   **COOKING TIME** 1 hour 15 minutes

1 bunch (about 550 g/1 lb 4 oz) rhubarb

250 g (9 oz) strawberries, hulled and thickly sliced

110 g (3¾ oz/½ cup) caster (superfine) sugar

2½ sheets (24 x 24 cm/9½ x 9½ inches) frozen butter puff pastry, thawed slightly

150 ml (5 fl oz) pouring (whipping) cream, lightly whipped

½ quantity crème pâtissière (see page 349), made using ½ vanilla bean

Icing (confectioners') sugar, to dust

1 Trim the rhubarb, discarding the leaves (you should have about 350 g/ 12 oz trimmed rhubarb). Cut the rhubarb into 1 cm (½ inch) pieces, then put in a saucepan with the strawberries and caster sugar and stir to combine. Cover and cook over medium–low heat, stirring occasionally, for 8–10 minutes or until the fruits are soft and have released their juices. Transfer the mixture to a sieve set over a bowl to drain, reserving the juices. Return the juices to the pan and bring to a simmer over medium heat. Simmer for 7–8 minutes or until reduced and syrupy. Pour into a heatproof jug and set aside to cool.

2 Meanwhile, preheat the oven to 200°C (400°F/Gas 6). Place each sheet of pastry on an unlined baking tray (see tip). Cut the whole pastry sheets into 8 evenly sized rectangles and the half sheet into 4 evenly sized rectangles *(pic 1)*. Cover the pastry rectangles on one of the trays with non-stick baking paper, then place another baking tray on top to weigh it down *(pic 2)*. Bake in the centre of the oven for 18 minutes or until the pastry is deep golden and crisp. Transfer to a wire rack to cool and repeat the covering, weighing and cooking process with the remaining pastry rectangles. Use a large sharp knife to trim the edges of the rectangles to neaten, if necessary.

3 Gently fold the cream into the cooled crème pâtissière until just combined. Place a pastry rectangle on each of six serving plates. Spoon half the crème pâtissière mixture over the pastries, dividing it evenly. Top with half the strained fruit, then drizzle over some of the reduced juices. Repeat the layering with the remaining pastry rectangles, crème pâtissière mixture, fruit and a little more juice, finishing with a pastry rectangle (you will have 2 pastry rectangles left over). Serve immediately, dusted with the icing sugar, and pass any remaining fruit syrup separately.

TIP If you cook all the pastry at once you will need 6 baking trays in total. Alternatively, you can bake one sheet at a time, which will only require 2 baking trays. Cool the trays completely before cooking each pastry sheet.

Cream cheese and cherry strudel

This is a cheat's version of a strudel, the filled and rolled pastry creation from Austria. Ready-made filo pastry is used instead of the traditional home-made stretched, thin dough, but it gives a similar result. Other popular fillings include apple and raisins, and cream cheese and cherries.

SERVES 6   **PREPARATION TIME** 40 minutes (+ cooling)   **COOKING TIME** 1 hour

2 x 415 g (14¾ oz) tins pitted black
   cherries in syrup
250 g (9 oz) cream cheese
110 g (3¾ oz/½ cup) caster
   (superfine) sugar
1 teaspoon natural vanilla extract
1 egg
1 egg yolk
2 tablespoons plain (all-purpose) flour
125 g (4½ oz) butter, melted
8 sheets filo pastry (see tip),
   at room temperature
70 g (2½ oz/⅔ cup) almond meal
35 g (1¼ oz/⅓ cup) flaked almonds
Icing (confectioners') sugar, to serve

1 Preheat the oven to 160°C (315°F/ Gas 2–3). Put the cherries in a sieve set over a bowl and drain well, reserving the syrup.

2 Meanwhile, put the cream cheese, caster sugar, vanilla, egg and egg yolk in a food processor bowl and process until just combined, scraping down the side of the bowl occasionally. Add the flour and process until just combined. Take care not to overprocess the mixture.

3 Lightly brush a large baking tray with some of the melted butter. Lay the filo on a work surface and cover with a slightly damp tea towel (dish towel). Place one sheet of filo on the greased tray, brush well with butter and sprinkle with 1 tablespoon of the almond meal.

Cover with another sheet of filo, brush with a little more butter and sprinkle with another tablespoon of almond meal *(pic 1)*. Continue layering with the remaining filo pastry, almond meal and butter — you should still have a little butter left at the end.

4 Use a rubber spatula to spread the cream cheese mixture down a long side of the pastry, about 5 cm (2 inches) in from the edge, to form a log shape. Press roughly one-quarter of the drained cherries gently into the mixture *(pic 2)*.

5 Carefully roll up the pastry to enclose the filling *(pic 3)*. Trim the edges of the strudel to neaten. Brush well with the remaining butter and sprinkle with the flaked almonds. Bake for 1 hour or until the pastry is crisp and deep golden and the filling is set. Cool on the tray.

6 Meanwhile, bring the reserved cherry syrup to the boil in a medium saucepan and simmer over medium–low heat for 15 minutes or until reduced by half and slightly syrupy. Remove from the heat, add the remaining cherries and cool.

7 To serve, use a serrated knife to slice the strudel. Serve dusted with icing sugar and with the cherries in the reduced syrup passed separately.

1

2

3

TIP Ready-made filo pastry is available both frozen and chilled. The chilled variety tends to be easier to handle and is less brittle than the frozen one. If using frozen filo, thaw it in the refrigerator overnight before using.

Croquembouche

The croquembouche is a spectacular French pastry creation that is served at special occasions. Its name is derived from the French words *croquet en bouche*, meaning 'crunch in the mouth'.

SERVES 20 **PREPARATION TIME** 2½ hours (+ cooling/chilling) **COOKING TIME** 1 hour 10–30 minutes

2 quantities choux pastry
  (see pages 40–41)
2 quantities crème pâtissière
  (see page 349)
125 ml (4 fl oz/½ cup) strained, freshly
  squeezed lemon juice
2 teaspoons finely grated lemon zest
495 g (1 lb 2 oz/2¼ cups) caster
  (superfine) sugar
175 g (6 oz/½ cup) light corn syrup
Fresh flowers, to decorate

1 Preheat the oven to 200°C (400°F/ Gas 6). Line 2 large baking trays with non-stick baking paper. Spoon the choux pastry into a large piping (icing) bag with a plain 1 cm (½ inch) nozzle and pipe 20 puffs, 2.5 cm (1 inch) in diameter, on each lined tray, allowing room for spreading. Use a wet finger to pat down the tip of each puff. Bake for 12–15 minutes or until puffed. Reduce the temperature to 180°C (350°F/Gas 4), swap the trays around and bake for 15 minutes or until golden and dry. Transfer to a wire rack to cool. Increase the temperature to 200°C (400°F/ Gas 6). Pipe another 20 puffs on each tray, pat down the tips and cook as before. Continue to cook a final tray of puffs. You'll need about 100 puffs.

2 Make the crème pâtissière, whisking in the lemon juice and zest with the second batch of milk. Refrigerate until completely chilled. Spoon into a piping (icing) bag with a 5 mm (¼ inch) plain nozzle. Use the tip of a sharp knife to make a hole in the base of each puff, then fill them three-quarters full.

3 Fill a large bowl with iced water. Put the sugar, corn syrup and 250 ml

(9 fl oz/1 cup) water in a small saucepan. Stir over medium–low heat, without boiling, until the sugar dissolves. Bring to a simmer, and simmer gently, without stirring, until light golden, brushing down the side of the pan regularly with a pastry brush dipped in water to avoid crystallisation. Cook for 20–25 minutes or until deep golden. Carefully remove from the heat and immerse the base of the pan in the bowl of iced water for 1–2 minutes, to stop the cooking process and cool the caramel slightly. Remove from the bowl and place on the benchtop *(pic 1)*.

4 Working with one profiterole at a time, dip the base in the caramel and place at the base of a 19 cm (7½ inch) diameter, 26 cm (10½ inch) high croquembouche cone, with the dipped side against the cone. As you place the profiteroles around the cone, ensure they sit snugly next to one another and completely cover the base of the cone. Continue dipping and layering profiteroles around the cone until you reach the top. Dip the base of the flowers in the caramel and arrange over the croquembouche.

5 Just before serving, gently reheat the caramel if it has hardened. Dip the prongs of a fork in the caramel, then rub against the back of another fork until the caramel begins to stick. Quickly pull the forks apart and arrange the web-like caramel around the croquembouche, reheating the caramel if it hardens. You can also hold the forks back to back, dip them in the caramel and drizzle it over the croquembouche *(pic 3)*. Serve immediately.

1

2

3

> **TIP** Unfilled profiteroles can be kept in an airtight container for up to 2 days or frozen in an airtight container for up to 2 weeks.

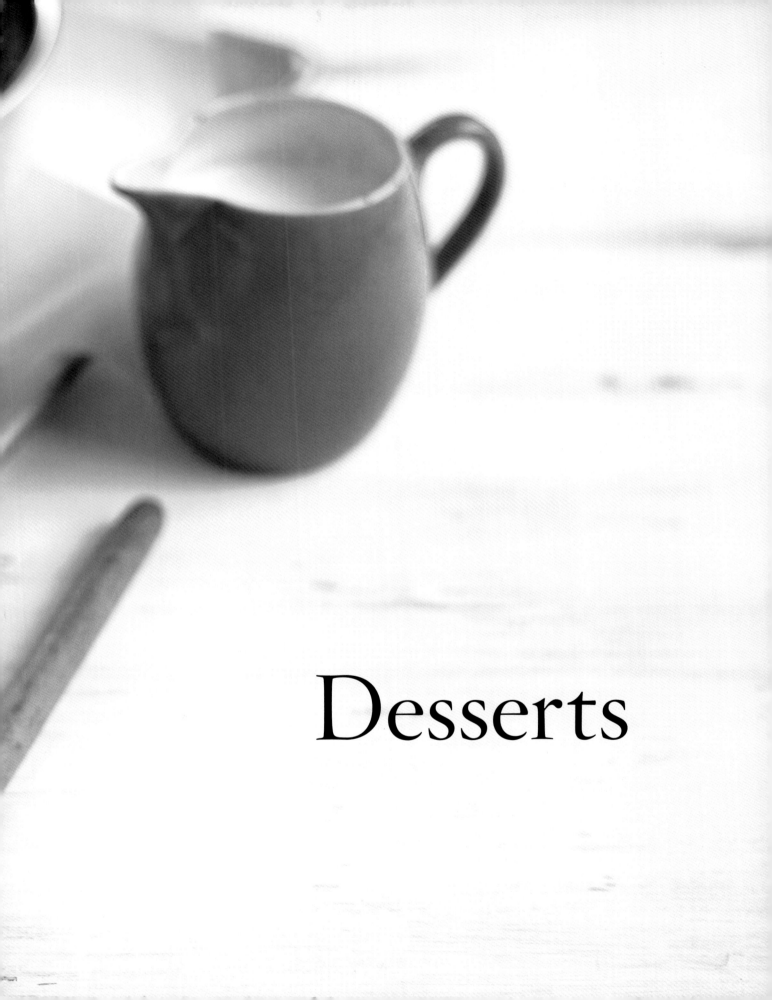

Desserts

Chocolate self-saucing puddings

This is one of those dishes that, when you're making it, doesn't seem like it could possibly work. It looks messy before cooking, but once in the oven it magically transforms into a wonderful cake-like topping over a rich chocolate sauce.

SERVES 4   **PREPARATION TIME** 20 minutes   **COOKING TIME** 25–30 minutes

150 g (5½ oz/1 cup) self-raising flour
220 g (7¾ oz/1 cup) caster (superfine) sugar
55 g (2 oz/½ cup) unsweetened cocoa powder
160 ml (5¼ fl oz/⅔ cup) milk
1 egg, lightly whisked
60 g (2¼ oz) butter, melted and cooled
60 g (2¼ oz) dark chocolate, finely chopped
250 ml (9 fl oz/1 cup) boiling water
Cream or vanilla ice cream, to serve

1 Preheat the oven to 180°C (350°F/ Gas 4). Lightly grease four 250 ml (9 fl oz/1 cup) ramekins or ovenproof cups (see tip).

2 Combine the flour, half the sugar and half the cocoa in a medium bowl and mix well. In another medium bowl or jug combine the milk, egg and butter and whisk until combined. Add the milk mixture to the flour mixture and use a large metal spoon to mix *(pic 1)* until combined and a smooth batter forms. Fold in the chopped chocolate.

3 Divide the mixture evenly among the greased ramekins or cups and place on a baking tray. Combine the remaining sugar and cocoa and sprinkle evenly over the top of the batter *(pic 2)*. Gently pour the boiling water over the back of a metal tablespoon evenly onto the batter *(pic 3)*.

4 Bake for 25–30 minutes or until the tops of the puddings have set and a sauce has formed underneath. Serve immediately with cream or ice cream.

1

2

3

TIP Deep ramekins, rather than wide shallow ones, work best for this pudding.

Bread and butter pudding

For this pudding to have the right texture when cooked you need to use the type of bread that will go stale after a day, such as a good rustic white loaf or baguette. Sliced white commercially produced bread lacks the body required to make a good bread and butter pudding.

SERVES 6–8   **PREPARATION TIME** 30 minutes (+ 30 minutes standing)   **COOKING TIME** 1 hour–1 hour 10 minutes

500 g (1 lb 2 oz) day-old crusty bread
75 g (2¾ oz) butter, softened
115 g (4 oz/⅓ cup) sweet orange
   marmalade
120 g (4¼ oz/⅔ cup) raisins (optional)
4 eggs, whisked
110 g (3¾ oz/½ cup) sugar, plus
   2½ tablespoons, for sprinkling
435 ml (15¼ fl oz/1¾ cups) milk
435 ml (15¼ fl oz/1¾ cups) pouring
   (whipping) cream
2 teaspoons natural vanilla extract
Whipped cream or pouring custard
   (see pages 348–49), to serve

1 Cut the bread into 1 cm (½ inch) thick slices and trim the crusts. Spread half the slices on one side with butter (you will have some butter left over) and then the marmalade *(pic 1)*, then place the remaining bread slices on the top to make sandwiches. Cut each sandwich into quarters.

2 Use some of the remaining butter to grease a 2 litre (70 fl oz/8 cup) ovenproof dish. Place half of the 'sandwiches' over the base of the dish, trimming as necessary to cover any gaps and form a neat layer *(pic 2)*. Scatter over half the raisins, if using.

3 Use a balloon whisk to whisk together the egg, sugar, milk, cream and vanilla until well combined. Ladle half the milk mixture over the bread in the dish. Place the remaining sandwiches over the top, unevenly and at angles. Scatter over the remaining raisins. Ladle the remaining milk mixture evenly over the top *(pic 3)*, trying to moisten as much of the bread as possible. Set the pudding aside for 30 minutes to allow the bread to absorb as much of the milk mixture as possible.

4 Preheat the oven to 170°C (325°F/ Gas 3).

5 Dot the remaining butter over the top of the pudding and sprinkle with the extra sugar. Bake for 1 hour to 1 hour 10 minutes or until deep golden and the custard is set in the middle. Serve hot, warm or at room temperature with whipped cream or custard.

VARIATION

Banana-toffee bread and butter pudding: Replace the marmalade with 3 ripe bananas, thinly sliced, to make banana sandwiches and scatter any remaining banana slices over the top. Combine 100 g (3½ oz) butter, 145 g (5½ oz) golden syrup and 100 g (3½ oz) caster (superfine) sugar in a saucepan and bring to a simmer. Cook for 2–3 minutes or until smooth and sticky, then pour over the pudding after standing and just before baking.

1

2

3

TIP You can replace the bread with a good-quality fruit bread and omit the raisins.

Steamed Christmas pudding

Good Christmas pudding recipes are hard to come by, unless you're lucky enough to have one passed down to you by a relative. This one, laden with both fresh and dried fruit, flavoured with orange and spices, and based on breadcrumbs, won't disappoint.

SERVES 8   **PREPARATION TIME** 40 minutes (+ 20 minutes standing)   **COOKING TIME** 5 hours

110 g (3¾ oz) fresh dates, pitted and chopped
120 g (4¼ oz/⅔ cup) raisins
115 g (4 oz/¾ cup) currants
120 g (4¼ oz/⅔ cup) sultanas (golden raisins)
55 g (2 oz/⅓ cup) mixed peel (mixed candied citrus peel)
115 g (4 oz) coarsely grated carrot
110 g (3¾ oz) coarsely grated, peeled apple
Finely grated zest of 1 orange
35 g (1¼ oz/¼ cup) slivered almonds
100 ml (3½ fl oz) brandy or dark rum
2 eggs, at room temperature, whisked
1 tablespoon treacle
110 g (3¾ oz/½ cup, firmly packed) dark brown sugar, plus 1 tablespoon, extra
120 g (4¼ oz) chilled unsalted butter, grated
110 g (3¾ oz/¾ cup) plain (all-purpose) flour
½ teaspoon mixed (pumpkin pie) spice
½ teaspoon ground nutmeg
½ teaspoon ground cinnamon
100 g (3½ oz) fine breadcrumbs, made from day-old white bread
20 g (¾ oz) unsalted butter, extra
1 tablespoon caster (superfine) sugar
Rich brandy sauce or pouring custard (see pages 348–49), to serve

1 Place the dried fruit, peel, carrot, apple, zest and almonds in a large heatproof mixing bowl. Heat the brandy in a small saucepan until warm, then pour over the fruit mixture, mix to combine and set aside for 20 minutes.

2 Add the egg, treacle and brown sugar to the soaked fruit and mix to combine. Stir through the grated butter.

Sift the flour and spices together over the mixture and stir to combine. Stir through the breadcrumbs.

3 Trace around the top and base of a 1.375 litre (48 fl oz/5½ cup) pudding basin onto non-stick baking paper, then cut out both rounds. Grease the basin with the extra butter. Put the smaller round of paper on the base. Spoon the pudding mixture into the basin, smooth the surface and cover with the larger round of paper.

4 Place a double sheet of foil on a work surface and fold the centre to make a pleat. Place on top of the pudding basin and use kitchen string to tie it securely below the rim *(pic 1)*. Use more string to make a long loop across the top, attaching it to the string already tied around the rim *(pic 2)* — this 'handle' will help you remove the basin from the saucepan later.

5 Place a small trivet or heatproof saucer in a saucepan large enough to hold the basin. Place the basin on the trivet, then add enough boiling water to the pan to reach two-thirds of the way up the side of the basin. Cover with a tight-fitting lid and bring to the boil over medium heat. Reduce the heat to low and cook for 5 hours, checking every hour *(pic 3)* and topping up the boiling water as needed.

6 Remove the basin from the pan. Remove the foil and paper and invert the pudding onto a serving plate. Remove the paper. Sprinkle over the combined extra brown sugar and caster sugar. Serve with brandy sauce or custard.

1

2

3

TIP You can make this pudding up to 2 months ahead. Cool it in the basin, cover tightly with plastic wrap and foil, then refrigerate. Remove from the refrigerator the night before serving. Reheat for 1 hour (follow method in step 5).

Chocolate fondant puddings

You may need to make these puddings a few times to get the feel for when they are perfectly cooked, as the timing will vary slightly depending on your oven. Be ready to serve them straight from the oven — if you leave them to stand in their moulds, the gorgeous gooey centre will disappear.

MAKES 10　**PREPARATION TIME** 20 minutes　**COOKING TIME** 12 minutes

Unsalted butter, melted, to grease
Unsweetened cocoa powder, to dust
250 g (9 oz) dark chocolate
   (70% cocoa solids), chopped
170 g (5¾ oz) unsalted butter, chopped
4 eggs, at room temperature
6 egg yolks, at room temperature
150 g (5½ oz/⅔ cup) caster
   (superfine) sugar
2 tablespoons pouring (whipping)
   cream or orange liqueur
   (such as Grand Marnier)
150 g (5½ oz/1 cup) plain
   (all-purpose) flour
Thick (double/heavy) cream or
   vanilla ice cream, to serve

1 Preheat the oven to 200°C (400°F/ Gas 6). Brush ten 125 ml (4 fl oz/ ½ cup) dariole moulds or ramekins well with melted butter and dust with cocoa, turning the ramekins to lightly coat and discarding any excess.

2 Put the chocolate and butter in a heatproof bowl over a saucepan of simmering water (make sure the base of the bowl doesn't touch the water) and stir occasionally until melted and smooth. Remove the bowl from the pan, and set aside.

3 Use an electric mixer with a whisk attachment to whisk the eggs, egg yolks and sugar in a medium bowl for 4 minutes or until very thick and pale *(pic 1)*. Add the chocolate mixture and use a balloon whisk to stir until combined. Add the cream or liqueur and whisk to combine. Sift the flour over the mixture and use a large metal spoon or spatula to fold together until just combined *(pic 2)*.

4 Spoon the mixture into the prepared moulds or ramekins *(pic 3)*, place on a baking tray and bake for 10–12 minutes or until set on top but still with some give if you gently press the centre of a pudding. Remove from the oven and turn out onto serving plates. Serve immediately, accompanied by thick cream or vanilla ice cream.

Golden syrup pudding with custard

This traditional steamed pudding is topped with golden syrup to create an intensely sweet sauce. Pouring custard, either home-made (see pages 348–49) or ready-made, complements it perfectly.

SERVES 6   **PREPARATION TIME** 20 minutes   **COOKING TIME** 1½ hours

115 g (4 oz/⅓ cup) golden syrup
2½ tablespoons lemon juice
30 g (1 oz/½ cup, lightly packed) fresh white breadcrumbs
150 g (5½ oz) unsalted butter, softened
150 g (5½ oz/⅔ cup) caster (superfine) sugar
1½ teaspoons natural vanilla extract
2 eggs
1 egg yolk
225 g (8 oz/1½ cups) self-raising flour, sifted
80 ml (2½ fl oz/⅓ cup) milk
1 quantity pouring custard (see pages 348–49), to serve

1 Lightly grease a 1.5 litre (52 fl oz/ 6 cup) pudding basin, then turn it upside down and trace around it onto a sheet of non-stick baking paper *(pic 1)*. Cut out the round of paper.

2 Put the golden syrup, lemon juice and breadcrumbs in a bowl and mix well to combine. Pour into the greased basin.

3 Use an electric mixer to beat the butter, sugar and vanilla until pale and creamy. Add the eggs and egg yolk one at a time, beating well after each addition. Use a large metal spoon to stir in the flour and milk until just combined. Spoon the mixture carefully into the pudding basin and smooth the surface with the back of the spoon.

4 Cover the pudding mixture with the round of non-stick baking paper *(pic 2)*. Cover the basin tightly with a lid or several layers of foil secured around the top of the basin with kitchen string.

5 Place the basin in a large saucepan filled with enough boiling water to come halfway up the side of the basin. Cook the pudding for 1½ hours, topping up the water as necessary to keep it at the halfway point and making sure the water is kept at a boil *(pic 3)*, or until the pudding is cooked through.

6 Carefully remove the basin from the pan and remove the lid or cover. Invert the pudding onto a serving plate and serve with the custard.

1

2

3

> **TIP** This pudding can easily be transformed into a jam pudding by replacing the golden syrup with 165 g (5¾ oz/½ cup) jam of your choice.

Creams, sauces and custards

Chantilly cream

MAKES 500 ml (17 fl oz/2 cups)

300 ml (10½ fl oz) thickened
   (whipping) cream
2 tablespoons pure icing
   (confectioners') sugar, sifted
1 vanilla bean, split lengthways and
   seeds scraped, or 1 teaspoon natural
   vanilla extract

1 Combine the cream, icing sugar and
vanilla seeds or extract in a medium
bowl and use a balloon whisk to whisk
until soft peaks form. Serve immediately.

VARIATIONS

Orange cream: Add 2 teaspoons orange
liqueur (such as Cointreau) to the cream
before whisking.

Rosewater cream: Replace the vanilla
with ½ teaspoon rosewater.

Chocolate cream: Replace the vanilla
with 2 tablespoons sifted unsweetened
cocoa powder.

Butterscotch sauce

MAKES 420 ml (14½ fl oz/1⅔ cups)

75 g (2¾ oz) butter
185 g (6½ oz/1 cup, lightly packed)
   light brown sugar
185 ml (6 fl oz/¾ cup) pouring
   (whipping) cream

1 Combine the butter, sugar and cream
in a small saucepan. Stir over low heat
until the sugar dissolves. Bring to the
boil, then reduce the heat and simmer
for 2 minutes. Serve warm.

Dark chocolate sauce

MAKES 300 ml (10½ fl oz)

150 g (5½ oz) dark chocolate, chopped
30 g (1 oz) chopped butter
185 ml (6 fl oz/¾ cup) pouring
   (whipping) cream

1 Combine the chocolate, butter and
cream in a small heatproof bowl over
a saucepan of simmering water (make
sure the base of the bowl doesn't touch
the water). Stir until the chocolate and
butter melt, and the sauce is smooth and
well combined. Serve warm.

Chocolate fudge sauce

MAKES about 500 ml (17 fl oz/2 cups)

200 g (7 oz) dark chocolate, chopped
50 g (1¾ oz) butter
185 ml (6 fl oz/¾ cup) pouring
   (whipping) cream
1 tablespoon golden syrup

1 Combine the chocolate, butter, cream
and golden syrup in a small saucepan.
Stir over low heat until the chocolate
and butter melt, and the sauce is smooth
and well combined. Serve hot or warm.

> **TIP** The butterscotch sauce, dark
> chocolate sauce and chocolate fudge
> sauce will each keep, in an airtight
> container in the refrigerator, for up to
> 4 days. Reheat gently to serve.

Pouring custard

MAKES 330 ml (11¼ fl oz/1⅓ cups)

3 egg yolks
2 tablespoons caster (superfine) sugar
375 ml (13 fl oz/1½ cups) milk
1 vanilla bean, split lengthways and
   seeds scraped

1 Use a balloon whisk to whisk
together the egg yolks and sugar in a
medium bowl until well combined.

2 Place the milk and vanilla seeds
and pod in a small saucepan over high
heat and bring to scalding point (small
bubbles will appear around the edge).
Stir if a skin starts to form. Remove
the vanilla pod, then pour into the egg
mixture, stirring with the balloon whisk
until well combined.

3 Clean the saucepan and return the
custard to the pan. Stir constantly with
a wooden spoon over the lowest possible
heat, making sure you stir through the
middle of the pan and around the edge,
where the custard is hottest, so it will
cook evenly. Keep the custard below
simmering point to prevent it curdling.
The custard is ready when it forms a
coating on the back of a spoon that
you can draw a line through with your
finger and which holds its shape.

4 When it is ready, pour the custard quickly through a sieve into a bowl or plunge the base of the pan into chilled water to stop the cooking process. If chilling the custard, lay a piece of baking paper or plastic wrap directly over the surface to prevent a skin forming. If keeping the custard warm, put it in a bowl over a saucepan of hot water. If storing, cover with plastic wrap and refrigerate for up to 2 days.

VARIATION

Rich brandy sauce: Increase the egg yolks to 4 and increase the caster sugar to 110 g (3¾ oz/½ cup). Replace the milk with 500 ml (17 fl oz/2 cups) pouring (whipping) cream and omit the vanilla bean. Stir over low heat for 5–6 minutes, until slightly thickened. Stir 60 ml (2 fl oz/¼ cup) brandy through the sauce before serving. Makes 810 ml (28 fl oz/3¼ cups).

> **Tip** You can replace the vanilla seeds in the custard with 2 teaspoons natural vanilla extract, stirred through the finished custard.
>
> If the custard curdles a little, remove it from the heat, add a teaspoon of chilled water and beat well. This will prevent further curdling, however it will not make a completely smooth custard.

Crème pâtissière (pastry cream)

MAKES 660 g (1 lb 7 oz/2⅔ cups)

1 vanilla bean, split lengthways and
   seeds scraped
250 ml (9 fl oz/1 cup) milk
250 ml (9 fl oz/1 cup) pouring
   (whipping) cream
4 egg yolks
150 g (5½ oz/⅔ cup) caster
   (superfine) sugar
2 tablespoons plain (all-purpose) flour
1 tablespoon cornflour (cornstarch)

1 Put the vanilla seeds, milk and cream in a medium heavy-based saucepan over medium heat and bring just to a simmer. Remove from the heat.

2 Use an electric mixer to whisk the egg yolks and sugar in a mixing bowl until thick and pale. Sift together the flour and cornflour, then stir into the yolk mixture until smooth and well combined. Pour about half the hot milk mixture onto the yolk mixture and stir until smooth, then stir in the remaining milk. Clean the pan. Return the mixture to the cleaned pan.

3 Stirring constantly with a balloon whisk to prevent lumps, bring the mixture slowly to the boil over medium heat. Reduce the heat and simmer, whisking often, for 2 minutes; the mixture will be thick and smooth. Remove from the heat. Transfer to a glass or metal bowl and place a cartouche (a round of non-stick baking paper) on the surface to prevent a skin forming. Cool to room temperature. Whisk with a balloon whisk until smooth before using as desired. The crème pâtissière can be refrigerated in an airtight container for up to 2 days.

Sticky date puddings

This popular dessert became famous in restaurants and cafés before people began making it in their own kitchens. Homely and decadently sweet, it's also low on fuss and requires only a few ingredients that aren't pantry staples (fresh dates and cream).

SERVES 6   **PREPARATION TIME** 20 minutes (+ cooling)   **COOKING TIME** 40 minutes

200 g (7 oz/1¼ cups) chopped pitted fresh dates
1 teaspoon bicarbonate of soda (baking soda)
80 g (2¾ oz) butter, softened
150 g (5½ oz/¾ cup, lightly packed) light brown sugar
2 eggs
150 g (5½ oz/1 cup) self-raising flour
Thickened (whipping) cream, to serve

BUTTERSCOTCH SAUCE

75 g (2¾ oz) butter
185 g (6½ oz/1 cup, lightly packed) light brown sugar
185 ml (6 fl oz/¾ cup) pouring (whipping) cream

1 Preheat the oven to 180°C (350°F/ Gas 4). Lightly grease a 6-hole 185 ml (6 fl oz/¾ cup) large muffin tin and line the bases with small rounds of non-stick baking paper.

2 Put the dates and 250 ml (9 fl oz/ 1 cup) water in a small saucepan over medium–high heat. Bring to the boil, then reduce the heat to medium–low and cook for 5 minutes *(pic 1)*. Remove from the heat, stir in the bicarbonate of soda and then set aside to cool to room temperature.

3 Use an electric mixer to beat the butter and sugar in a medium bowl until pale and creamy. Add the eggs and beat well. Use a large metal spoon or spatula to gently stir in the flour and the date mixture until just combined. Divide the mixture evenly among the muffin holes *(pic 2)*. Bake for 30 minutes or until the puddings are risen and just firm to the touch (they will still be slightly sticky in the middle). Immediately run a palette knife around the side of each pudding to loosen it from the tin and then turn them out onto a wire rack.

4 Meanwhile, to make the butterscotch sauce, stir the butter, sugar and cream in a small saucepan over low heat until the butter melts and the sugar dissolves *(pic 3)*. Bring to the boil, then reduce the heat and simmer for 2 minutes.

5 Place the warm puddings on serving plates. Drizzle with the hot butterscotch sauce and serve immediately, accompanied by the cream.

1

2

3

TIP These puddings can also be cooked in 6 greased and lined 185 ml (6 fl oz/¾ cup) ramekins.

Raspberry and lemon soufflés

There's no reason to be daunted by a hot soufflé. Soufflés rise because air incorporated into egg whites expands in the heat of the oven. So the trick is to use a light hand when folding the whisked egg whites through the raspberry mixture, and then serve them without delay.

SERVES 10   **PREPARATION TIME** 20 minutes (+ cooling and chilling)   **COOKING TIME** 18 minutes

300 g (10½ oz) fresh or thawed
   frozen raspberries
Finely grated zest and juice of 1 lemon
110 g (3¾ oz/½ cup) caster
   (superfine) sugar, plus 150 g
   (5½ oz/⅔ cup), extra
3 teaspoons cornflour (cornstarch)
30 g (1 oz) butter, softened
5 egg whites, at room temperature
Icing (confectioners') sugar, to dust
150 g (5½ oz) fresh raspberries,
   extra, to serve

1 Put the raspberries in a food processor bowl and process until puréed. Use a large spoon to push the purée through a fine sieve set over a bowl. Discard the pips. Measure 125 ml (4 fl oz/½ cup) sieved raspberry purée.

2 Place the measured raspberry purée in a small saucepan with 1 tablespoon strained lemon juice, the caster sugar and 2 tablespoons water and stir over low heat until the sugar dissolves. Increase the heat to medium and bring to the boil. Remove from the heat. Combine the cornflour with 3 teaspoons water and add to the raspberry mixture while whisking constantly. Return to medium heat and cook for 1 minute, whisking constantly. Remove from the heat, transfer to a large heatproof bowl and allow to cool slightly, then refrigerate until well chilled.

3 Preheat the oven to 200°C (400°F/ Gas 6). Grease ten 185 ml (6 fl oz/ ¾ cup) soufflé dishes with the softened butter — the best way to do this is to use a pastry brush to brush the base, then make upward strokes around the side *(pic 1)*. Dust with 75 g (2¾ oz/ ⅓ cup) of the extra sugar, turning the dishes to lightly coat and discarding any excess. Place the dishes on a baking tray.

4 Put the egg whites in a clean, dry large mixing bowl and use an electric mixer with a whisk attachment to whisk until soft peaks form. Gradually add the remaining 75 g (2¾ oz/⅓ cup) of extra sugar, whisking well after each addition, until thick and glossy. Remove the raspberry and lemon mixture from the refrigerator. Add one-third of the egg white mixture and use a large metal spoon or spatula to gently fold together *(pic 2)* until almost combined. Add the remaining egg white mixture and the lemon zest and gently fold through until just combined.

5 Spoon the mixture into the prepared soufflé dishes and use a large palette knife to level off the tops. Lightly tap each dish on the bench to expel any air pockets. Run the tip of your thumb around the inside of each dish to create an edge *(pic 3)* — this will help the soufflé rise evenly.

6 Place the dishes on a baking tray and bake for 12 minutes or until the soufflés have risen and are golden. Remove from the oven, dust with icing sugar and serve immediately with fresh raspberries.

Rhubarb, apple and strawberry crumble

If you haven't put these winter fruits together before, you're in for a treat. They pair up beautifully in this warming crumble, with the slightly tart flavour offset perfectly by the sweet, cinnamon-infused topping.

SERVES 6–8   **PREPARATION TIME** 15 minutes   **COOKING TIME** 30–35 minutes

600 g (1 lb 5 oz) granny smith apples
2 teaspoons lemon juice
350 g (12 oz) trimmed rhubarb
250 g (9 oz) strawberries, hulled, large berries halved
1 vanilla bean, split lengthways and seeds scraped
140 g (5 oz/⅔ cup) sugar
Vanilla ice cream, to serve

CRUMBLE TOPPING
75 g (2¾ oz/¾ cup) rolled (porridge) oats
75 g (2¾ oz/½ cup) plain (all-purpose) flour
110 g (3¾ oz/½ cup) sugar
½ teaspoon ground cinnamon
90 g (3¼ oz) chilled unsalted butter, diced

1 Preheat the oven to 200°C (400°F/ Gas 6).

2 Peel the apples and cut into 1.5–2 cm (⅝–¾ inch) pieces. Toss the apples and lemon juice together in a large bowl. Cut the rhubarb into 2.5 cm (1 inch) lengths *(pic 1)*. Add to the apple with the strawberries, vanilla seeds and sugar and toss to combine *(pic 2)*. Transfer to six 250 ml (9 fl oz/1 cup) heatproof ramekins or dishes.

3 To make the crumble topping, put the oats, flour, sugar and cinnamon in a medium bowl and mix to combine. Use your fingertips to rub in the butter *(pic 3)* until well combined. Sprinkle the crumble topping evenly over the fruit in the ramekins or dishes.

4 Bake for 30–35 minutes, until golden and bubbling. Cover with foil if the topping is browning too quickly. Serve with vanilla ice cream.

1

2

3

TIP You can also cook this crumble in a 1.5 litre (52 fl oz/ 6 cup) ovenproof dish. Cook at the same temperature for 50–60 minutes.

Crème brulée

This heavenly combination of chilled baked custard with a brittle topping of caramelised sugar is a staple on most bistro menus. Translated literally as 'burnt cream' it's surprisingly simple to make at home (particularly if you have a kitchen blowtorch, though this is not essential).

MAKES 6   **PREPARATION TIME** 15 minutes (+ 20 minutes standing and 3 hours chilling)   **COOKING TIME** 25 minutes

750 ml (26 fl oz/3 cups) pouring (whipping) cream
1 vanilla bean, split lengthways and seeds scraped
6 egg yolks
75 g (2¾ oz/⅓ cup) caster (superfine) sugar, plus 110 g (3¾ oz/½ cup), extra, to sprinkle

1 Preheat the oven to 160°C (315°F/ Gas 2–3). Place six 160 ml (5¼ fl oz/ ⅔ cup) heatproof ramekins in a large roasting pan.

2 Put the cream and vanilla seeds in a medium saucepan and bring almost to the boil. Remove from the heat.

3 Use a balloon whisk to whisk the egg yolks and sugar in a large bowl until combined. Whisk in the hot cream mixture until just combined (you don't want it to be frothy). Strain the custard into a jug and divide evenly among the ramekins. Use a tablespoon to remove any air bubbles from the surface of each custard *(pic 1)*.

4 Add enough boiling water to the roasting pan to reach halfway up the sides of the ramekins. Bake for 20 minutes or until the custards are set, but still a little wobbly in the centre when the ramekins are shaken gently.

Transfer the custards to a wire rack and set aside for 15 minutes to cool slightly, then place in the refrigerator, uncovered, for 3 hours or until well chilled.

5 Sprinkle the custards evenly with the extra sugar *(pic 2)* and use a kitchen blowtorch (see tip) to caramelise the sugar *(pic 3)*. Set aside for 5 minutes to allow the caramel to cool and set before serving. If you don't have a blowtorch, put the extra sugar and 2 tablespoons water in a small heavy-based saucepan over low heat and cook, stirring, for 2 minutes, until the sugar dissolves. Bring to the boil, brushing down the side of the pan often with a pastry brush dipped in water to remove any sugar crystals. Cook, without stirring, for 5 minutes or until the syrup is deep golden. Remove from the heat and allow the bubbles to subside. Pour evenly over the chilled custards and set aside for 1 minute or until the caramel sets.

VARIATION

Vanilla and strawberry crème brulée: Spread 2 teaspoons of strawberry jam over the base of each ramekin before adding the custard mixture.

1

2

3

TIP The most efficient way to caramelise the sugar layer on top of a crème brulée is by scorching it with a small kitchen blowtorch. These are available from speciality kitchenware stores.

Vanilla baked custard with drunken muscatels

Just one mouthful of this rich and velvety baked custard will transport you back to the family meals of your childhood, though the drunken muscatels anchor it firmly in the grown-up present. Simply omit them or replace with fresh fruit to give your kids a baked custard to remember.

SERVES 6–8　　**PREPARATION TIME** 15 minutes (+ 2 hours chilling)　　**COOKING TIME** 40–45 minutes

750 ml (26 fl oz/3 cups) milk

250 ml (9 fl oz/1 cup) pouring (whipping) cream

1 vanilla bean, split lengthways and seeds scraped

6 eggs, at room temperature

110 g (3¾ oz/½ cup) caster (superfine) sugar

DRUNKEN MUSCATELS

100 g (3½ oz) muscatel raisins

125 ml (4 fl oz/½ cup) Pedro Ximenez or Marsala

1 Preheat the oven to 160°C (315°F/ Gas 2–3). Grease a shallow 18 x 25 cm (7 x 10 inch), 1.5 litre (52 fl oz/6 cup) ovenproof dish and place in a large roasting pan.

2 Combine the milk, cream and vanilla seeds in a medium saucepan and bring almost to the boil.

3 Use a balloon whisk to whisk the eggs and sugar in a large bowl until combined. Whisk in the hot milk mixture until combined. Strain into the prepared dish *(pic 1)*. Add enough boiling water to the roasting pan to come halfway up the sides of the dish.

Bake for 35–40 minutes or until the custard is set on top but still slightly wobbly in the centre when the dish is lightly shaken. Remove from the oven and set aside to cool *(pic 2)*. Cover and refrigerate for 2 hours or until chilled.

4 Meanwhile, to make the drunken muscatels, combine the muscatels, Pedro Ximenez or Marsala and 2 tablespoons water in a small saucepan. Bring to a simmer over low heat *(pic 3)*. Remove from the heat and set aside for 2 hours to macerate.

5 Serve the baked custard topped with the drunken muscatels and their liquid.

VARIATIONS

Chocolate baked custard: Omit the vanilla seeds and melt 100 g (3½ oz) dark chocolate, chopped, in the hot milk and cream mixture.

Coffee baked custard: Omit the vanilla seeds and replace 80 ml (2½ fl oz/⅓ cup) of the milk with freshly brewed, strong espresso coffee.

1

2

3

Crème caramel

If you're out to impress, this dish will do the trick. It's another classic French dessert, though there are variations on this silky smooth baked custard from both Spain (flan) and Italy (crema caramella).

SERVES 6   **PREPARATION TIME** 15 minutes (+ 30 minutes standing, cooling, and 2 hours chilling)   **COOKING TIME** 50 minutes

220 g (7¾ oz/1 cup) caster
   (superfine) sugar
600 ml (21 fl oz) milk
1 vanilla bean, split lengthways
   and seeds scraped
4 eggs
2 egg yolks

1 Combine 175 g (6 oz) of the sugar with 80 ml (2½ fl oz/⅓ cup) water in a small saucepan and stir over low heat until the sugar dissolves. Increase the heat to medium–high and bring to the boil. Boil for 6–7 minutes or until the mixture turns a deep caramel colour. Working quickly and taking care as the mixture will spit, remove the pan from the heat and add 2 tablespoons cold water. Return the pan to the heat and bring to a simmer, swirling the pan to combine well, and cook for 2 minutes or until smooth. Place six 185 ml (6 fl oz/¾ cup) dariole moulds or heatproof ramekins in a roasting pan and divide the caramel evenly among them *(pic 1)*. Set aside for 30 minutes to allow the caramel to set. Preheat the oven to 160°C (315°F/Gas 2–3).

2 Heat the milk and vanilla seeds in a small saucepan over medium heat until almost simmering. Remove from the heat. Use a balloon whisk to whisk the eggs and egg yolks together in a large bowl until combined. Add the remaining sugar and the hot milk and stir to combine well. Strain the mixture through a fine sieve into a jug *(pic 2)*.

3 Divide the mixture among the moulds, then fill the roasting pan with enough hot water to come halfway up the sides of the moulds. Bake for 35 minutes or until the custards are set, but still a little wobbly in the centre when the moulds are shaken gently. Remove from the pan and cool to room temperature. Cover each mould with plastic wrap, then refrigerate for 2 hours or until chilled.

4 To serve, use your fingertip to gently press all around the top of a custard to loosen it from the side of the mould *(pic 3)*. Invert onto a serving plate and shake quickly, but gently, until the custard is released from the mould. Repeat with the remaining crème caramels. Serve immediately.

VARIATIONS

Orange crème caramel: Stir the finely grated zest of 1 orange into the strained custard before baking.

Rum crème caramel: Use 540 ml (18½ fl oz) milk and stir 80 ml (2½ fl oz/⅓ cup) rum into the custard before baking.

Espresso crème caramel: Heat 20 g (¾ oz/¼ cup) finely ground espresso beans with the milk, then stand for 30 minutes to infuse. Strain the milk through a fine sieve before adding to the egg mixture.

1

2

3

Apricot clafoutis

Hailing from the Limousin region of France, this traditional dessert is a fabulous way to make use of fresh seasonal fruit. Apricots, cherries, peaches, plums and other stone fruit all pair beautifully with the luscious baked custard-like batter. This recipe has almond meal added to the batter for extra richness.

SERVES 8–10   **PREPARATION TIME** 10 minutes   **COOKING TIME** 25–35 minutes

400 g (14 oz) ripe apricots,
   halved and stoned
1½ teaspoons icing (confectioners')
   sugar, plus extra, to dust
125 g (4½ oz/1¼ cups) almond meal
220 g (7¾ oz/1 cup) caster
   (superfine) sugar
2 tablespoons plain (all-purpose) flour
500 ml (17 fl oz/2 cups) pouring
   (whipping) cream
4 eggs, at room temperature
6 egg yolks, at room temperature

1 Preheat the oven to 180°C (350°F/ Gas 4). Grease a square 24 cm (9½ inch), 2 litre (70 fl oz/8 cup) ovenproof dish with butter. Place the apricots in the dish, some cut-side up and others cut-side down *(pic 1)*. Sift the icing sugar over the fruit.

2 Put the almond meal, caster sugar and flour in the bowl of a food processor and process for 5 seconds. Add the cream, eggs and egg yolks and process until smooth *(pic 2)*. Transfer to a jug.

3 Pour the batter over and around the apricots in the dish *(pic 3)*.

4 Bake the clafoutis for 25–35 minutes or until puffed, golden and just set in the centre, checking after 20 minutes.

5 Serve immediately, dusted with the extra icing sugar.

TIP This clafoutis can also be made using 400 g (14 oz) cherries, pitted. The cooking time will be the same.

Berry and passionfruit pavlova

Every cook should be able to whip up a pavlova. They are a great standby recipe, as they require few ingredients, the preparation is quick and uncomplicated, and they're universally popular. You can top the cream with whatever fruit is in season or simply sprinkle with grated dark chocolate.

SERVES 8   **PREPARATION TIME** 20 minutes (+ cooling)   **COOKING TIME** 1 hour 20 minutes

4 egg whites, at room temperature
220 g (7¾ oz/1 cup) caster
   (superfine) sugar
1 tablespoon cornflour (cornstarch)
1 teaspoon white vinegar

TOPPING

300 ml (10½ fl oz) thickened
   (whipping) cream
2 passionfruit, halved, pulp removed
250 g (9 oz) strawberries,
   hulled and sliced
125 g (4½ oz/1 cup) raspberries

1 Preheat the oven to 110°C (225°F/ Gas ½). Mark a 20 cm (8 inch) circle on a piece of non-stick baking paper. Turn the paper over and place it on a baking tray. Brush the paper with a little melted butter and dust with a little flour *(pic 1)*.

2 Place the egg whites in a clean, dry, large mixing bowl. Use an electric mixer with a whisk attachment to whisk until soft peaks form. With the motor running, gradually add the sugar, whisking well after each addition. Continue to whisk for 6–7 minutes, until the mixture is very thick and glossy.

3 Fold the sifted cornflour and the vinegar through the meringue mixture *(pic 2)*. Spoon the mixture onto the tray and use a spatula to spread it out, using the marked circle as a guide *(pic 3)*. Smooth the sides or create swirls, as desired.

4 Bake for 1 hour 20 minutes or until the meringue is crisp, but not coloured. Turn the oven off. Cool completely in the oven, with a wooden spoon keeping the door slightly ajar.

5 To serve, use an electric mixer with a whisk attachment or a balloon whisk to whisk the cream in a medium bowl until soft peaks form. Spread the cream over the top of the pavlova and then spoon half the passionfruit pulp over the cream. Top with half the strawberries and raspberries. Drizzle the remaining passionfruit pulp over the top and serve accompanied by the remaining berries.

1

2

3

TIP It is best to make pavlova on a dry day with low humidity, as humidity in the air can cause the meringue to 'weep'.

Mini pavlovas with caramelised figs

These simple-to-make mini pavlovas have just the right amount of wow factor. The meringue is infused with a caramel flavour courtesy of the brown sugar and the caramelised figs make an elegant topping.

SERVES 4   **PREPARATION TIME** 30 minutes (+ 2–3 hours cooling)   **COOKING TIME** 35 minutes

3 egg whites, at room temperature
110 g (3¾ oz/½ cup) caster
   (superfine) sugar
60 g (2¼ oz/¼ cup, firmly packed)
   light brown sugar
½ teaspoon natural vanilla extract
1 teaspoon white vinegar
250 ml (9 fl oz/1 cup) thickened
   (whipping) cream
Icing (confectioners') sugar, to dust
2 tablespoons slivered almonds, toasted

CARAMELISED FIGS

20 g (¾ oz) butter
1 tablespoon light brown sugar
4 fresh figs, trimmed, cut into thirds

1 Preheat the oven to 160°C (315°F/ Gas 2–3). Grease 2 baking trays and line with non-stick baking paper.

2 Use an electric mixer with a whisk attachment to whisk the egg whites in a clean, dry medium bowl until soft peaks form. Gradually add the combined sugars, 1 tablespoon at a time, whisking well after each addition *(pic 1)*, until the mixture is thick and glossy. Add the vanilla and vinegar and whisk for 30 seconds or until combined.

3 Use a metal spoon to drop one-quarter of the meringue mixture onto a prepared tray. Use the back of the spoon to spread the mixture out slightly and then make a slight indent in the top *(pic 2)*. Repeat with the remaining meringue mixture to make 4 mini pavlovas in total.

4 Bake for 30 minutes or until they are crisp and sound hollow when tapped on the base. Turn the oven off. Cool completely in the oven, with a wooden spoon keeping the door slightly ajar.

5 Use an electric mixer with a whisk attachment to whisk the cream in a medium bowl until soft peaks form. Cover and refrigerate until needed.

6 To make the caramelised figs, melt the butter in a medium frying pan over medium–high heat until foaming. Add the sugar and cook, stirring, for 1 minute or until it dissolves. Add the figs, cut side down, and cook for 3–4 minutes each side or until caramelised *(pic 3)*. (The cooking time will depend on the ripeness of the figs.)

7 To serve, place the mini pavlovas on serving plates, dust lightly with icing sugar, top with the cream and figs and sprinkle with the almonds.

1

2

3

TIP The pavlovas can be made up to 4 days ahead. Keep in an airtight container in a cool place.

Meringue and berry torte

A true crowd-pleaser, this spectacular torte is a bit like a three-tiered pavlova. Three meringue discs are topped with whipped cream and berries, so it's not complicated to pull together but you do need to get the meringue right for it to hold its shape well.

SERVES 8–10   **PREPARATION TIME** 20 minutes (+ cooling)   **COOKING TIME** 45 minutes

6 egg whites, at room temperature
330 g (11½ oz/1½ cups) caster (superfine) sugar
1 teaspoon natural vanilla extract
1 tablespoon cornflour (cornstarch)
300 ml (10½ fl oz) pouring (whipping) cream, whipped
2 tablespoons icing (confectioners') sugar, plus extra, to dust
500 g (1 lb 2 oz) mixed fresh berries

1 Preheat the oven to 120°C (235°F/ Gas ½). Line 3 baking trays with non-stick baking paper and draw a 22 cm (8½ inch) diameter circle on each piece (*pic 1*), then turn them over.

2 Use an electric mixer with a whisk attachment to whisk the egg whites in a clean, dry large bowl on medium speed until soft peaks form. Gradually add the caster sugar, 1 tablespoon at a time, whisking well after each addition. Continue whisking until the sugar has dissolved and the meringue is very thick and glossy. Whisk in the vanilla and cornflour.

3 Divide the mixture evenly among the marked circles and use a spatula or palette knife to carefully spread it to the edge of each circle (*pic 2*). Bake for 40–45 minutes, swapping the trays around halfway through cooking, or until the meringues are crisp. Turn off the oven and leave the meringues to cool in the oven with the door ajar.

4 To make the filling, use an electric mixer with a whisk attachment to whisk the cream and icing sugar in a small bowl until firm peaks just form.

5 Place a cooled meringue disc on a serving plate, spread with half the whipped cream and top with half the berries (*pic 3*). Place another meringue disc on top and repeat with the remaining cream and berries. Top with the last meringue disc. Dust with the extra icing sugar and serve immediately.

1

2

3

Tip To ensure egg whites whisk to their greatest potential volume, use eggs that are at room temperature and a clean, dry mixing bowl.
 Keep the meringue discs in an airtight container, layered with baking paper, for up to 4 days.

Hazelnut and chocolate meringue torte

This beautiful torte, combining chocolate, meringue and hazelnuts, is highly appealing. It's a terrific do-ahead dessert and one that family and friends are bound to request time and again.

SERVES 6 **PREPARATION TIME** 1 hour (+ cooling/standing and overnight chilling) **COOKING TIME** 35 minutes

135 g (4¾ oz/1 cup) roasted and
skinned hazelnuts
4 egg whites, at room temperature
220 g (7¾ oz/1 cup) caster
(superfine) sugar
1 teaspoon natural vanilla extract
1 teaspoon white vinegar
200 g (7 oz) dark chocolate (70% cocoa
solids), melted

CHOCOLATE MOUSSE
150 g (5½ oz) dark chocolate,
finely chopped
375 ml (13 fl oz/1½ cups) thickened
(whipping) cream

1 Preheat the oven to 160°C (315°F/ Gas 2–3). Line 2 large baking trays with non-stick baking paper. Draw two 10 x 25 cm (4 x 10 inch) rectangles on one lined tray, leaving a little room between for spreading, and one rectangle on the other. Turn both pieces of paper over.

2 Finely chop 115 g (4 oz/¾ cup) of the hazelnuts. Coarsely chop the remaining nuts and put in an airtight container.

3 Use an electric mixer with a whisk attachment to whisk the egg whites in a medium bowl until soft peaks form. Gradually add the sugar, a little at a time, whisking well after each addition. Whisk for a further 2–3 minutes or until very thick and glossy. Add the vanilla and vinegar and whisk for 30 seconds or until combined. Use a large metal spoon or spatula to gently fold in the finely chopped hazelnuts.

4 Divide the meringue mixture among the marked rectangles and use a palette knife to spread it out evenly. Bake for 30 minutes or until dry to touch. Turn the oven off. Cool completely in the oven, with a wooden spoon keeping the door slightly ajar.

5 Spread three-quarters of the melted chocolate over the cooled meringue rectangles and leave to set. Reserve the remaining melted chocolate.

6 To make the chocolate mousse, put the chocolate in a heatproof bowl. Bring 100 ml (3½ fl oz) of the cream just to a simmer, then pour over the chocolate. Stand for 1 minute, then stir gently until melted and well combined. Set aside at room temperature until the mixture has cooled completely.

7 When the chocolate mixture has cooled, use an electric mixer with a whisk attachment to whisk the remaining cream until soft peaks form (*pic 1*) (do not whisk the cream past soft peaks or it will curdle later). Add the chocolate mixture and use a spatula or large metal spoon to fold together until just combined (*pic 2*). Refrigerate for 1 hour or until firm.

8 Place a meringue rectangle on a serving platter. Spread with half the chocolate mousse (*pic 3*). Continue to layer the remaining meringue rectangles and mousse, finishing with meringue. Warm the reserved chocolate until it is melted again, then drizzle over the torte and refrigerate overnight.

9 Remove from the refrigerator 1 hour before serving. Serve sprinkled with the coarsely chopped hazelnuts.

1

2

3

Raspberry and vanilla vacherin

We have the French to thank for the impressive, yet simple, dessert of vacherin, which is made by layering meringue discs and ice cream. This recipe uses ready-made ice cream, but you can substitute your favourite home-made ice cream (chocolate with roasted hazelnuts is a good flavour combination).

SERVES 10   **PREPARATION TIME** 40 minutes (+ cooling and standing)   **COOKING TIME** 2 hours 15 minutes
FREEZING TIME 3 hours

3 egg whites, at room temperature
220 g (7¾ oz/1 cup) caster (superfine) sugar
600 ml (21 fl oz) vanilla ice cream
125 g (4½ oz) frozen raspberries
125 ml (4 fl oz/½ cup) thickened (whipping) cream
2 tablespoons pistachios, toasted and finely chopped
125 g (4½ oz/1 cup) fresh raspberries, to serve
Icing (confectioners') sugar, to dust

RASPBERRY COULIS
250 g (9 oz) frozen raspberries
2 tablespoons caster (superfine) sugar
1 tablespoon lemon juice

1 Preheat the oven to 150°C (300°F/Gas 2). Mark two 18 cm (7 inch) circles on a piece of non-stick baking paper. Turn the paper over and place on a large baking tray.

2 Use an electric mixer with a whisk attachment to whisk the egg whites and 2 tablespoons of the caster sugar until soft peaks form. With the motor running, add 110 g (3¾ oz/½ cup) of the remaining caster sugar, 1 tablespoon at a time, whisking well after each addition, until very thick and glossy. Use a spatula or large metal spoon to fold in the remaining caster sugar until well combined.

3 Divide the meringue between the two marked circles and use a palette knife to spread evenly *(pic 1)*. Bake for 8 minutes, until starting to set. Reduce the oven temperature to 90°C (190°F/Gas ½) and

bake for a further 2 hours, until crisp and dry all the way through. Transfer to a wire rack to cool.

4 Meanwhile, to make the raspberry coulis, put all the ingredients in a medium saucepan over medium heat and cook, covered, for 3 minutes. Stir until the sugar dissolves and the raspberries break down. Increase the heat and bring to the boil. Reduce the heat to low and simmer for 5 minutes.

5 Line a round 20 cm (8 inch) spring-form cake tin with non-stick baking paper. Place a meringue disc in the tin, trimming to fit if necessary *(pic 2)*.

6 Scoop the ice cream into a large bowl and set aside at room temperature for 5–10 minutes, until softened slightly but not melted. Add the frozen raspberries and quickly stir through until evenly distributed. Spoon the mixture into the tin, gently pressing down with the back of the spoon to remove any air pockets *(pic 3)*. Top with the remaining meringue disc, trimming to fit if necessary. Cover with plastic wrap and freeze for 3 hours or until firm.

7 To serve, use an electric mixer with a whisk attachment to whisk the cream until soft peaks form. Remove the vacherin from the freezer, remove from the tin and transfer to a chilled serving plate. Spread with the whipped cream, sprinkle with the pistachios and top with the fresh raspberries. Dust with icing sugar and serve with the coulis.

1

2

3

TIP You may need to stand the vacherin at room temperature for 5–10 minutes to allow it to soften slightly before serving. Use a large sharp knife, dipped in hot water and dried, to cut it.

New York cheesecake

Americans adore cheesecakes, especially the version they lay claim to, the New York cheesecake. Creamy, smooth and dense, this style of cheesecake often has a rich sour cream topping.

SERVES 10–12 **PREPARATION TIME** 30 minutes (+ cooling and overnight chilling) **COOKING TIME** 35 minutes

250 g (9 oz) plain sweet biscuits,
  broken into pieces
100 g (3½ oz) butter, melted
Freshly grated nutmeg, to dust
Passionfruit pulp, to serve

FILLING

750 g (1 lb 10 oz) cream cheese,
  at room temperature
150 g (5½ oz/⅔ cup) caster
  (superfine) sugar
2 eggs, at room temperature
1 tablespoon lemon juice

TOPPING

370 g (13 oz/1½ cups) sour cream
2 tablespoons caster (superfine) sugar
¼ teaspoon natural vanilla extract

1 Preheat the oven to 190°C (375°F/ Gas 5). Lightly grease a round 23 cm (9 inch) spring-form cake tin.

2 Place the biscuits in a food processor bowl and process to fine crumbs. Add the butter and process until combined. Use a flat-based glass to press the crumb mixture evenly over the base and side of the greased tin, coming 5 cm (2 inches) up the side *(pic 1)*. Refrigerate while making the filling.

3 To make the filling, use an electric mixer to beat the cream cheese and sugar until smooth. Add the eggs, one at a time, beating well after each addition *(pic 2)*. Beat in the lemon juice. Pour the cream cheese mixture over the biscuit base and use a spatula to spread evenly. Bake for 30 minutes or until just set. Remove from the oven and set aside to cool to room temperature.

4 Increase the oven to 220°C (425°F/ Gas 7). To make the topping, use an electric mixer to beat the sour cream, sugar and vanilla until smooth *(pic 3)*. Pour over the cooled cheesecake and use a small spatula to spread evenly. Bake for 3 minutes or until glazed and shiny. Transfer to a wire rack and cool completely in the tin. Cover and refrigerate overnight.

5 Dust the top of the cheesecake lightly with nutmeg and spoon over some passionfruit pulp. Serve immediately.

2

1

3

TIP This cheesecake also pairs well with strawberries, sliced banana, thin wedges of plum or a drizzle of honey.

White chocolate and raspberry cheesecake

SERVES 8–10   **PREPARATION TIME** 20 minutes (+ 10 minutes cooling)   **COOKING TIME** 1 hour 5 minutes

180 g (6¼ oz) white chocolate, chopped
1 orange
650 g (1 lb 7 oz) cream cheese,
   at room temperature
220 g (7¾ oz/1 cup) caster
   (superfine) sugar
1 vanilla bean, split lengthways and
   seeds scraped
3 eggs, at room temperature,
   lightly whisked
125 g (4½ oz/1 cup) raspberries
Icing (confectioners') sugar, to dust

1 Preheat the oven to 170°C (325°F/ Gas 3). Grease an 18 x 28 cm (7 x 11¼ inch) slice tin and line with non-stick baking paper, extending above the sides.

2 Place the chocolate in a heatproof bowl over a saucepan of simmering water (make sure the base of the bowl doesn't touch the water) and use a metal spoon to stir occasionally *(pic 1)* until melted and smooth. Set aside for 10 minutes to cool.

3 Meanwhile, finely grate the zest from the orange and set aside. Juice the orange and strain. Measure 80 ml (2½ fl oz/⅓ cup) of the juice.

4 Put the cream cheese, caster sugar, vanilla seeds and orange zest in a medium bowl and use an electric mixer to beat for 2 minutes or until smooth. Gradually add the egg, beating well after each addition *(pic 2)*. Add the orange juice and white chocolate and beat until combined and smooth. Pour into the prepared tin and smooth the surface with the back of a spoon. Place the raspberries on top *(pic 3)*.

5 Bake for 30 minutes (the cheesecake is quite puffed at this stage but it will collapse after cooking), then carefully turn the tin and cook for a further 30 minutes or until light golden and just set in the middle. Place on a wire rack and cool completely in the tin.

6 Dust with icing sugar and serve at room temperature (it is very delicate and soft, so slice it with a sharp knife) or refrigerate before serving for a firmer texture.

TIP You can melt the chocolate in the microwave. Place in a microwave-safe bowl and heat on 50% (medium) for 1 minute bursts, stirring in between each burst, until melted and smooth.

Italian ricotta cheesecake with red wine figs

This cheesecake has a lighter texture than most, thanks to the ricotta. Use the fresh one that is sold in rounds. The orange, pine nuts and figs create a sublime combination of flavours and textures.

SERVES 8   **PREPARATION TIME** 40 minutes (+ 2 hours standing, 2 hours cooling and 3 hours chilling)
COOKING TIME 1 hour 20 minutes

1 kg (2 lb 4 oz) firm, fresh ricotta cheese
115 g (4 oz/⅓ cup) honey
75 g (2¾ oz/⅓ cup) caster
   (superfine) sugar
2½ teaspoons finely grated orange zest
60 ml (2 fl oz/¼ cup) strained, freshly
   squeezed orange juice
4 eggs, at room temperature,
   lightly whisked
35 g (1¼ oz/¼ cup) plain
   (all-purpose) flour, sifted
65 g (2¼ oz) pine nuts

RED WINE FIGS
375 g (13 oz) dried figs, stems trimmed
250 ml (9 fl oz/1 cup) boiling water
250 ml (9 fl oz/1 cup) red wine
2 tablespoons Marsala
75 g (2¾ oz/⅓ cup) caster
   (superfine) sugar
Large pinch of ground cloves

1 To make the red wine figs, put the figs in a small heatproof bowl and pour over the boiling water, then stand for 1 hour or until softened.

2 Combine the undrained figs, wine, Marsala, sugar and cloves in a medium saucepan and bring to a simmer over medium heat. Cook, uncovered, for 20 minutes or until the figs are very tender (*pic 1*). Remove from the heat and cool to room temperature.

3 Preheat the oven to 170°C (325°F/Gas 3). Lightly grease and flour a round 18 cm (7 inch) spring-form cake tin.

4 Combine the ricotta, honey, sugar, orange zest and juice in the bowl of a food processor (*pic 2*) and process until smooth and well combined. Add the egg and process to combine. With the motor running add the flour and process briefly until just combined. Pour the mixture into the prepared tin (*pic 3*) and smooth the surface with the back of a spoon. Sprinkle with the pine nuts.

5 Bake for 1 hour or until light golden and the cheesecake wobbles just a little in the centre when the tin is shaken lightly. Turn off the oven and cool the cheesecake in the oven with a wooden spoon keeping the door slightly ajar for 2 hours or until cooled to room temperature. Cover and refrigerate for at least 3 hours or until well chilled.

6 Remove the cheesecake from the refrigerator 1 hour before serving to bring to room temperature. Serve in wedges with the figs and some of their syrup spooned over.

1

2

3

TIP The red wine figs can be cooked up to 4 days in advance and stored in an airtight container in the refrigerator.

Conversion charts

OVEN TEMPERATURE		
C	F	Gas
70	150	¼
100	200	½
110	225	½
120	235	½
130	250	1
140	275	1
150	300	2
160	315	2–3
170	325	3
180	350	4
190	375	5
200	400	6
210	415	6–7
220	425	7
230	450	8
240	475	8
250	500	9

LENGTH	
cm	inches
2 mm	1/16
3 mm	⅛
5 mm	¼
8 mm	⅜
1	½
1.5	⅝
2	¾
2.5	1
3	1¼
4	1½
5	2
6	2½
7	2¾
7.5	3
8	3¼
9	3½
10	4
11	4¼
12	4½
13	5
14	5½
15	6
16	6¼
17	6½
18	7
19	7½
20	8
21	8¼
22	8½
23	9
24	9½
25	10
30	12
35	14
40	16
45	17¾
50	20

WEIGHT	
g	oz
5	⅛
10	¼
15	½
20	¾
30	1
35	1¼
40	1½
50	1¾
55	2
60	2¼
70	2½
80	2¾
85	3
90	3¼
100	3½
115	4
120	4¼
125	4½
140	5
150	5½
175	6
200	7
225	8
250	9
280	10
300	10½
350	12
375	13
400	14
450	1 lb
500	1 lb 2 oz
550	1 lb 4 oz
600	1 lb 5 oz
700	1 lb 9 oz
800	1 lb 12 oz
900	2 lb
1 kg	2 lb 3 oz

LIQUID	
ml	fl oz
30	1
60	2
80	2½
100	3½
125	4
160	5¼
185	6
200	7
250	9
300	10½
350	12
375	13
400	14
500	17
600	21
650	22½
700	24
750	26
800	28
1 L	35
1.25 L	44
1.5 L	52

Index

A

almond biscotti 69
almond filling 224
almond macaroons 74
angel food cake 141
angel food cake tins 17
Anzac biscuits 62
apple and rhubarb tart,
  free-form 273
apple pie, double-crust 286
apple popovers 190
apple tarte Tatin 282
apple turnovers 321
apricot clafoutis 362

B

babka 224
  chocolate and cinnamon 236
bagels 216
baking equipment *see also* mixing techniques
  bakers' friends 13
  bakeware 16–7
  conversion charts 380
  cutting and grating 14
  measuring 12
  mixing 12
  ovens 12, 380
baking paper 122–3
baking powder 10
baklava 313
banana bread 193
banana muffins 158
banana–toffee bread and butter pudding 341

basil pesto 254
beignets, lemon 325
berries
  freezing 55
  frosting 55
  storing 55
berry and passionfruit
  pavlova 365
berry tarts 277
bicarbonate of soda 10
biscotti, almond 69
biscuits
  almond biscotti 69
  digestive 81
  parmesan 89
  vanilla 70
  wheatmeal 81
blind baking 30–1, 44
blowtorch 357
blueberry and almond friands 145
brandy sauce, rich 349
bread *see also* pizza
  bagels 216
  banana 193
  challah 228
  cornbread 177
  definitions of terms 44–5
  feta and olive pull-apart 203
  focaccia 207
  four-seed 199
  fruit 248
  gozleme 223
  grissini 211
  Irish soda 182
  naan 208

pitta 212
pretzels 215
rye 200
rye damper, seeded 174
skillet 181
sourdough, cheats' 204
white, basic 196
wholemeal 196
bread making
smooth and elastic texture 45
techniques 46–7
using bread maker 47
bread and butter pudding 231
brioche 231
orange, cardamom and
plum jam 235
brownies 103
buns see also brioche
hot cross 251
sticky pecan 227
butter 10
buttercake, vanilla 120
buttercream 72
buttercream icings 22–3
butterfly 164
buttermilk 10
buttermilk scones 166
butterscotch sauce 348, 351

C

cake cutting 131
cake handling 130–1
cake tins
preparing 122–3
types and uses 16–7
calzone 219
candied citrus zest 52, 72
caramel apple cake 153
caramel-coated fruits 51
caramel making 50
caramel praline 51
caramelised figs 366
cartouche 44
challah 228
Chantilly cream 348
cheats' sourdough 204
cheddar and walnut soda bread 182
cheese naan 208

cheese scones 166
cheesecake
Italian ricotta, with red wine
figs 378
New York 374
white chocolate and raspberry 377
cherry and hazelnut friands 145
cherry clafoutis 362
cherry tarts 277
chicken, bacon and mushroom
vol-au-vents 302
choc chip biscuits 70
choc-coconut slice 108
chocolate and blackberry muffins 161
chocolate and cinnamon babka 236
chocolate and hazelnut praline
roll 150
chocolate and prune loaf 244
chocolate and raisin banana
bread 193
chocolate and raspberry
cheesecake 377
chocolate baked custard 358
chocolate biscuits 70
chocolate cake
flourless 133
simple 116
chocolate caramel slice 104
chocolate cream 82, 348
chocolate croissants 318
chocolate decorations
coating 72, 82
curls 49, 116
drizzle 72
frosting 116
glacé icing 309
scrolls and shards 49
chocolate éclairs 309
chocolate fondant puddings 345
chocolate fudge cookies, jumbo 58
chocolate fudge sauce 348
chocolate ganache 99, 100, 164, 278
chocolate mousse 370
chocolate mud cake, white 134
chocolate muffins 158
chocolate sauce
dark 348
hot 164
chocolate self-saucing puddings 338

chocolate tart, rich 278
Christmas mince pies 322
Christmas pudding, steamed 342
citrus biscuits 70
citrus zest
    candied 52, 72
    removing 53
    segmenting citrus 53
clafoutis, apricot 362
cocoa powder 10, 244
coconut jam slice 111
coconut macaroons 74
coffee
    coffee and walnut cake 138
    coffee baked custard 358
    coffee buttercake 120
    espresso crème caramel 361
    espresso meringue kisses 99
conversion charts 380
cookies, jumbo chocolate fudge 58
coriander and garlic naan 208
corn tortillas 178
cornbread 177
cornflour 10
Cornish pasties 305
cornstarch 10
coulis, raspberry 373
cream cheese and cherry strudel 333
cream cheese frosting 164
cream pastries 293
creams
    Chantilly 348–9
    chocolate 82, 348
    hazelnut 82
    types of 10
crème brulée 357
crème caramel 361
crème pâtissière 349
crescents, Greek almond 65
crimping 44
croissants 318
croquembouche 334
croquet en bouche 334
crumbing 44
crumble, rhubarb, apple and strawberry 355
crumble topping 355
crumpets 189
crust 44
cupcakes 142

patty pan tins 16
toppings 142, 164
currant and rum savarin 239
custard
    pouring 348–9
    rice 294
    vanilla baked, with drunken
        muscatels 358
custard tarts, Portuguese 293

D

damper, seeded rye 174
dariole moulds 16
date crumble slice 112
date puddings, sticky 351
date scones 166
decorative finishes *see also* chocolate decorations;
  icings; toppings
    candied citrus zest 52–3, 72
    caramel-coated fruits 51
    for cupcakes 142
    frosted fruits 55
    icing sugar 72
    praline 51
detrempe 44
digestive biscuits 81
doughnuts, jam 243
drunken muscatels 358

E

Eccles cakes 317
éclairs 309
eggs
    egg wash 44
    using 10
    whisking whites 21
    whisking with sugar 21
espresso crème caramel 361
espresso meringue kisses 99

F

fennel and pepper grissini 211
feta
    feta and olive pull-apart 203
    spinach and feta muffins 162

spinach and feta pie 257
spinach and feta quiche 261
figs
    caramelised 366
    mascarpone and fig sponge 119
    pistachio and fig tart 285
    red wine 378
fillings 72
filo pastry 43, 333
filo rolls, honey and nut 310
financier 145
fingers
    hazelnut meringue and chocolate 107
    shortbread 78
flan 361
flan tins 17
Florentines 85
flour 10, 178
focaccia 207
four-seed bread 199
frangipane, pistachio and
    rosewater 285
freezing 18
    berries 55
friands, blueberry and almond 145
frosted fruits 55
frosting, cream cheese 164
fruit bread 248
fruit cake, rich 125
fruit mince 322

G

garlic and oregano grissini 211
ginger cake, double, with lime
    frosting 146
gingerbread people 77
gingernuts 61
glacé icing 22–3, 164
glaze 44
gluten 44
golden syrup 11
golden syrup pudding with
    custard 346
gozleme 223
greasing 44, 122
Greek almond crescents 65
grissini 211

H

ham and cheese croissants 318
hazelnut caramel spread 164
hazelnut creams 82
hazelnut meringue and chocolate fingers 107
hazelnut praline 150
honey 11
honey and nut filo rolls 310
honey spice Swiss roll 137
hot chocolate sauce 164
hot cross buns 251

I

icing sugar 11, 72
icings *see also* decorative finishes; toppings
    buttercream 22–3, 72
    chocolate glacé 309
    glacé 22–3, 164
Irish soda bread 182
Italian meringue 281
Italian ricotta cheesecake with red
    wine figs 378

J

jam doughnuts 243
jam pudding 346
jelly roll
    honey spice Swiss roll 137
    rolling 131

K

khubz 212
kneading 44, 46
knocking back 44, 47
kugelhopf 232
kugelhopf tins 17
kulich 247

L

lemon and apricot savarin 239
lemon beignets 326
lemon buttercake 120
lemon curd and strawberry sponge 119

lemon daisy cupcakes 142
lemon filling 281
lemon macaroon and strawberry
  mousse cake 154
lemon meringue pie 281
lemon tart 270
lime frosting 146
lime tart 270
lining 123
Linzertorte 274
loaf tins *see* cake tins

M

macarons 100
macaroons
    almond 74
    coconut 74
    lemon macaroon and strawberry
      mousse cake 154
malt and chocolate chunk
  brownies 103
marble cake 129
masa harina 178
mascarpone and fig sponge 119
meat pies 258
melting moments 90
meringue *see also* pavlova; torte
    angel food cake 141
    espresso kisses 99
    Italian 281
    lemon meringue pie 281
    making 94
    orange and almond 96
    raspberry and vanilla
      vacherin 373
    rosewater and pistachio 96
    vanilla 96
milk 11
mille feuille, strawberry, rhubarb
  and vanilla 330
mince pies, Christmas 322
mixing techniques
    creaming 19
    folding 20
    melt and mix 19
    rubbing in 20
    whisking 21
Monte creams 66

mousse
    chocolate 370
    strawberry 154
mud cake, white chocolate 134
muffins
    banana 158
    chocolate 158
    muffin tins 16
    orange 158
    spinach and fetta 162
    toppings 142, 164
    white chocolate and blackberry 161
muscatels, drunken 358
mushroom calzone 219

N

naan 208
nectarine and almond cake 149
New York cheesecake 374
nuts
    making nut meal 48
    skinning hazelnuts 48
    toasting 48
nutty biscuits 70

O

oil 11
olive, green, and oregano focaccia 207
onion tart, roast 269
orange and almond meringues 96
orange, cardamom and plum jam brioche 235
orange cream 348
orange crème caramel 361
orange liqueur syrup 126
orange muffins 158
oven temperature
    conventional and fan-forced 12
    conversion charts 380
ovenproof dishes 16

P

palmiers, walnut, cinnamon and brown
  sugar 325
pancetta and zucchini quiche 261
Paris Brest 329
parmesan biscuits 89

parmesan grissini 211
passionfruit cream 126
passionfruit genoise 126
pastéis de nata 293
pasties, Cornish 305
pastry *see also* shortcrust pastry
    choux (pâte à choux) 40–1
    choux, piping/shaping 42
    Cornish pasties 305
    definitions of terms 44–5
    filo 43, 333
    flaky 34–5
    laminated 45
    puff 32–3
    puff, leavened 38–9
    puff, rough 36–7
    shortcake 289
pastry cream 349
pavlova *see also* torte
    berry and passionfruit 365
    mini, with caramelised figs 366
peach pie 289
pear and honey tarte Tatin 282
pecan buns, sticky 227
pecan pie 290
pesto
    basil 254
    pesto, tomato and parmesan
      pull-apart 203
pies
    apple, double-crust 286
    Christmas mince 322
    lemon meringue 281
    meat 258
    peach 289
    pecan 290
    pie tins 17
    silverbeet 257
piping bags 45
pissaladière 262
pistachio and fig tart 285
pitta bread 212
pizza
    calzone 219
    pizza stones 17
    three-cheese and sage 220
    tomato, salami and mozzarella 220
popovers, apple 190
pork, apple and fennel sausage rolls 298

Portuguese custard tarts 293
potato and pea samosas 301
potato, sage and pecorino
  focaccia 207
pound cake 129
prawn and avocado tartlets, mini 266
preheating 45
pretzels 215
profiteroles 334
proving 45, 47
puddings
    bread and butter 341
    chocolate fondant 345
    chocolate self-saucing 338
    Christmas, steamed 342
    golden syrup, with custard 346
    pudding basins 17
    sticky date 351
    Yorkshire 185
pull-apart, feta and olive 203

Q

quiches
    Lorraine 261
    tomato and fennel, with basil pesto 254

R

raisin and custard spirals 306
raisin and rosemary soda bread 182
ramekins 16
rasberry and pistachio friands 145
raspberry and lemon soufflés 352
raspberry and vanilla vacherin 373
raspberry brownies 103
raspberry coulis 373
raspberry-filled scones 173
red wine figs 378
resting 45
rhubarb, apple and strawberry crumble 355
rice custard 294
ricotta and raisin strudel 314
ricotta and spinach calzone 219
ricotta cheesecake, Italian, with red
  wine figs 378
ring tins 17
rising 45, 46
rosemary and honey rice-custard tart 294

rosemary and parmesan brioche 231
rosemary, sugar and clove twists 325
rosewater and pistachio meringues 96
rosewater cream 348
rubbing in 45
rum crème caramel 361
rye bread 200
rye damper, seeded 174

S

salt 11
samosas, potato and pea 301
sauces
    brandy, rich 349
    butterscotch 348, 351
    chocolate, dark 348
    chocolate fudge 348
    chocolate, hot 164
    tomato 220
sausage rolls, pork, apple and fennel 298
savarin, lemon and apricot 239
scones
    plain 166
    raspberry-filled 173
    rich 169
    variations 166
Scottish shortbread 78
seeded rye damper 174
shortbread fingers 78
shortbread, Scottish 78
shortcake pastry 289
shortcakes, strawberry 170
shortcrust pastry 24–5
    blind baking 30–1, 44
    making in food processor 28
    pâte brisée 26
    pâte sucrée 27
    rolling out 28
    sweet 25
silverbeet pie 257
skillet bread 181
slices
    choc-coconut 108
    chocolate caramel 104
    coconut jam 111
    cutting 112
    date crumble 112
soda bread, Irish 182

soufflés, raspberry and lemon 352
sourdough, cheats' 204
spanakopita 257
spinach and feta muffins 162
spinach and feta pie 257
spinach and feta quiche 261
spirals, raisin and custard 306
sponge, classic 119
spring-form tins 17
steamed Christmas pudding 342
sticky date puddings 351
stollen 240
stone fruit
    clafoutis 362
    lemon and apricot savarin 239
    nectarine and almond cake 149
    peach pie 289
    peeling 54
strawberries and cream cupcakes 142
strawberry essence 86
strawberry mousse 154
strawberry, rhubarb and vanilla mille
    feuille 330
strawberry shortcakes 170
strudel
    cream cheese and cherry 333
    ricotta and raisin 314
sugar 11
sultana scones 166
sweet hearts 86
Swiss roll
    honey spice 137
    rolling 131
syrup
    for baklava 313
    for filo rolls 310
    for savarin 239

T

tarts see also torte
    apple and rhubarb, free-form 273
    berry 277
    chocolate, rich 278
    lemon 270
    pistachio and fig 285
    Portuguese custard 293
    prawn and avocado tartlets,
        mini 266

roast onion 269
rosemary and honey rice-custard 294
tart tins 17
tarte Tatin 282
tomato, caramelised 265
temperature
    conversion charts 380
    ovens, conventional and
      fan-forced 12
three-cheese and sage pizza 220
tomato and fennel quiches with basil pesto 254
tomato, salami and mozzarella
  pizza 220
tomato sauce 220
tomato tart, caramelised 265
toppings *see also* decorative finishes; icings
    cheesecake 374
    crumble 355
    for muffins and cupcakes 142, 164
    pavlova 365
torte *see also* pavlova
    hazelnut and chocolate
      meringue 370
    Linzertorte 274
    meringue and berry 369
tuiles 93
turnovers, apple 321
twists, rosemary, sugar and clove 325

V

vacherin, raspberry and vanilla 373
vanilla and strawberry crème brulée 357
vanilla baked custard with drunken
  muscatels 358
vanilla beans 11
vanilla bean paste 11

vanilla biscuits 70
vanilla buttercake 120
vanilla essence 11
vanilla extract 11
vanilla meringues 96
vanilla sparkle cupcakes 142
vegetarian mince pies 322
vol-au-vents, chicken, bacon and
  mushroom 302

W

walnut, cinnamon and brown sugar palmiers 325
weights and measures 380
Welsh cakes 186
wheatmeal biscuits 81
white chocolate and blackberry muffins 161
white chocolate and raspberry cheesecake 377
white chocolate mud cake 134

Y

yeast 11
Yorkshire puddings 185

ABOUT THE AUTHOR

Anneka Manning has spent more than 22 years in the food print media as a food writer and editor. She has worked for a range of leading food publications in Australia such as *Australian Gourmet Traveller*, *VOGUE Entertaining + Travel*, *australian good taste* (which she helped to launch and make one of Australia's most successful food magazines), *The Australian Women's Weekly* and *Good Living* (Sydney Morning Herald). In addition, Anneka has also compiled and written a number of successful, award-winning books, including *good food* and *more good food*. Anneka believes that the best food is simple food done well, relying on sound basics, simple techniques and good ingredients. Her food reflects the way she cooks, eats and entertains in her busy life. It is good food – realistic, yet inspiring.

Published in 2013 by Murdoch Books, an imprint of Allen & Unwin.

This edition published 2013 for Index Books

Murdoch Books Australia
83 Alexander Street
Crows Nest NSW 2065
Phone: +61 (0) 2 8425 0100
Fax: +61 (0) 2 9906 2218
www.murdochbooks.com.au
info@murdochbooks.com.au

Murdoch Books UK
Erico House, 6th Floor
93–99 Upper Richmond Road
Putney, London SW15 2TG
Phone: +44 (0) 20 8785 5995
Fax: +44 (0) 20 8785 5985
www.murdochbooks.co.uk
info@murdochbooks.co.uk

Publisher: Anneka Manning
Editor: Anna Scobie
Design concepts: Susanne Geppert
Designers: Susanne Geppert and Tania Gomes
Project Manager: Alice Grundy
Photographers: Alan Benson, Louise Lister, Julie Renouf
Stylists: Jane Hann, Kate Nixon, Cherise Pagano
Food editors: Anneka Manning and Leanne Kitchen
Recipe development: Sonia Greig, Leanne Kitchen, Cathie Lonnie,
    Lucy Nunes and the Murdoch Books Test Kitchen
Food preparation for photography: Grace Campbell, Dixie Elliot,
    Caroline Jones, Sharon Kennedy, Lucy Lewis and Sabine Spindler
Production Controller: Joan Beal

For Corporate Orders & Custom Publishing please contact
Noel Hammond, National Business Development Manager.

Printed by C&C Offset Printing Co. Ltd, China.
Reprinted 2012 (twice), 2013

The Publisher and Stylist would like to thank Breville
(www.breville.com.au) for their generous support with equipment
for use and photography.

They would also like to thank The Essential Ingredient
(www.theessentialingredient.com.au), Izzi & Popo (izziandpopo.com.au)
and Wüsthof (www.wusthof.com.au) for supplying equipment for use and
photography.

IMPORTANT: Those who might be at risk from the effects of salmonella poisoning (the elderly, pregnant women, young children and those suffering from immune deficiency diseases) should consult their doctor with any concerns about eating raw eggs.

CONVERSION GUIDE: You may find cooking times vary depending on the oven you are using. For fan-forced ovens, as a general rule, set the oven temperature to 20°C (35°F) lower than indicated in the recipe. We have used 20 ml (4 teaspoon) tablespoon measures. If you are using a 15 ml (3 teaspoon) tablespoon, add an extra teaspoon for each tablespoon specified. We have used 60 g (Grade 3) eggs in all recipes.